ADVANCE PRAISE

Joel Richardson has written a very important and hard-hitting book. His arguments against replacement theology, or supersessionism, are powerful and solid. I have greater optimism of the final end of the age on the tribulation. However, the basic thrust of this book is right and true and a wonderful contribution.
—DANIEL JUSTER, TH. D. TIKKUN INTERNATIONAL, JERUSALEM

This latest book by Joel Richardson is desperately needed and a must read for the serious Christian. His characteristic scholarship and diligence is long overdue on this very crucial perspective for everyone that claims the name of Christ. The inevitable rise of criticism will simply underscore the reality that these issues lie at the very centroid of all doctrines of a Biblical faith and include a crucial re-examination of the eschatological issues on our immediate horizon. Indeed, a pivotal contribution for us all.
—CHUCK MISSLER, KOINONIA HOUSE

This book draws the reader through foundational biblical and historical issues regarding the restoration of the Jewish people, as well as the speckled and sometimes glorious history of the body of Messiah vis-à-vis Israel's destiny. Thoughtful, respectful, helpful, edifying.
—AVNER BOSKEY, FINAL FRONTIER MINISTRIES, BEERSHEVA, ISRAEL

There are numerous points of light that illuminate the canvas on which the history of the church is rendered. However, these points of light shine against a shadowy backdrop rendered in dark crimson. The vitriol and bloodlust displayed by many nations toward the people that birthed God's Son has dimmed the light of God and obscured the path of love he came to reveal. In this work Joel lays bare the historic roots of this hatred as well as revealing God's plan for His ancient chosen people—Israel. This book will open your eyes and engage your heart with the love God has for those whom He first chose and called according to His purposes.

—BURT YELLIN, PASTOR / RABBI, ROEH ISRAEL, DENVER

In a season where it is becoming increasingly popular to delegitimize Israel—whether in the press, in politics, or even in the pulpit—along comes this refreshing, faith-building, and biblically centered book that will challenge every honest reader to embrace God's unchanging heart for His people.

—SCOTT VOLK, TOGETHER FOR ISRAEL

WHEN A
JEW
RULES *the* WORLD

WHEN A
JEW
RULES *the* WORLD

WHAT *the* BIBLE REALLY SAYS
ABOUT ISRAEL *in the* PLAN OF GOD

JOEL RICHARDSON

WND Books

WHEN A JEW RULES THE WORLD

Published by WND Books, Washington, D.C. WND Books is a registered trademark of WorldNetDaily.com, Inc. ("WND")

Unless otherwise noted, all scripture quotations are from the New American Standard Bible®, Copyright © 1960, 1962, 1963, 1968, 1971, 1972, 1973, 1975, 1977, 1995 by The Lockman Foundation Used by permission. (www.Lockman.org) Scripture quotations marked ESV are taken from the English Standard Version. © 2001 by Crossway Bibles, a division of Good News Publishers. Scripture quotations marked NIV are taken from the Holy Bible, New International Version®, NIV®. Copyright © 1973, 1978, 1984, 2011 by Biblica, Inc.™ Used by permission of Zondervan. All rights reserved worldwide. www.zondervan.com. Scripture quotations marked NKJV are taken from the NEW KING JAMES VERSION˙. Copyright © 1982 by Thomas Nelson. Used by permission. All rights reserved.

Book designed by Mark Karis

WND Books are available at special discounts for bulk purchases. WND Books also publishes books in electronic formats. For more information call (541) 474-1776 or visit www.wndbooks.com.

Hardcover ISBN: 978-1-938067-71-6
eBook ISBN: 978-1-938067-72-3

Library of Congress Cataloging-in-Publication Data
Richardson, Joel.
When a Jew rules the world : what the Bible really says about Israel in the plan of God / Joel Richardson.
pages cm
ISBN 978-1-938067-71-6 (hardcover)
1. Judaism--Relations--Christianity--History. 2. Christianity and other religions--Judaism--History. 3. People of God--Biblical teaching. 4. Israel (Christian theology)--Biblical teaching. I. Title.
BM535.R475 2015
261.2'6--dc23
2014029612

Printed in the United States of America
14 15 16 17 18 19 MPV 9 8 7 6 5 4 3 2 1

DEDICATED TO

The Jewish people, the descendants of Abraham, Isaac, and Jacob. Take comfort, the Lord GOD will come with might, with His arm ruling for Him. His reward will be with Him, and His recompense before Him.

CONTENTS

ACKNOWLEDGMENTS

First and highest thanks must go, of course, to Jesus of Nazareth, the King of Kings, Lord of Lords, and the longing of my heart. After Jesus, no one deserves my gratitude more than my wife. You are a woman of such deep beauty, strength, and character. I am blessed. The "well done, good and faithful servant" that you'll receive from Him will be more than you could ever imagine. I so hope I can see the look in your eyes on that day. It's going to be awesome.

Much thanks to the handful of supporters who have blessed me these past few years. You truly have made this book possible.

Thanks also to Samuel Clough, Paul Blake, Shane Meredith, Stephen Holmes, Julie Loomis, Aaron Maendel, Dax Cabrera, Avner Boskey, Brock Hollett, Nick Uva, and Dan McCarthy for looking at the early manuscript and giving me feedback.

Finally I want to express my deep gratefulness to Joseph and Elizabeth Farah for your support. Thanks also to the whole WND team. Thanks to Geoff Stone, the editorial director, for all of your work, as well as your input and advice on the manuscript. Thanks to Renee Chavez and Kelsey Whited, my editors. Great is your reward in heaven! Thanks to Mark Karis for contributing your gift of design. I always love your stuff. Thanks also to Michael Thompson and Amanda Prevette, the marketing coordinators. What a great team to work with. Thanks again and many blessings to you all.

PART 1

WHAT THE BIBLE REALLY SAYS ABOUT ISRAEL IN THE PLAN OF GOD

1

THE WARNING:

IGNORANCE AND ARROGANCE

Just three years before his death in 1546, Martin Luther, the great Protestant reformer, wrote an anti-Jewish treatise titled *On the Jews and Their Lies*. For more than a thousand years, Christians throughout Europe had debated among themselves about how they should treat the Jews living in their midst. By Luther's day, some argued that the "problem" of the Jews called for a definitive solution. Luther's treatise offered his solution in no unclear terms. I'll allow his own words to speak for themselves:

What then shall we Christians do with this damned, rejected race of Jews? . . . First, their synagogues should be set on fire, and whatever does not burn up should be covered or spread over with dirt so that no one may ever be able to see a cinder or stone of it. And this ought to be done for the honor of God and of Christianity in order that God may see that we are Christians. . . .

Secondly, their homes should likewise be broken down and destroyed. For they perpetrate the same things there that they do in their synagogues. For this reason they ought to be put under one roof or in a stable, like gypsies, in order that they may realize that they are not masters in our land, as they boast, but miserable captives. . . .

Thirdly, they should be deprived of their prayer-books and Talmuds in which such idolatry, lies, cursing, and blasphemy are taught. . . .

Fourthly, their rabbis must be forbidden under threat of death to teach any more. . . .

To sum up, dear princes and nobles who have Jews in your domains, if this advice of mine does not suit you, then find a better one so that you and we may all be free of this insufferable devilish burden—the Jews. . . . Next to the devil, a Christian has no more bitter and galling foe than the Jew. [1]

Most Christians who read Luther's words for the first time are shocked. Tragically, Luther was far from alone among notable Christian leaders in his hatred and abuse of the Jews. As we will see, his attitude was actually quite common among Christians throughout an overwhelming majority of Church history.

Even more tragically, roughly five hundred years after Luther wrote his hateful treatise, Adolf Hitler would rely heavily on Luther's proposals as the basis of his own "final solution," resulting in the death of two-thirds of the roughly nine million Jews who were living in Europe at the time.

How did it all come to this? How did Christianity, whose adherents claim to follow a *Jewish* Messiah, become a *Gentile*-dominated religion that persecuted the Jews no matter where they were found? How did those Christians who claimed to worship the God of Israel come to hate the children of Israel so deeply, so passionately, and so relentlessly? To answer that question, we must begin with the words of the apostle Paul in chapter 11 of his letter to the Romans. It is there that Paul issued a most solemn warning—one specifically intended for Gentile Christians. First, Paul warned them against being *arrogant* toward the Jews, reminding his readers of the ongoing calling and election of Israel—*including unbelieving Israel*—as the people of God. Second, he also warned Gentile believers not to become conceited about their own standing before God. Instead, they were exhorted to "fear." Let us read Paul's warning:

[D]o not be arrogant toward the [natural] branches; but if you are arrogant, remember that it is not you who supports the root, but the root supports you. You will say then, "Branches were broken off so that I might be grafted in." Quite right, they were broken off for their unbelief, but you stand by your faith. *Do not be conceited, but fear*; for if God did not spare the natural branches, He will not spare you, either. Behold then the kindness and severity of God; to those who fell, severity, but to you, God's kindness, *if you continue in His kindness; otherwise you also will be cut off.* (Rom. 11:18–22; emphasis added)

This is an absolutely profound statement. Put another way, a failure to be both informed and humble concerning unbelieving Israel could very well result in believing Gentile Christians being "cut off" from God. The word Paul used here is the Greek *ekkoptō*. It is the same word John the Baptist used as he warned those coming to him to be baptized: "The axe is already laid at the root of the trees; therefore every tree that does not bear good fruit is *cut down and thrown into the fire*" (Matt. 3:10; emphasis added). On the night that I came to faith and surrendered my life to Jesus, it was these very words that the Lord used to confront me about my sin, convicting me that unless I repented, my eternal destiny would be in hell. It's not surprising, then, that Paul would call on Gentile believers to recognize and ponder "the severity of God."

Paul and John the Baptist were not alone in issuing such stern warnings. Jesus also used precisely the same term as John in His exhortation: "Every tree that does not bear good fruit is *cut down and thrown into the fire*" (Matt. 7:19; emphasis added).

Today, as we look back two thousand years to Paul's warning, a terrifying reality immediately grips us. When we take an honest look at the Gentile-dominated Christian Church throughout its history, right up to this present day, most believers have utterly failed to heed Paul's warnings. The vast majority of the Church from very early on, from the top down, fell headlong into wrong ideas and arrogance toward unbelieving Israel. How quickly they forgot about the promises of God and Israel's ongoing role in His plan! And the results have been horrific.

One of the results of the Church's ignorance of Israel's role in the plan of God is the profound blindness of much of the Church concerning unfolding prophecy. Many Christians have heard of "the sons of Issachar," mentioned in 1 Chronicles 12:32. We are told that they were "men who understood the times, with knowledge of what Israel should do." Today the Church is in desperate need of understanding concerning the times and the ability to properly respond. The Jewish prophets, apostles, and Jesus Himself have given us such a profound gift in that their words contain a tremendous amount of information concerning what we will witness in the days ahead. Throughout the pages of Scripture, the future, like the past, is laid out in great detail on a divinely revealed timeline. Understanding the times and recognizing where we are on this timeline is of tremendous strategic benefit to the Church as it seeks to fulfill its divine mandate. But when the Church fails to acknowledge and recognize the consistent thread of the people and the land of Israel that runs through the entire timeline, it quickly becomes distorted beyond understanding, resulting in a thick fog of confusion settling over the vision of the Church. Such is the state of the Church today. This timeline, the great strategic blueprint that the Lord has given to His people, has essentially been scribbled over, defaced with the errant doctrines of a Gentile-dominated Church. Not only are vast segments of the Church fundamentally unaware of where they presently sit on God's prophetic timeline; many reject the idea that such a clear timeline even exists. If the Church is to ever truly blow the fog away, if it is to ever regain the clarity and prophetic spirit it needs to navigate the dark days ahead, then it must both identify and thoroughly reject those false doctrines and wrong ideas that crept into the Church early on. This process of cleansing must begin by acknowledging Israel as the essential thread that runs throughout the Lord's unfolding promise-plan of redemption. It is my deepest hope that this book will accomplish this in an easy-to-understand way, clearing away nearly two thousand years of confusion for any who are willing to give the matter the serious consideration that it demands.

Another negative result of the Church's ignorance concerning Israel is her relative impotence and inability to articulate accurately the full gospel message, most particularly to the Jewish people. Far too many Christians view the Gospel, or "the good news," in the most minimalistic of terms, something along the lines of "Jesus died for your sins so that someday, when you die, you can go to heaven forever." The fact of the matter, however, is that the good news as it was proclaimed by Jesus and the apostles was so much more than this. It involved the full testimony of God, from creation to the great covenants of God, to the atoning death and resurrection of the Messiah, to His return to judge the earth and restore the kingdom of Israel. All of these things and so much more are integral parts of the Gospel. Because of the Church's minimizing and sanitizing of any Jewish dimensions of the Gospel message, however, it has forgotten so much of what Jesus and the apostles actually proclaimed. Bluntly stated, as the title of this book reminds us, if the Gospel that one preaches does not culminate with a Jewish man ruling the world, then it is not the Gospel of the New Testament. The Gospel today has been reduced to a simplified formula whereby one might "get saved," but it has been fundamentally detached from the coming kingdom that we are saved unto. Whenever Peter, Paul, and Stephen preached the Gospel, they did so by placing the listeners within the context of the larger biblical story, a very specific story rooted in the Creation, the covenants of God, and the history and suffering of the Jewish people and culminating with the day of judgment and the kingdom of God that follows. Until the Church reclaims the full biblical story it was entrusted with and recognizes the central and ongoing role of Israel in this story, it will remain relatively impotent in its ability to effectively and fully communicate the true Gospel, especially to the Jewish people.

My hope is that this book will help Christians to better understand the Gospel in its actual Jewish context. Perhaps you yourself are Jewish and do not believe that Jesus (Yeshua) is the Messiah, but have stumbled upon or have been given this book. I promise that if you read it through, you will find much more that you agree with than you could have imagined.

A third result of the Church's ignorance and pride toward Israel is the long and bloody history of anti-Semitism demonstrated not only by individual Christians, but often by official Church sanction. This fact is one that few Christians have the desire or the courage to face. Yet according to Paul, the alternative to facing our sins, of remaining in ignorance and making excuses for the truly evil actions of the Church, places us in danger of being cut off. Alternatively, if the Church desires to walk in fullness and maturity, then it must begin by confronting and repenting of its dark, anti-Semitic past, the evidence of which is overwhelming. Such calls to repentance, of course, are easy to make, but they are not as easily received. Although I am absolutely convinced that one of the premier needs of the Church in this hour, as we approach the last days, is a deep, widespread, and thorough repentance for its long history of hatred and mistreatment of the Jewish people, the reality is that at the very root of our collective sins are some very specific doctrines, ideas, and theologies that much of the Church today still believes. Not only are these wrong ideas foundational to the historical traditional churches, but they are also part of the very fabric of the Protestant Reformation and were heartily espoused by virtually all of the great and notable Reformers. These doctrines—specifically, super-sessionism, preterism, and amillennialism, which we will discuss later—are not going to go away on their own or be expelled from the Church without a tremendous fight. But again, we must very soberly remember the alternative that Paul spoke of. I trust that as you read this book through and give it serious consideration, you will see why the Church must fundamentally reject these doctrines.

Sadly, the Church's arrogance toward Israel also has consequences that are yet to be seen—acts of evil that will be committed in the days ahead. God has ordained that in the last days the hearts of all men will be tested by their response to "Jacob's distress" a time of unparalleled tribulation for the Jewish people (see Jer. 30:7). As sad as it is to consider today, no one can deny that the overwhelming majority of European Christians failed the Jewish people during the Holocaust. What makes anyone think we will respond differently if another time of suffering should ever befall the Jews? To date, few in the Church have committed to do the painful and introspective "soul-work" necessary to identify and root out the wrong doctrines and attitudes they have harbored for so long. It was these very views that allowed the Church to sit by idly or even stand in approval as those whom the Lord called "the apple of His eye" (Zech. 2:8) were literally slaughtered by the millions. The Scriptures are clear that in the last days world events will culminate with the full rage of Satan against God's plan to restore the nation of Israel. Simply put, if the Church does not identify and thoroughly purge the thinking that caused it to fail so miserably during the Holocaust, then its future sins and failures will far surpass anything in its past. Of course, I pray this is not the case. I pray that the Church will get it right next time. My most earnest prayer is that this book will awaken some to embrace a humble posture before the Lord concerning the Jewish people and awaken even more to our responsibility as followers of Jesus in the difficult days ahead. While I certainly hope that many who read this will be strengthened in the convictions they already have on these matters, finding greater clarity and resolve to do what is right in the sight of God, I also pray that others will be stirred and challenged to reconsider formerly held positions concerning the Jewish people that are not in accordance with the Scriptures. For far beyond merely arguing concerning theological propositions, I want this book to change hearts and affect the practices and actions of the Christian Church. If only one reader is changed and one heart touched with the Father's heart for His people, then writing this book will have been beyond worth it. If just one soul hears the message of this book and truly repents of those beliefs that Paul warned would lead to being "cut off," then this will have been among my greatest accomplishments.

2

RESTORATIONISM VERSUS SUPERSESSIONISM

For the past two thousand years, the overwhelming majority of the Christian Church has held the view that the Jewish people, because of their rejection of Jesus as Messiah, have in turn been corporately rejected by God as His people. While there were indeed numerous groups such as the Moravians, numerous Puritans, and various Lutheran Pietists who looked for a future restoration of Israel and the salvation of the Jewish people, for the most part, these groups are a minority in Church history. One of the most significant movements that would dramatically change this began in 1827, when several groups of Anglican Christians gathered to meet in Dublin, Ireland, for informal Bible study and sharing the Lord's Supper. With the conviction that the Bible was their ultimate source of authority, this group began conducting formal meetings, which eventually resulted in the formation of what came to be known as the Plymouth Brethren. This group believed that the Anglican Church had abandoned many of the ancient doctrines of the apostolic Church, particularly those concerning the ongoing role of Israel in the plan of God and the future glorious restoration of the Jewish people and their kingdom. This movement eventually crossed the ocean to the United States, where it caught on like wildfire. In time, large segments of Christendom came to reject the long-held view that Israel has been cast off and spurned by God and replaced by the Christian Church. Since the rebirth of the state of Israel in 1948, these numbers have swelled even larger. In more recent years, however, the old controversy seems to have been reignited, and it will no doubt continue to rage until the return of Jesus. This chapter will briefly introduce and explain the positions of the two conflicting camps.

THE RESTORATIONIST CAMP

Before defining the specific tenets of what I am calling "restorationism," it is important to explain how this camp views and interprets the Bible. Restorationists begin with the conviction that the Bible should simply be taken at face value. It calls for a straightforward, natural reading of the Scriptures, a rational literalism, if you will. Restorationists believe that although portions of the Bible are sometimes difficult to understand, it is most certainly not beyond the average person's ability to read and comprehend. One does not need an ascended guru to teach him how to understand the Bible. This is not to devalue the importance of teachers and responsible scholarship within the body of Christ—no doubt, we need more responsible scholars. But the Bible was not written exclusively for ivory-tower theologians, who then teach it to the average person. The Bible was ultimately written for any common believer who diligently and humbly applies himself or herself to understanding its words, context, and meaning. It is out of this view of the Scriptures that restorationists hold to the following three eschatological doctrines:

> **RESTORATIONISM.**[1] This view believes that the promises made to the sons of Israel through the great covenants are yet to be fulfilled. When Jesus returns, all Israel will be saved and the kingdom of Israel will be restored in the land that was promised to Abraham. Jesus will rule over the Jewish people as their king and as sovereign of all the earth.

> **FUTURISM.** This view sees the overwhelming emphasis of biblical prophecy as pertaining to the future events that

surround the return of Jesus. We might divide these events into the following three categories: (1) the events that precede the coming of Jesus, (2) the actual return of Jesus, and (3) the establishment of Jesus's kingdom for one thousand years. This view was shared by the prophets, Jesus, the apostles, and the earliest Christians.

PREMILLENNIALISM. This is the view that all of the descriptions throughout the Bible of the coming kingdom of God that will be established here on this earth after Jesus returns are to be taken literally. As we will see, this also was the position held by the prophets, Jesus, the apostles, and the earliest Christians.

Restorationists affirm that it is only by interpreting the Scriptures through the lens of these three perspectives that the Bible in general, and biblical prophecy specifically, truly makes sense. Whenever the Church loses an Israel-centric, restorationist, futurist, premillennialist understanding of the Scriptures, not only does it quickly lose proper vision of the Lord's prophetic calendar; it also loses an understanding of the very Gospel and deviates from fulfilling its primary mandate in the earth. We will discuss all of these things in more detail as we move forward.

THE SUPERSESSIONIST CAMP

In stark contrast to those who embrace restorationism, futurism, and premillennialism are those who tend to take a much more non-literal, allegorical approach to understanding the Scriptures. It is out of this view of the Scriptures that this camp holds to the following three theological positions:

SUPERSESSIONISM. This view, commonly known as "replacement theology," holds that the Christian Church has superseded or replaced Israel as the people of God. In fact, according to a popular document written in 2002 and posted on the website of Knox Theological Seminary, "the inheritance promises that God gave to Abraham . . . do not apply to any particular ethnic group, but to the church of Jesus Christ, the true Israel."[2] The document was signed by hundreds of prominent evangelical leaders, pastors, and professors.

As articulated by Albertus Pieters, a frequently cited supersessionist: "The Visible Christian Church being now the new covenant Israel, those whom we call "The Jews" are outsiders, cut-off branches, having no more connection with either promises or prophecies than any Gentile group. Those now called 'Jews,' . . . have . . . no prophetic destiny, except a continuance of their sad and bitter state . . . The closed book of Israel's history will not be reopened."[3]

While not every modern supersessionist is this blunt or harsh when articulating his or her views, Pieters has very accurately described the historical supersessionist position. According to this perspective, as the "New Israel," the Church has now become the inheritor of all of the promises and blessings (but not any of the curses) that were formerly given to Israel. Supersessionism holds that Israel's lack of faithfulness to God was so persistent that eventually the Lord permanently stripped her of the unique calling and election that she held throughout the Old Testament period. Other terms sometimes used to describe supersessionism (by those who have sought to create less offensive varieties of supersessionism) are "fulfillment theology" or "inclusion theology." Supersessionism stands in direct conflict with restorationism.

PRETERISM. This is the belief that the overwhelming majority of biblical prophecy has already been fulfilled. Preterism interprets most of the passages that speak of the "last days" or the "end times" as having been fulfilled in the events that surrounded AD 70 when the Roman legions destroyed

Jerusalem and the Jewish Temple. Preterists are not in agreement among themselves concerning exactly how much has already been fulfilled in the past, so some embrace "partial preterism" while others believe in "full preterism." Preterism most often holds that there is no future "great tribulation," no "Antichrist," no "mark of the beast," no "great apostasy," or many of the other things often associated with the last days before the return of Jesus. All of these things are often seen as having been fulfilled in AD 70. Full preterism even goes so far as to say the return of Jesus metaphorically occurred in that year. Preterism stands in sharp conflict with futurism as described earlier.

AMILLENNIALISM. People who hold this view point reject the idea that after Jesus returns, there will be a millennial (one-thousand-year) period wherein Jesus will rule over the nations on the throne of David from Jerusalem to fulfill all of God's promises made to the Jewish people through the Abrahamic covenant. Amillennialism interprets the various references to the millennial period in the Scriptures allegorically or spiritually. Because these passages are not interpreted literally, amillennialism holds that the Church is essentially now in the Millennium. A more optimistic and triumphalist variation of amillennialism, called *postmillennialism*, holds that the Church is moving beyond the persecution of the first century to a triumphal and victorious state, progressively conquering and Christianizing the world before Jesus returns. Both perspectives (amillennialism and postmillennialism) stand in fundamental conflict with premillennialism.

It is essential to recognize that while each of these doctrinal views (supersessionism, preterism, and amillennialism) relate to different issues within scripture, they are in fact, all logically connected and inseparably linked. If one holds to supersessionism—and if he is consistent—one will also hold to preterism and amillennialism. It is also important to understand that because these doctrines are so connected, if one is shown to be in clear and direct conflict with the Scriptures, then all three collapse together. Let's consider the relationship of supersessionism to both preterism and amillennialism.

THE SUPERSESSIONIST ROOTS OF PRETERISM

If one holds to the notion that God has essentially divorced Israel from her status as the elect people of God, as supersessionism does, some glaring difficulties immediately arise. For example, all of the biblically prophesied wars and battles that occur just before the return of Jesus take place specifically in and around Jerusalem and Israel. As we will see going forward, a broad range of scriptures thoroughly testify to this fact. This is an insurmountable problem for supersessionism. After all, what sense would it make for the nations of the earth, driven by Satan, to go to war against Israel, a nation that no longer has any special relevance to God whatsoever? If God is done with Israel, then why would Satan have such a specific and focused intention to destroy them? If supersessionism were true, then Satan's rage would be almost exclusively directed at Christians, not Israel. Not only is this contrary to the present global reality, but it is also not at all the story that the Scriptures tell.

Preterism as a method of interpreting the Scriptures was created out of necessity to support supersessionism. It is simply the application of supersessionism to the events that precede the return of Jesus. Preterism seeks to reinterpret the prophetic Scriptures that speak of the last-days gathering of the nations against Jerusalem as having already taken place in history, most often in AD 70, when the Roman armies destroyed Jerusalem and the Temple. Within the worldview of supersessionism, the events of that year define the moment in history when God declared his final decree of divorce from the corporate Nation of Israel and transferred all of his favor to the Christian Church. If you consider the various sermons and books of any number of supersessionist-preterist teachers, you will find an extremely lopsided emphasis on AD 70 and almost no emphasis whatsoever on our "blessed hope" (Titus 2:13), the return of Jesus. Instead of emphasizing the coming salvation and restoration of Israel (Acts 1:6–7; Rom. 11:26), supersessionists-preterists emphasize the alleged divorce of, and dissolution of, national Israel. For this reason, among the various names that one could use to refer to supersessionism, "divorce theology" would be both fair and accurate.

Reality, of course, has not made it easy for supersessionists-preterists. Since 1948 they have had to face the embarrassing problem of the miraculous rebirth of the State of Israel. Supersessionist-preterists must reject any suggestion that the modern-day State of Israel has anything to do with the sovereignty or the will of God. No doubt, Israel is truly a briar in the side of those who hold to this view. We will explore these matters in much more detail as we proceed.

THE SUPERSESSIONIST ROOTS OF AMILLENNIALISM

Amillennialism is also a logical extension of supersessionism. Whereas preterism is simply the application of supersessionism to the events that come before the return of Jesus, amillennialism is the application of supersessionism to the events that follow Jesus's return. The reason again is clear. While the prophets all speak with such great detail and specificity of a time when Jesus the Jewish King will rule from the throne of David in Jerusalem over a restored Jewish kingdom, such a reality can have absolutely no place in a supersessionist world, where Israel has been forever rejected by God.

The following chart shows the relationship of supersessionism and restorationism to the correlating doctrines that they logically require and produce:

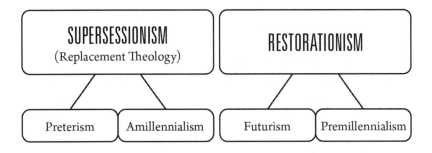

DOES THE NEW TESTAMENT REINTERPRET THE OLD TESTAMENT?

An essential difference between the two camps is the general manner in which they interpret the Bible and view the relationship of the Old and New Testaments. As already stated, restorationism approaches the Bible in a natural way, according to the manner and order in which it was revealed. Restorationists realize that to properly understand the New Testament, one must first understand the Old Testament.

The supersessionist method of interpretation, however, approaches the Bible in reverse. It begins with the New Testament and then seeks to reinterpret or completely revise the original meaning of the Old Testament. Because supersessionists begin with the view that God is done with the Jews, when they look to the many promises made to the Jewish people throughout the Old Testament, they see a clear conflict with the New Testament. To resolve this, they turned to the Greek method of allegorizing or spiritualizing any passage in conflict with their supersessionist worldview.

Although supersessionism holds that "Israel" in the Old Testament is to be reinterpreted as being an advance metaphor for the Church, this process of "reinterpretation" actually applies to several other related issues, such as (1) the land of Israel, (2) Jerusalem, and (3) the Jewish Temple. Consider the words of N. T. Wright, a prominent supersessionist theologian, who discusses his belief that Jesus altered the meaning of the land of Israel and the kingdom of God:

[Jesus] had not come to rehabilitate *the symbol of the holy land, but to subsume it within a different fulfillment of the kingdom,* which would embrace the whole creation. . . . Jesus spent his whole ministry redefining what the kingdom meant. He refused to give up the symbolic language of the kingdom, but filled it with such *new content* that, as we have seen, *he powerfully subverted Jewish expectations.*[4]

Commenting on Wright's interpretive approach, Dalton Thomas unpacks some of the profound implications:

According to Wright, [the promise of the Old Testament] has been emptied of its original substance and "filled" with another; something "new." That which was promised to Abraham was never intended to be conceived the way it was declared but rather, as a "symbol" that has been "redefined." This "redefinition" is so radical that thousands of years of "Jewish expectation" of the fulfillment of God's immutable word and purposes have been "powerfully subverted."[5]

According to the *Merriam-Webster's Dictionary,* the meaning of "subvert" is "to overturn or overthrow from the foundation" or "to pervert or corrupt by an undermining of . . . faith."[6] While very few supersessionists like to admit it, the view they espouse is precisely that: *an effort to overturn, undermine, and overthrow the promises of the Old Testament to the Jewish people.* Needless to say, Jesus did not come to "subvert" the Old Testament promises of God. He came the first time to provide atonement for humankind. When He returns, however, He will bring the promises made to Abraham, Isaac, Jacob, and David to fruition, taking them from mere promises to established reality.

I have a firm conviction that there is a fundamental unity of the Scriptures, a consistency between the New and the Old Testaments. The two in no way are in conflict. The same God who inspired the Old Testament inspired the New Testament. As the old adage goes,

"The New is in the Old concealed; the Old is in the New revealed." The New Testament expands upon and more fully reveals what was introduced in the Old Testament. This is absolutely true. But to say that something was hinted at in the Old Testament but more fully explained in the New Testament is far different from saying that the New Testament actually changes, abrogates, "redefines," "subverts" or "overthrows" the Old Testament promises to Israel. On this point, I find myself in complete agreement with J. C. Ryle, the eighteenth-century reformed expositor who perfectly articulated the problem with the supersessionist method of (re)interpreting the Scriptures: "What I protest against is, the habit of allegorizing plain sayings of the Word of God concerning the future history of the nation of Israel, and explaining away the fullness of the contents in order to accommodate them to the Gentile Church. I believe the habit to be unwarranted by anything in Scripture, and to draw after it a long train of evil consequences."[7]

We will consider these "evil consequences" as we move forward. For now, however, let us simply say that the job of any responsible teacher of the Word of God is to help fellow believers better understand the meaning of Scripture more clearly—not to deconstruct, reinterpret, and modify what it is obviously saying. Let us conclude with another comment from J. C. Ryle. I believe it is a very appropriate exhortation for all of us, and one we will seek to adhere to throughout this book:

> Cultivate the habit of reading prophecy with a single eye to the literal meaning of its proper names. Cast aside the old traditional idea that Jacob, and Israel, and Judah, and Jerusalem, and Zion must always mean the Gentile Church, and that predictions about the second Advent are to be taken spiritually, and first Advent predictions literally. Be just, and honest, and fair. If you expect the Jews to take the 53rd of Isaiah literally, be sure you take the 54th and 60th and 62nd literally also.[8]

In other words, if we expect Jews to take literally the prophecy of Isaiah 53, which so clearly speaks of a suffering Messiah who makes atonement for the sins of His people, then we must be consistent and take the prophecies of Isaiah 54, 60, and 62, which speak of the future restoration of the Jewish Kingdom in an equally literal manner. Supersessionists are quick to apply all of Israel's blessings to the Church (themselves), but do not apply Israel's judgments—or even the mere threat of judgment—to the Church. In this sense, supersessionism is a deeply inconsistent approach to interpreting the Bible.

In the next three chapters, we will see how the restorationist camp and the supersessionist camp interpret the great covenantal promises of God in two radically different ways.

THE ABRAHAMIC COVENANT

Before anyone can truly understand the meaning of the New Testament, there are some foundational issues in the Old Testament that must first be understood. Hands down, premier among these issues are the four great biblical covenants. I am speaking of (1) the Abrahamic covenant, (2) the Mosaic covenant, (3) the Davidic covenant, and (4) the new covenant. Amazingly, though the covenants are the very foundation of the entire biblical story, the majority of Christians know very little about them. If the Church were properly informed concerning these great biblical covenants—what their purposes are, how they relate to one another, and how they differ—then the entire debate and controversy between restorationism and supersessionism would dissolve. We will begin with the most foundational covenant of all, the one upon which all the others are built.

GOD MADE A PROMISE

To understand not only where Israel's story began, but where God's entire plan of redemption began, realize that it is summarized in one simple statement: *God made a promise.* This promise, it is fair to say, is one of the most significant and fundamental themes of the entire Bible, dominating the pages of the Old and New Testaments alike. Not only is the Abrahamic covenant the very foundation for the Lord's plan of redemption, but it has also become the hinge of history—

the primary driving factor behind the single most prominent global spiritual and geopolitical conflict in the earth today.

The promise was made to Abram, who would later be renamed Abraham—which of course is why it has come to be called "the Abrahamic covenant." There are three critical aspects of the Abrahamic covenant that must be recognized:

1. The Abrahamic covenant is a promise that was made specifically to the descendants of Abraham, through Isaac, and then Jacob (who was later renamed Israel).

2. The primary emphasis of the promise concerned a very specific and literal piece of land on this earth.

3. The promise made through the Abrahamic covenant is ongoing, irrevocable, and everlasting.

Supersessionism, it should be mentioned, in varying degrees denies one or even all three of these elements of the Abrahamic covenant. But as we will see, the broad scriptural testimony concerning each of these issues is clear, consistent, and complete.

THE COVENANT WITH ABRAHAM

As most who are familiar with the story know, the Lord called Abram out of the land of Ur in Chaldea, or in modern terms, Iraq. Sometime after leaving Ur, we are told, "The word of the LORD came to Abram in a vision, saying, 'Do not fear, Abram, I am a shield to you; your reward shall be very great'" (Gen. 15:1). Of course, upon hearing that he would be given a "very great" reward, Abram asked God how he could obtain it, since he didn't have any son to pass his reward on to. The Lord responded and assured Abram that his great reward would not be given to any mere servant in his household, but would in fact be given to his own flesh-and-blood son "who will come forth from your own body" (v. 4). What happened next is beautifully poetic. The Lord took Abram outside under the night sky and had him "look toward the heavens" (v. 5). I imagine the sky that night was radiant with the glow of ten million shining ambassadors of promise. Twenty years ago, I spent a few nights with an Arab Bedouin family out in the Jordanian desert, in what is called *Wadi Rum*. The name means "Valley of the Moon," because its dramatic, jutting mesas look like the surface of the moon. But having seen the stars at night from such diverse places as mountain peaks far from the city lights to miles offshore in the Atlantic Ocean long before daybreak, never before have I seen such a marvelously spectacular number of stars as when sitting on the desert floor in Wadi Rum. The stars there are as thick as a mighty river flooding over its banks, silently sweeping across the sky. I imagine that what Abram saw that night was no different. As an uncountable number of stars glittered above him, the Lord said to Abram, "One who will come forth from your own body, he shall be your heir . . . Now look toward the heavens, and count the stars, if you are able to count them. So shall your descendants be" (vv. 4–5).

According to the Scriptures, at that moment, not only did Abram believe God that he would have a son and many descendants, but Abram actually trusted God and put his faith in the one who would come forth from his own loins, accomplishing all that God had just promised. As a result of Abram's trust, the Lord, "reckoned it to him as righteousness" (v. 6). It is this episode that the apostle Paul used as the basis for his overwhelming emphasis, throughout his epistles, on salvation being attained through faith (Rom. 4:3; Gal. 3:6).

After this, God had Abram bring Him "a three year old heifer, and a three year old female goat, and a three year old ram, and a turtle-dove, and a young pigeon" (Gen. 15:9). Abram brought these and as instructed, he "cut them in two" (v. 10), arranging the halves opposite each other, essentially creating a path between them. As the sun was setting, "a deep sleep fell upon Abram; and behold, terror and great darkness fell upon him" (v. 12). Then, out of the darkness, the Lord appeared in the very strange form of "a smoking oven and a flaming torch" (v. 17), and He walked between the pieces of the dead animals.

A very important aspect of this story that every Christian must be aware of is that only God walked down the aisle. As all of this was taking place, Abram had fallen into "a deep sleep" (v. 12). The point is that this was not a bilateral agreement made between two parties. It was a unilateral and unconditional promise made by God to Abraham's descendants. As such, God will be faithful to His promise. It is not contingent on the faithfulness of Abraham's descendants, to whom the promise was made. Additionally, although the promise would pass through his son Isaac—and Isaac's son Jacob—the ultimate heir of the promises was actually Jesus the Messiah. He was the one in whom Abraham placed his faith. We will discuss this much more as we move forward.

It's interesting that while Christian theologians most often simply refer to this covenant as "the Abrahamic covenant," among Jews it is often referred to as the *Brit bein HaBetarim*, which means the "covenant between the parts." But what was God's reason for cutting the animals in half and walking in between them? Why did He use such a graphic and bloody display?

GOD'S COVENANT UNTO DEATH

Walter C. Kaiser Jr. is truly a shining light among conservative evangelical Old Testament scholars. Having authored and published more than forty books, Dr. Kaiser served as the academic dean and professor of Old Testament at Trinity Evangelical Divinity School for more than twenty years and then as president of Gordon-Conwell Theological Seminary. He is respected by all within the theological community, so it was a tremendous honor for me to be able to visit with Dr. Kaiser to discuss, among other things, the issue of supersessionism/replacement theology and the Abrahamic covenant.

As I pulled up to the Kaisers' family farm less than a mile from the shores of Lake Michigan, Walter and his wife, Margaret, sat chatting on the front porch, enjoying a gorgeous late summer afternoon. Roaming through the yard were several variously colored llamas who apparently also call the Kaiser farm their home.

Once inside, to my extreme delight, Margaret invited me to peruse Dr. Kaiser's personal library. As I scanned the rows of tightly arranged shelves, I thought about the profound impact this man has had in the field of Old Testament studies and about the many students who have had the benefit of sitting under him. Dr. Kaiser walked in, darted around the shelving, and then reemerged to hand me a fresh copy of his two latest books. Despite being retired from his formal role as president of Gordon-Conwell, and now in his eighties, his mind, wit, and productivity remain as focused as ever. We went into his living room and sat down.

Soon our conversation turned to the issue of the Abrahamic covenant. With a smile, he took a quick breath and then like a laser, cut directly to heart of the matter, addressing the vividly graphic and emphatic manner in which God made his promise to Abraham: "In Genesis 15, it was God Himself who walked in between the pieces," he said. "They cut a covenant. The word to make a covenant is to 'cut' a covenant. And they cut the pieces, one half of the animal on each side, forming an aisle down the middle. So there were three cut animals and then two birds. And God walked between the pieces and said, in effect, 'May I, God, die like these animals if I do not keep what I have promised here.' So when the Church brought in replacement theology and embraced a supersessionist mentality in which they sat now in the chair that belonged to Abraham, Isaac, Jacob, and his descendants, they took away what God had promised on the pledge of his life!" He paused briefly, then finished with, "*So I think God is going to fulfill that.*"

In choosing to carry out the covenant in such a visually bloody and graphic manner, the Lord was making a profound and deeply emphatic statement. Dr. Kaiser's comments confirmed all of my own feelings. Believing that God will fulfill His promises to Abraham is to affirm the very integrity, reliability, and faithfulness of God to His word and to His promises. Simply stated, if any Christian desires to be called *a child of Abraham*, then believing the things that Abraham believed is a basic requirement. (See Romans 4:6; Galatians 3:7; 1 Peter 3:6.) God is going to give the land to Abraham's descendants. If we say that God is not going to literally fulfill His promises to the faithful remnant among the Jewish people, how then can we as Christians turn around and claim to trust Him with regard to our own salvation? I agree with Dr. Kaiser, and I hope you do as well. I believe that God is going to fulfill His promises. He is a promise keeper.

But what exactly did God promise? This is where it becomes essential to examine His actual words very carefully.

WHERE IS THE PROMISED LAND?

As the covenant-making ceremony ended, the Lord defined the region that he was giving to Abraham and his descendants. The boundaries of the land that was promised were incredibly precise, and it encompassed an area far greater than the relatively small segment of land that is today called the State of Israel. Here is the specific land that the Lord promised: "From the river of Egypt as far as the great river, the river Euphrates: the Kenite and the Kenizzite and the Kadmonite and the Hittite and the Perizzite and the Rephaim and the Amorite and the Canaanite and the Girgashite and the Jebusite" (Gen. 15:18–21).

Based on these descriptions, and other passages where the boundaries are reiterated, it is easy to define the "promised land" according to modern national and natural markers. The promised land is defined according to the following boundary:

The northwestern boundary of the promised land is simply the "Great Sea" or the "Western Sea." This is, of course, the Mediterranean (cf. Numbers 34:6; Ezekiel 47:20).

The southwestern boundary of the promised land is defined by "the river of Egypt" (Hebrew: *Nachal Mitzrayim*). Scholars are divided concerning the identification of this river. Some Bible commentaries identify it with Wadi el-Arish, or the "brook of Egypt," and some parallel passages seem to confirm this (Ex. 23:31; Ezek.

47:19). Wadi el-Arish flows from the southern border of Taba, just south of the modern Israeli city of Eilat, and extends north to the city of Arish, which sits on the Mediterranean Sea, roughly forty miles west of the Gaza Strip in the Sinai Peninsula. In other words, this would mean that the promised land does not include the majority of the Sinai Peninsula. There are some problems with this view however, and the more likely view is that the brook of Egypt is what is called the Pelusian arm of the Nile—an arm that no longer runs with water. If this is the case, then the promised land would include virtually all of the Sinai Peninsula.

The northern boundary of the promised land extends from the Mediterranean Sea at least as far north as Sidon (perhaps to Beirut) in Lebanon, and then through Syria eastward to the Euphrates river (cf. Gen. 15:18; Deut. 11:24; Ezek. 47:17; Josh. 1:4).

The eastern boundary of the promised land seems to extend from the Euphrates in the north, southwest through Syria, along the eastern side of the Sea of Galilee, (or "Lake Kinneret," sometimes translated "Sea of Chinnereth" or the "eastern sea") including much of southern Syria and all the Golan Heights. From the southern end of the Sea of Galilee, the boundary lines follow the Jordan River, which flows south to the Dead Sea. (cf. Num. 34:11–12; Ezek. 47:18).

Within the various passages that detail the boundaries of the promised land, there are some reference points that we cannot be entirely sure of, but the general parameters are fairly clear. And while most believe that the "promised land" only includes the modern-day State of Israel, the truth is that the promise also included a large segment of the Sinai Desert, much of modern-day Lebanon, a large segment of southern Syria, a large portion of Jordan, all of the Golan Heights, as well the West Bank and Gaza.

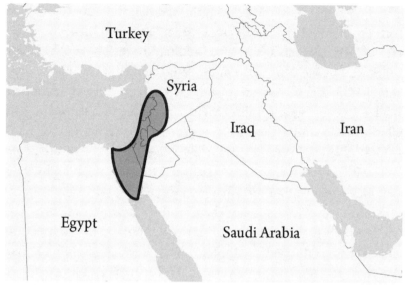

Map of Actual Land Promised

WHEN AND WHERE WILL THE PROMISES BE FULFILLED?

Anyone familiar with the geography and national boundaries of the Middle East knows that never before in the history of the Jewish people have they ever actually possessed all of the land promised by the Lord through the Abrahamic covenant. When considering this prophecy, then, the believer is faced with four possible conclusions:

1. The Lord simply failed to keep His promises.

2. The Lord never intended to literally keep His promises. The land promises were always intended to be understood spiritually, referring to the blessings of being in Christ.

3. The promise will never be fulfilled literally according to the specifications given by the Lord, but will instead be fulfilled spiritually in "heaven" or in some heavenly "New Earth" that has no direct correlation to the present earth or any of the regions specified within the actual covenant.

4. While the Lord has not yet fulfilled His promises literally, He remains committed to doing so in the future when He returns.

Of these options, the only feasible one is the fourth. This is the view of restorationism, which sees the Lord as being a genuinely faithful promise keeper. Only this view acknowledges the Lord to be a God whose integrity and word can be trusted. The fulfillment of the Lord's promises within the Abrahamic covenant to the Jewish people continue to await their yet-future fulfillment on this present earth.

ON EARTH OR IN HEAVEN?

When faced with the abundantly clear promises of God concerning the promised land, supersessionists-amillennialists must perform a bit of theological contortionism. Many of the old-school amillennialists argue that the Lord has no plan to give any actual earthly land to anyone, but is simply planning on giving "heaven" to those who inherit His promises. One such "heavenly amillennialist" is theologian Gary M. Burge, a professor at Wheaton College and an outspoken proponent of supersessionism and amillennialism. In his book *Jesus and the Land*, Burge refers to the Jerusalem which Abraham looked forward to as being "in heaven—not an earthly city."[1] To support his case Burge cites Hebrews 11:13–16:

> All these died in faith, without receiving the promises, but having seen them and having welcomed them from a distance, and having confessed that *they were strangers and exiles on the earth.* For those who say such things make it clear that they are seeking a country of their own. And indeed if they had been thinking of that country from which they went out, they would have had opportunity to return. But as it is, they desire a better country, that is, *a heavenly one.* Therefore God is not ashamed to be called their God; for He has prepared a city for them. (Emphasis added)

Is Burge correct? What is this passage intending to convey when it says that Abraham was a stranger and exile on the earth, while looking for a "heavenly" city? The answer is actually quite simple. The Hebrew or biblical worldview holds that when Jesus returns, He will destroy the present sinful and corrupt systems as well as the satanic principalities that govern and hold sway over the earth and establish His own divine rule over the whole world. The elimination of these wicked systems and the establishment of his own divine government is what is meant by the age to come as being "heavenly." It is not speaking of the location of the coming kingdom, but the nature of the coming kingdom. Make no mistake: the Scriptures are quite clear that Jesus will indeed restore and redeem this present physical earth. Consider how clearly the apostle Paul spoke concerning this very matter:

> For *the anxious longing of the creation waits eagerly* for the revealing of the sons of God. For *the creation was subjected to futility*, not willingly, but because of Him who subjected it, in hope that *the creation itself also will be set free from its slavery to corruption into the freedom of the glory of the children of God.* For we know that *the whole creation groans and suffers the pains of childbirth together until now.* And not only this, but *also we ourselves*, having the first fruits of the Spirit, even we ourselves groan within ourselves, *waiting eagerly for our adoption as sons, the redemption of our body.* (Rom. 8:19-23; emphasis added)

According to Paul, it is *this present physical creation* that is groaning, anxiously awaiting the time when it will no longer be subject to "futility" but will instead be "set free . . . into the glory of the children of God." Even as there is a direct correlation between the bodies we presently possess and the immortal bodies that we will possess after Jesus returns (see 1 Corinthians 15:35–44), so also is there a direct correlation between the present earth and the future earth that Jesus will rule, "set free," and redeem. The earth will be under new management, as it were; the old earthly and sinful systems will be done away with as it comes under the full sway and control of the heavenly King. This is the meaning of the "heavenly" city that Abraham longed for. In no way does this mean that Abraham's inheritance will be anywhere other than on this actual planet. The meek will "inherit *the earth*," says Matthew 5:5 (emphasis added). If the Lord promised Abraham's descendants the actual land between the River of Egypt and the Euphrates, then that is exactly what the Lord will give to them in the age to come.

CHANGING GOD'S WORDS

While Burge's celestial vision of the coming kingdom is still popular among some amillennialists, many others, those more up to speed on the problems with classic amillennialism, call themselves "earthly amillennialists." They argue that the Lord will in fact rule on the earth. The problem, however, is that they also argue that the earth He will rule will be *fundamentally different* from the land He actually promised. In his book *Kingdom Come*, well-known pastor and author Sam Storms, in referring to the Abrahamic covenant, states, "I believe this promise will be *literally* fulfilled, but not merely or even primarily in the land of Canaan."[2] I scratched my head when I read this statement. How can one say that the promises will be "literally" fulfilled, but in way *completely different* from how God spoke them? This is an oxymoron. Supersessionist-amillennialists such as Storms believe that after Jesus returns, we will immediately enter into the "eternal state" without an intervening transitional period. The inheritance, according to Storms, will not merely be the promised land, but in fact the whole earth, albeit a very different earth from the one on which we now find ourselves. But if this is the case, if the land that will be provided by the Lord does not literally correlate to the specific land promised, then why in the world did the Lord even bother to so precisely define the land using such literal and natural boundary markers as the Euphrates, the Great Sea, and the River of Egypt? Why would He use all of these very specific markers if none of them will even exist? For example, Storms says that immediately after Jesus returns, there will no longer be any literal sea. We must ask then, why would the Lord specifically use "the Great Sea" as a distinct boundary for the promised land if it won't even exist during the time that His promises are fulfilled? This doesn't make any sense. Several other such examples could be considered. This is just one example of how the amillennialist position simply cannot be reconciled with the biblical testimony. By claiming that He will not literally fulfill what He promised, amillennialists portray the Lord as either incredibly confusing at best or as a deceiver and a waffling promise breaker at worst.

To defend his case, Storms appeals to an argument used by G. K. Beale, another well-known supersessionist-amillennialist. In his book *The Temple and the Church's Mission*, Beale begins by describing a father who in 1900 makes a promise to his young son to buy him a horse and buggy when he grows up and gets married. Years later, when his son is actually grown and married, he doesn't actually buy him a horse and buggy, but instead buys him an automobile. This is where the bending of all sound logic begins:

> During the early years of expectation, the son reflects on the particular size of the buggy, its contours and style, its beautiful leather seats and the size and breed of horse that would draw the buggy. Perhaps the father had knowledge from early experimentation elsewhere that the invention of the automobile was on the horizon, but coined the promise to his son in terms that his son would understand. Years later, when the son marries, the father gives the couple an automobile, which has since been invented and mass-produced . . . Is this not a "literal" fulfillment of the promise?[3]

The answer is a resounding *no*. In no way could it be considered a "literal" fulfillment of his promise. Let me share a more accurate analogy. If I specifically promise my son all of Colorado Springs, but instead give him the entire state of Montana, I have not literally fulfilled my promise, no matter how much bigger my gift may be.

If I very specifically promise my daughter a 2006 Ford Focus, but instead give her a 2014 Maserati, I have not *literally* fulfilled my promise. Making something bigger or better does not make it literal. If the Lord very specifically promised the descendants of Abraham the land of Canaan "from the River of Egypt" and the "Great Sea to the Euphrates," but instead gives them another world altogether— one that doesn't even include these bodies of water—then He has not *literally* fulfilled His promises. Yet it is precisely this kind of flowery-yet-fallacious argument that so often passes as *profound* among those who seek to defend the theology of supersessionism and amillennialism.

Further, as egregious as it is to alter the clear meaning of the Lord's promises as amillennialists do, what is even worse is that after employing such fallacious arguments, they then scorn a more straightforward reading of the Bible. British scholar N.T Wright unapologetically mocks the literalist interpretation of those who look for the literal fulfillment of God's promises using the derisive phrase "crass literalism."

TO WHOM WERE THE PROMISES MADE?

Now that we know *where* the promise will be fulfilled, we must ask for *whom* will they be fulfilled? As we have already seen, the promises made to Abraham concerned his physical descendants. But did that include *all* of them? No, for as Genesis 25 shows, Abraham had eight sons altogether. But according to the Scriptures, the promises were only made to the descendants of his one son Isaac (see Genesis 17:15–21; 21:9–13). The Lord specifically told Abraham that it would be Isaac and not Ishmael through whom his descendants would inherit the land promised. Later the promise was extended to Isaac's son Jacob/Israel (see Genesis 28:13) but not to his brother, Esau. While it is clear that the Lord loves the descendants of Ishmael, the land promises of the Abrahamic covenant were made solely to the direct descendants of Jacob, the corporate family or nation of Israel.

In an effort to undermine the Lord's ongoing commitment to the modern-day Jewish people, the descendants of Abraham through Isaac and Jacob's line, many determined supersessionists and anti-Israel activists seek to conceal or distort the scriptural testimony on these matters. Carl Medearis, a popular author, sought-after speaker, and outspoken proponent of the anti-Israel movement, provides us with a good example of fairly brazen vandalism of the Scriptures. On his ministry blog, in answering the question, "What is your position on Israel?" Medearis shockingly responded, "The land was given to the descendants of Abraham—his descendants are Isaac and Ishmael. The descendants of Abraham, do in fact, live in the land. God has fulfilled this promise!"[4]

I've met Carl on a few occasions. He is a tremendously personable guy and an amazing storyteller, and I am confident that he loves Jesus. But it pains me to say so bluntly that his theology is truly abysmal and even dangerous. Unfortunately, the comment I just cited is only one example of the kind of distortion of the biblical testimony that many supersessionists must employ in order to justify their position.

So did God promise, as Medearis claims, to give the land of Israel to both Isaac and Ishmael? Even the most basic review of the passages that address these matters reveal the answer to be no. In fact, if we go back to the Genesis 17 account, we find that Abraham specifically entreated the Lord concerning Ishmael, requesting that he be the recipient of the Lord's promises. But the Lord flatly rebuffed his request:

"And Abraham said to God, "Oh that Ishmael might live before You!" But God said, *"No, but Sarah your wife will bear you a son, and you shall call his name Isaac; and I will establish My covenant with him for an everlasting covenant for his descendants after him.* "As for Ishmael, I have heard you; behold, I will bless him, and will make him fruitful and will multiply him exceedingly. He shall become the father of twelve princes, and I will make him a great nation. *"But My covenant I will establish with Isaac, whom Sarah will bear to you at this season next year."* (Gen. 17:18–21; emphasis added)

Years later, when Ishmael was fourteen and Isaac was still just a baby, Sarah saw that Ishmael was mocking (or "persecuting," as Paul wrote in in Galatians 4:29) his younger brother, Isaac: "Therefore she said to Abraham, 'Drive out this maid [Hagar] and her son, for the son of this maid shall not be an heir with my son Isaac.' The matter distressed Abraham greatly because of his son" (Gen. 21:10–11). If Ishmael were in fact the coheir or co-recipient of the Lord's promises, then of course, the Lord would have intervened against Sarah's wishes. But instead, the Scriptures reveal He actually agreed with Sarah and commanded Abraham to expel both Hagar and her son, Ishmael, permanently out of the family camp: "But God said to Abraham, 'Do not be distressed because of the lad and your maid; whatever Sarah tells you, listen to her, *for through Isaac your descendants shall be named.* And of the son of the maid I will make a nation also, because he is your descendant'" (Gen. 21:12–13; emphasis added. See also Gen. 28:10–16).

It would be difficult to be any more clear. The Lord repeatedly told Abraham that it would be Isaac and not Ishmael through whom his descendants would inherit the land promise. Later the promise was made to Jacob/Israel (see Genesis 28:13) but not to his brother, Esau. Again, while it is clear that the Lord loves all people, the land promises of the Abrahamic covenant were only to the corporate family or nation of Israel.

THE EVERLASTING COVENANT

As I said earlier, it is difficult to overstate the place of prominence and foundational importance that the Abrahamic covenant and the associated land promises hold within the biblical narrative. The Abrahamic covenant is the foundation upon which the Lord's entire plan of redemption is built. This is why, long after Abraham's death, the Lord's promises would be repeated a multitude of times throughout the Scriptures. After the sons of Israel had long been slaves in Egypt, it was out of faithfulness to His covenant that the Lord responded to their misery. In the midst of their suffering, the Lord identified Himself to Moses as the one who had "appeared to Abraham, Isaac, and Jacob" and established His "covenant with them, to give them the land of Canaan, the land in which they sojourned" (Ex. 6:3–4). And then, in very clear and direct fashion, the Lord promised to give that very land to "the sons of Israel" as "an everlasting possession." (vv. 5–8). Later, in 1 Chronicles 16:13–18 and Psalm 105:6–12, we are told that the Abrahamic covenant has been made with the "Sons of Jacob, His chosen ones." More important, the covenant is described as "the word which He commanded to a thousand generations . . . to Israel as an everlasting covenant." In 1 Kings 8:35–36, Israel is described as the Lord's people, to whom He has given his land as an inheritance. In Isaiah 14:1–3, the land promise is specified as having been made to the corporate "house of Jacob" and "the house of Israel." In Ezekiel 11, the Lord speaks to "the whole house of Israel, all of them"—many of whom were living in exile—and promises them, "I will gather you from the peoples and assemble you out of the countries among which you have been scattered, and I will give you the land of Israel" (vv. 15, 17). Through the prophet Amos, the Lord spoke of the eschatological restoration of "My people Israel" to "their land which I have given them" (Amos 9:14–15), never to be rooted out again.

The bottom line is that any survey of the Old Testament will reveal the clarity, specificity, and driving emphasis of God's promises as He repeated them over and over again. All in all, in the book of Deuteronomy alone, the Lord reiterated the land promises to Israel nearly seventy times. Altogether, the promises are reiterated in one way or another more than two hundred times throughout the Scriptures. There can be no question that the land promises made to the children of Israel are among the most thoroughly repeated and emphasized realities within all of the Bible.

Understanding then the prominence of the Abrahamic covenant within the biblical testimony, we are once again stunned and saddened by the comments of Carl Medearis, whose opinions this time come from a CNN online article titled "My Take: Jesus would support Palestinian statehood bid." Referring to the Abrahamic covenant promises, which, as we have just seen, dominate the biblical testimony, Medearis asks, "Rather than allowing *obscure Old Testament promises* to dictate our foreign policy, what if we stuck to the clear commands of God—love your neighbor, your enemy and the foreigner in your midst—which appear in Exodus, Leviticus and three of the four gospels?[5]

According to Medearis, the Abrahamic covenant, wherein the God of Heaven and Earth literally made a vow unto death, is little more than an "obscure Old Testament promise." Such a statement is truly grievous. If we value the biblical testimony and the words of God, then the Lord's promises to Abraham are anything but "obscure." Again, they are the very foundation for the entire plan of redemption. Medearis also seeks to create conflict where there is none. The Abrahamic covenant and the commandments to love our neighbors and our enemies are not at odds. To suggest that they are is simply a false dichotomy. The same God who made the Abrahamic covenant also gave the commandments to love our neighbors. Ultimately, Medearis's comments should not be surprising, for as was mentioned at the beginning of this chapter, a majority of Christians are largely ignorant concerning the covenants. While the Abrahamic covenant may be "obscure" to many Christians, from the emphasis placed on this foundational promise of God, it is anything other than obscure. This is why it is so essential that the Church recover a solid understanding of these most crucial matters.

CONCLUSION

In summary, God Himself made a covenant promise to Abraham. He later reiterated the promise hundreds of times throughout the

Scriptures. The primary promise He made was very specific. It was not abstract or obscure or stated in difficult-to-understand language. God promised the land from the Mediterranean Sea in the west to the Euphrates River in the northeast to the River of Egypt in the southwest. The promise was made to Abraham's physical descendants specifically through his son Isaac and then through Isaac's son Jacob/Israel. Despite the fact that God made this promise with a vow upon His very life, supersessionists-amillennialists claim that He never planned to make good on it. Instead, they argue, God will deliver on something very different from what He specified or that He never planned to give the "land" to Abraham's descendants at all, but to another people entirely. We began this chapter by stating how absolutely essential is it for all believers to understand the Abrahamic covenant. We are now beginning to understand the dramatic ramifications of remaining ignorant about this most foundational element of the grand biblical story.

4

THE MOSAIC AND DAVIDIC COVENANTS

THE MOSAIC COVENANT

Four hundred thirty years after the Abrahamic covenant was made, the Lord made another covenant with Israel, this time through Moses. The Mosaic covenant was profoundly different from the Abrahamic covenant. While the Abrahamic covenant was an unconditional, one-sided promise made by God, the Mosaic covenant was very much a two-sided legal agreement between the Lord and all of Israel. While the Abrahamic covenant is defined by the Lord repeatedly declaring "I will," the Mosaic covenant is repeatedly defined by, "If you . . . then I . . ."

Some wrongly believe that in the Mosaic covenant the Lord somehow reneged on the land promise made in the Abrahamic covenant. There is no truth to this whatsoever. Within the Mosaic covenant were the regulations and requirements to not only possess the land, but to remain in it: "Now, O Israel, listen to the statutes and the judgments which I am teaching you to perform, so that you may live and go in and take possession of the land which the LORD, the God of your fathers, is giving you. You shall not add to the word which I am commanding you, nor take away from it, that you may keep the commandments of the LORD your God which I command you" (Deut. 4:1–2).

If on the other hand, the Israelites violated the various laws detailed in the Mosaic covenant, then the Lord would *temporarily* remove them from the land. For example, in Deuteronomy 4, Moses warned the sons of Israel that if they acted corruptly in the land and fell into idolatry, then "you will surely perish quickly from the land where you are going over the Jordan to possess it. You shall not live long on it, but will be utterly destroyed. The LORD will scatter you among the peoples, and you will be left few in number among the nations where the LORD drives you" (vv. 26–27). But *after* such a season of exile, Moses declared, in time God would remember His promise made to them through the Abrahamic covenant and would bring them back to their land: "When you are in distress and all these things have come upon you, in the latter days you will return to the LORD your God and listen to His voice. For the LORD your God is a compassionate God; He will not fail you nor destroy you *nor forget the covenant with your fathers which He swore to them*" (vv. 30–31; emphasis added). This point is absolutely critical. While the Jews' permanent residency in the land was contingent upon their obedience to the laws given in the Mosaic covenant, the Lord *never reneged* on the initial gift of His land to His corporate people Israel as made through the Abrahamic covenant. But what if they were disobedient and the Lord expelled them from the land? Did that mean that the land was no longer theirs? Not at all. Even if they became disobedient and the Lord expelled them from the land, "their unbelief [would] not nullify the faithfulness of God . . . May it never be!" the apostle Paul wrote. "Rather, let God be found true, though every man be found a liar" (Rom. 3:3–4).

Paul's point is simple. God made an unconditional promise, and God cannot lie. The promised land belongs to the sons of Israel not because of their goodness or faithfulness, but because of God's faithfulness. Despite the stipulations of the Mosaic covenant, the Lord has never changed His mind or forgotten His promises. Biblical history shows that through the Assyrian and Babylonian invasions, Abraham's descendants indeed suffered the consequences of their disobedience and were expelled from the land, only to return in time. Later, in AD 70, through the Romans, the Jews were again exiled from the land. But in our very day, we have seen the Jewish people once more return to their land.

THE "OLD COVENANT"

One of the most common ways in which the Church's ignorance concerning the covenants is seen, is in the conflation of the Abrahamic and Mosaic covenants into one generalized, composite "old covenant." Survey a few supersessionist discussions of the covenants and you will find many vague claims that the new covenant replaces "the old covenant." Such statements, however, betray a fundamental lack of familiarity with the actual covenants. Let's consider just a couple of examples.

Alex Awad is pastor of the East Jerusalem Baptist Church, professor at Bethlehem Bible College, and one of the primary organizers of the bi-annual Christ at the Checkpoint conference. When asked, "What is the problem with American evangelicals?" Awad answered, "They are more interested in endorsing the state of Israel as God's prophetic instrument than in calling out the injustices that are being done to the Palestinian people. The message of Christianity is a universal one that is not interested in ethnicity or territory. The new covenant ushered in by the coming of messiah made the old covenant obsolete."[1]

Notice the vague reference to the "old covenant" being made obsolete by the new. Gary Burge, professor of New Testament at Wheaton College, similarly speaks of the "new covenant that abrogates the old" without qualification as to what he means by "old."[2] Neither Burge nor Awad makes any distinction between the Abrahamic covenant and the Mosaic covenant—they are simply combined into one "old covenant." However, because both Awad and Burge were specifically discussing the issue of land and Israel and not the regulations of the Mosaic covenant, we must assume they are claiming that the new covenant makes the Abrahamic covenant obsolete. As we have already seen, any such claim is simply absurd. In no way do the Scriptures allow for this. Yet it is precisely this kind of biblical illiteracy that is so common among those who are viewed as leading voices within the growing supersessionist, anti-Israel movement.

One may indeed rightly say that through the new covenant, the regulations for righteousness in the Mosaic covenant are "obsolete" (see Hebrews 7:22; 8:13), but nowhere does the New Testament even hint at the notion that the Abrahamic covenant has been laid aside or abrogated. In fact, Paul very specifically rebuffed such a claim: "What I am saying is this: the Law, which came four hundred and thirty years later, does not invalidate a covenant previously ratified by God, so as to nullify the promise. For if the inheritance is based on law, it is no longer based on a promise; but God has granted it to Abraham by means of a promise" (Gal. 3:17–18).

Beyond this, as we will see in the next chapter, the new covenant thoroughly affirms the Abrahamic covenant. It is through the new covenant that the Abrahamic covenant will be fulfilled, but that time is yet to come. Before we turn to the new covenant, however, it is essential that we first stop and consider the biblical testimony concerning the Davidic covenant.

THE DAVIDIC COVENANT

The Davidic covenant was delivered through Nathan the prophet to King David. Like the Mosaic covenant, the Davidic covenant also begins with a reiteration of the land promises made through the Abrahamic covenant: "I will also appoint a place for My people Israel and will plant them, that they may live in their own place and not be disturbed again, nor will the wicked afflict them any more as formerly, even from the day that I commanded judges to be over My people Israel; and I will give you rest from all your enemies" (2 Sam. 7:10–11).

But how will the Lord give Israel rest from her enemies in the land that He has promised? This will only come through Jesus the Messiah. For immediately following the words above, the Lord promised that a descendant of David would inherit the royal dynasty that would endure forever:

> "The Lord also declares to you that the Lord will make a house for you. When your days are complete and you lie down with your fathers, I will raise up your descendant after you, who will come forth from you, and I will establish his kingdom. He shall build a house for My name, and I will establish the throne of his kingdom forever . . . Your house and your kingdom shall endure before Me forever; your throne shall be established forever." (vv. 11b–16)

Later the covenant was summarized in 1 Chronicles 17:11–14 and 2 Chronicles 6:16. Needless to say, this covenant will be fulfilled when Jesus, a descendant of the line of David, takes the throne of David in Jerusalem. This is why the gospel of Matthew begins by declaring that Jesus is "the Son of David" (Matt. 1:1). Peter also preached that Jesus was a fulfillment of God's covenant to David (Acts 2:29–36). It is through Jesus the Messiah that the land promises of the Abrahamic covenant and the promises of a Davidic King will find their fulfillment together. Today, we continue to await that future fulfillment.

We should also highlight the fact that like the Abrahamic covenant, the Davidic Covenant is unconditional. It has not been annulled or "fulfilled." The surety of the promises made rests solely on God's faithfulness and does not depend at all on David's or Israel's obedience. The fulfillment of God's promises are something that He will bring about according to *His* everlasting faithfulness.

SUMMARY

In summary, the Abrahamic and Davidic covenants are unconditional, unilateral promises made by God to man, while the Mosaic covenant is a conditional and bilateral agreement between God and man. It is absolutely essential that the Church comes to recognize the profound difference between the promises of God as expressed in the Abrahamic and Davidic covenants and the two-way contract of the Mosaic covenant. According to Carl Medearis, "The promises of God to Israel from Deuteronomy through the prophets were always conditional."[3] This is simply not true. The promises that God made to Abraham, Isaac, Jacob, and David—to the people of Israel—are unconditional. When God makes a promise, He keeps it. Bilateral agreements may be conditional, but God's unilateral promises are not. Heaven and earth may pass away, but God's promises will never fail.

The initial land promise made through the Abrahamic covenant has become the foundational promise upon which every other covenant since that time has been built. The Mosaic covenant provides Israel with the conditions and regulations necessary to maintain unbroken occupancy of the land. The Davidic covenant, built upon the Abrahamic covenant, promised a King who will rule over Israel at the time when she inherits the land. As we will see in the next chapter, the new covenant is built on the foundation of the Abrahamic and Davidic covenants and was also made specifically with the people of Israel.

We end this chapter with a simple chart detailing the distinctions between the three covenants that we have considered thus far:

COVENANT	MADE TO	WHAT	CONDITIONAL OR UNCONDITIONAL	UNILATERAL OR BILATERAL
Abrahamic	Abraham and his descendants	God will give the land of Israel to the people of Israel forever, and all of the Gentile nations will be blessed as well.	Unconditional	One-way promise
Mosaic	The corporate nation of Israel	God issued the regulatory conditions for Israel to maintain permanent occupancy of the land	Conditional	Two-way agreement
Davidic	King David	God will raise up a descendant of King David to sit on the throne of Israel	Unconditional	One-way promise

THE NEW COVENANT

ow that we've reviewed the Abrahamic, Mosaic, and Davidic covenants, let us turn to the final covenant, known as the "new covenant." As we will see, the new covenant is the culmination and grand capstone of all the other covenants. The new covenant does not replace the Abrahamic or Davidic covenants; instead, it builds upon and establishes them. It is through the new covenant that the Lord will give His people Israel a new heart and a new spirit so they can receive the unconditional promises made in the Abrahamic and Davidic covenants.

Though many might assume that the new covenant is found only in the New Testament, it was, in fact, announced and spoken of many times throughout the Old Testament by the prophets Isaiah, Jeremiah, and Ezekiel.

THE NEW COVENANT IN ISAIAH

The first announcement of the new covenant is found in the prophet Isaiah. In this fascinating passage, before the new covenant is announced, it is preceded by a thoroughly apocalyptic description of the time of the Lord's return, when the Lord will execute justice on behalf of His people, Israel, and vengeance against the unrighteous Gentiles. "He put on righteousness like a breastplate, and a helmet of salvation on His head; and He put on garments of vengeance for clothing and wrapped Himself with zeal as a mantle. According to their deeds, so He will repay, wrath to His adversaries, recompense to His enemies; to the coastlands He will make recompense" (Isa. 59:17–18).

The first element of the prophecy that should be highlighted is the fact that it encompasses the time of the Lord's "vengeance" and "recompense" against "His adversaries." In Isaiah, this language is always used to point ultimately to the time of the Lord's return and the Day of the Lord (see Isaiah 34:8; 35:4; 61:2; 63:3–4). The Lord's vengeance among the nations, however, will have a thoroughly redemptive effect. Isaiah informs us that as a result of His chastisements, the nations will turn to Him and fear His name: "So they will fear the name of the LORD from the west and His glory from the rising of the sun, for He will come like a rushing stream which the wind of the LORD drives" (Isa. 59:19). It is out of this context that the Scriptures first announce the new covenant. Although it is not specifically referred to here as the "new covenant," it is certainly *a* new covenant, and yet future in Isaiah's day, ruling out any of the previous covenants. This new covenant was different from other covenants, first, because it was connected to the coming Messiah-Redeemer who would come to mount Zion, and second, because it entailed the Lord's Spirit forever remaining with the people of Israel. Pay special attention to this passage, as we will return to it at the end of this chapter:

> "A Redeemer will come to Zion, and to those who turn from transgression in Jacob," declares the LORD. "As for Me, this is My covenant with them," says the LORD: "My Spirit which is upon you, and My words which I have put in your mouth shall not depart from your mouth, nor from the mouth of your offspring, nor from the mouth of your offspring's offspring," says the LORD, "from now and forever." (Isa. 59:20–21)

As we will see, both the prophets Jeremiah and Ezekiel elaborated on this same covenant, describing it in great detail. And each time they mentioned or alluded to the new covenant, they repeated the themes of the Lord placing His Spirit, His words, or His heart into Israel for her salvation.

THE NEW COVENANT IN JEREMIAH

Through the prophet Jeremiah, the Lord revealed that His ultimate reason in making the Abrahamic covenant was about much more than the mere possession of land. It is in Jeremiah's prophecies that the Lord first specifically used the phrase "a new covenant." In this new covenant, we discover that the reason the Lord gave the promised land to the Jewish people was to provide a location where they could live in fellowship with Him eternally. But for this to become a reality, the Lord promised to write His Law upon their hearts so they could serve Him with absolute and complete obedience. Let's read the passage in full, as it is one of the most important passages in all of the Old Testament:

> "At that time," declares the LORD, "I will be the God of all the families of Israel, and they shall be My people. . . . Behold, days are coming," declares the LORD, "when I will make a new covenant with the house of Israel and with the house of Judah, not like the covenant which I made with their fathers in the day I took them by the hand to bring them out of the land of Egypt, My covenant which they broke, although I was a husband to them," declares the LORD. "But this is the covenant which I will make with the house of Israel after those days," declares the LORD, "I will put My law within them and on their heart I will write it; and I will be their God, and they shall be My people. They will not teach again, each man his neighbor and each man his brother, saying, 'Know the LORD,' for they will all know Me, from the least of them to the greatest of them," declares the LORD, "for I will forgive their iniquity, and their sin I will remember no more." (Jer. 31:1, 31–34)

It is essential to note that the specific recipients of this new covenant are "all the families of Israel," "the house of Israel," and "the house of Judah," whom the Lord also refers to as, "My people." As we consider the state of global Jewry today, with so many living in rebellion from God, and the vast majority not living as servants of their Messiah, it is clear that this promise is yet to be fulfilled. The Lord specifically says that the new covenant will not be like the Mosaic covenant, in which the house of Israel was unfaithful. But like the Abrahamic covenant, the new covenant would be something that the Lord Himself would oversee and accomplish within His people. Like the Abrahamic and Davidic covenants, the new covenant was also an unconditional promise made by God to Israel. The Lord Himself would place His law within their hearts. Then He would forgive their sins and forget their iniquities. As such, they would go on to "know the Lord . . . from the least of them to the greatest." Through the new covenant, the Lord will empower His people to live according to the holiness that fellowship with God requires.

In the next chapter, Jeremiah once again prophesied concerning the time when Israel would be regathered to their land.

> "Behold, I will gather them out of all the lands to which I have driven them in My anger, in My wrath and in great indignation; and I will bring them back to this place and make them dwell in safety. They shall be My people, and I will be their God; and I will give them *one heart* [LXX: "new heart"] *and one way*, that they may fear Me always, for their own good and for the good of their children after them. *I will make an everlasting covenant with them* that I will not turn away from them, to do them good; and I will put the fear of Me in their hearts so that they will not turn away from Me. I will rejoice over them to do them good and will faithfully plant them in this land with all My heart and with all My soul. For thus says the LORD, 'Just as I brought all this great disaster on this people, so I am going to bring on them all the good that I am promising them. (Jer. 32:37–42; emphasis added)

Consider the power and relevance of this particular prophecy. Jeremiah describes a regathering to the land that cannot be correlated with Israel's condition after their return from the Babylonian exile or even Israel's present condition. According to Jeremiah, a Jewish regathering to the land of Israel is coming that will be accompanied specifically by the following conditions:

- Israel will "dwell in safety."

- They will receive a "new heart" (LXX).

- They will "fear [the Lord] always."

- The Lord will "put the fear of [Him] into their hearts."

- The Lord will "will rejoice over them to do them good and will faithfully plant them in this land with all [His] heart and with all [His] soul."

Although in Israel today there is a growing remnant of believing (Messianic) Jews, the overwhelming majority have not received a "new heart," nor does the nation today possess a unified heart that fears the Lord. In fact, visitors are often astonished when they go to the Holy Land for the first time to find it so similar to other nations in its utter lack of holiness. One might be surprised, for example, to get out of the cab in Tel Aviv and find oneself surrounded by nightclubs, strip clubs, drug-addled youth, and prostitution. To be clear, I'm not putting Israel down as any worse in this regard than my own nation or so many others; I'm simply highlighting the fact that the condition of Israel today, more than sixty-five years after the nation was born, simply does not correlate with the regathering that Jeremiah described. Jeremiah's prophecy of regathering is in a thoroughly eschatological context wherein the people have received a new heart, and thus the Lord says He will "make with them an everlasting covenant." This day is yet future. The prophet Jeremiah specifically linked Israel's permanent possession of the promised land with the promise of a new heart. It is in these passages that the Abrahamic covenant and the new covenant are seen to merge together as the singular and ultimate goal of the Lord's magnificent plan of redemption for His people.

THE NEW COVENANT IN EZEKIEL

Later yet, the prophet Ezekiel also spoke of this time when the nation of Israel would receive both a new spirit and a new heart along with both the desire and the ability to walk in complete obedience and holiness to God: "And I will give them one heart, and put a new spirit within them. And I will take the heart of stone out of their flesh and give them a heart of flesh, that they may walk in My statutes and keep My ordinances and do them. Then they will be My people, and I shall be their God" (Ezek. 11:19–20).

Then in chapter 36, Ezekiel again reiterated the same promise. This time, however, like Jeremiah, Ezekiel also clearly connected the land promise of the Abrahamic covenant with the promise of a new heart associated with the new covenant. And notice again, this promise is addressed to the "house of Israel":

> "Therefore say to the house of Israel, 'Thus says the Lord GOD. . . . 'I will take you from the nations, gather you from all the lands and bring you into your own land. Then I will sprinkle clean water on you, and you will be clean; I will cleanse you from all your filthiness and from all your idols. Moreover, I will give you a new heart and put a new spirit within you; and I will remove the heart of stone from your flesh and give you a heart of flesh. I will put My Spirit within you and cause you to walk in My statutes, and you will be careful to observe My ordinances. You will live in the land that I gave to your forefathers; so you will be My people, and I will be your God.'" (Ezek. 36:22–28)

This passage brings truly profound insight into the concept of the new covenant in the New Testament and how it would have been understood by the apostles and the early Jewish believers. While so many Christian theologians view the new covenant made through the blood of Jesus as only providing for the forgiveness of sins, what this passage so powerfully reveals is that the new covenant is integrally connected to the land promise of the Abrahamic covenant. It is the new heart and the new spirit promised through the new covenant that will empower the people of Israel to walk in a manner worthy of inheriting the land as promised to Abraham. The Lord's ultimate purpose was always to have a people who loved Him fully and served Him with gladness and joy, specifically in the land that He promised to give them. This continues to be God's intention today, and in the days ahead, the Lord will see to it that all of these promises are completely fulfilled.

THE NEW COVENANT IN THE NEW TESTAMENT

While the new covenant was announced in the Old Testament, its actual inauguration is recorded in the New Testament when the body of Jesus the Messiah was broken for the sins of His people:

> And when He had taken a cup and given thanks, He said, "Take this and share it among yourselves; for I say to you, I will not drink of the fruit of the vine from now on until the kingdom of God comes." And when He had taken some bread and given thanks, He broke it and gave it to them, saying, "This is My body which is given for you; do this in remembrance of Me." And in the same way He took the cup after they had eaten, saying, "This cup which is poured out for you is the new covenant in My blood. (Luke 22:17–20)

It is in the new covenant that we have the grand prophetic crescendo of the Lord's previous promises and covenants. Whereas the Lord Himself made a covenant unto death with Abraham, emphatically declaring that He would not renege on His word, it is in the new covenant that the Lord Himself endured death, laying down His human body as the sacrifice and making the promise possible. Whereas the Lord used the many various sacrifices of the Mosaic covenant to help the penitent look upon the gruesome result of sin and the great cost of life necessary to remove it, it was at the cross that the Lord Himself made the ultimate payment for the sins of His people Israel.

THE MYSTERY OF GENTILE INCLUSION

Up until this point, we have seen that all of the covenants—including the new covenant—were made specifically to and for Israel. In none of the passages that we've examined so far have the Gentiles been overtly stated to be the primary recipients of the promises. While it has always been possible for Gentiles to find salvation (see Ezekiel 18:20-21), before the apostolic age, apart from joining themselves to the people of Israel, it would have been extremely rare. The apostle Paul, in describing the spiritual condition of Gentiles prior to the cross, said they were "vessels of wrath prepared for destruction" (Rom. 9:22) and were "excluded from the commonwealth of Israel, and strangers to the covenants of promise, having no hope and without God in the world" (Eph. 2:12). This is precisely why the opening up of the Gospel to the Gentiles, as recorded in the New Testament, was such a revolutionary concept for many. This is why Peter and all of the early Jewish believers were so shocked when the Spirit was poured out on Cornelius and his non-Jewish household (see Acts 10–11). Although many of the Jewish believers were doubtful at first, after Peter explained how the Holy Spirit had been given to the whole Gentile household of Cornelius as promised in the new covenant, we are told the skeptics "quieted down and glorified God, saying, 'Well then, God has granted to the Gentiles also the repentance that leads to life'" (Acts 11:18). Although the swarming in of the Gentiles had been hinted at in the Prophets, the floodgates had not truly burst open until that moment. This is why Paul refers to the inclusion of Gentiles as "the *mystery* . . . which in other generations was not made known to the sons of men, as it has now been revealed to His holy apostles and prophets in the Spirit; to be specific, that the Gentiles are fellow heirs and fellow members of the body, and fellow partakers of the promise in Christ Jesus through the gospel" (Eph. 3:4–6; emphasis added).

The good news is that any individual, whether Jew or Gentile, is freely welcomed into the family of God through repentance and placing their trust in Jesus (Mark 1:15, 6:12, John 3:16, Acts 2:21, 2:38, 3:19, 10:42–43, 17:30, 26:20). Conversion to Judaism, circumcision, and adherence to the Mosaic law are not requirements for salvation (Acts 15).

ROMANS 11: THE MYSTERY OF ISRAEL

At this point many Christians become confused in terms of understanding how Israel fits into God's plans. And perhaps understandably so, for according to the Scriptures, at the present time, there are two spiritual realities that may seem to be in conflict. First, the Scriptures are clear that only a remnant of Israel will be saved (see Romans 9:27). But at the same time, there is also the reality that "all Israel will be saved" (Rom. 11:26). Only a remnant will be saved, yet all Israel will be saved? How are these two seeming contradictions resolved? Paul addressed this question quite directly in Romans 9–11, which are the most important portions of Scripture that specifically address these matters. Paul's solution to these two seemingly contradictory realities is to recognize that from the time of Jesus's public ministry, the Lord has chosen to partially and temporarily harden the majority of the Jewish people to the Gospel and the identity of their own Messiah. At the proper time, however—specifically, when Jesus Himself returns—that partial and temporary hardening will be permanently removed and "all Israel," at that moment, will be saved. Paul's explanation culminates with his critical explanation of the "mystery" of this unfolding reality. Romans 11:25–27 are among the most important verses in all of Scripture that must be understood if one is to properly comprehend the plans of God for both the Jews and the Gentiles. Paul began by warning Gentiles not to remain uninformed concerning this "mystery":

> For I do not want you, brethren, to be uninformed of this mystery—so that you will not be wise in your own estimation—that a partial hardening has happened to Israel until the fullness of the Gentiles has come in; and so all Israel will be saved; just as it is written, "The Deliverer will come from Zion, He will remove ungodliness from Jacob. This is my covenant with them, when I take away their sins."

There are five crucial components of Paul's message that we must acknowledge.

1. The hardening of Israel is partial—not affecting all Jews.

2. This partial hardening of Israel is temporary—not permanent.

3. This hardening will be lifted at a very specific time in the future.

4. It will be specifically lifted after "the fullness of the Gentiles has come in."

5. At that time, "all Israel will be saved."

SUPERSESSIONIST OBJECTIONS

In his book *Kingdom Come*, Sam Storms, in presenting the traditional supersessionist perspective, seeks to deconstruct the notion that this is what Paul was actually saying and argues that when Paul said "all," he was only referring to the relatively small percentage of Jews who have come to faith throughout history. He denies any "future restoration in mass of ethnic Jews."[1] Storms takes a full chapter—*thirty-two pages*—to argue his case.

The bulk of Storms's argument revolves around Paul's teaching that not all Jewish people are truly Israel: "For they are not all Israel who are descended from Israel" (Rom. 9:6). His argument is that while there may someday be a revival among Jews, their present condition, with only a small remnant of believers, will in all likelihood be permanent. Storms argues that it is unlikely that the hardening of Israel will be lifted at some specific period of time. Specifically, he contends that Paul does not teach that "a mass turning of Jews to faith in Christ will occur in conjunction with the return of Christ at the close of history."[2]

There are some insurmountable problems with this supersessionist argument. Throughout Romans 9-11, the apostle Paul unequivocally, systematically, and thoroughly repudiates any claim that God has rejected corporate, national Israel and affirms the notion that a mass conversion of "all Israel" will occur when Jesus returns. Let us consider some of Paul's inspired arguments.

PAUL'S DILEMMA

To understand Romans 11, we must recognize that Paul sought to explain the glaring problem—*the scandal, even*—of the condition of the Jewish people in his day wherein the majority had rejected Jesus, their prophesied Messiah. While many Jewish *individuals* were coming to faith, the actual covenants speak of the Lord saving *all of Israel in a corporate sense.* Paul sought to address the difficulty of reconciling the language of the covenants with the scandal of Jewish unbelief by discussing the difference between the condition of Jews in his day and their condition at the end of the age, when Jesus returns. Let us begin by discussing the issue of individual versus corporate calling and salvation.

To truly understand the "mystery of Israel," it is absolutely critical to understand that in Paul's day, as in ours, *whosoever*—whether Jew or Gentile—comes to the Lord in repentance and places their faith in Jesus will be saved and brought into the family of God. In fact, this is the only way anyone will ever be saved. But Paul also knew that the specific wording of the covenants speak of a calling upon Israel on a corporate, national level. This calling rests upon the physical bloodline descendants of Abraham, Isaac, and Jacob, precisely according to the manner in which the Lord made His promises in the Abrahamic, Davidic, and new covenants. The promises of God were not made to individuals, but always to the whole nation of Israel. In the following examples, consider to whom exactly the promises were made:

- "the sons of Israel" (Ex. 6:2–8; Ezek. 43:7; 44:9)

- "all the families of Israel" (Jer. 31:1)

- "the house of Israel" and "the House of Judah," (Isa. 14:1–3; Jer. 31:31; Heb. 8:8)

- "the whole house of Israel, all of them" (Ezek.11:15; 20:40; 39:25; 45:6)

- "the sons of Jacob, His chosen ones" (1 Chron. 16:13–18; Ps. 105:6–12)

- the house of David and on the inhabitants of Jerusalem (Zech. 12:10–11)

Numerous other examples could be cited. Throughout the hundreds of times that God pledged Himself to the future salvation of Israel, His words were always directed to a corporate people. Paul's answer to this problem was to draw a distinction between his day, wherein some individuals were coming into the body of Messiah, and the last days, when Jesus returns and the whole house of Israel would be saved.

WHEN WILL "ALL" ISRAEL BE SAVED?

The structure of Paul's argument in Romans 11 clearly contrasts the present condition of the Jews in his day with their future condition at the time of Jesus's return. Thus, today, we can say along with Paul that "at the present time [there is] a remnant according to God's gracious choice" (v. 5). His flow of thought moves forward, however, to a clear climax, with Paul jubilantly declaring that after the temporary hardening is lifted, "all Israel" will be saved! Let's discuss some of the reasons why we know that Paul had in mind a mass conversion of the children of Israel specifically when Jesus returns.

THE DELIVERER WILL COME FROM ZION

First, we know Paul was speaking of the time of Jesus's return because he cited Isaiah 59:17–18, where God made a covenant with Israel, promising to place His Spirit on them and His words in their mouths forever. When Paul cited this passage, he tied it directly to the salvation of all Israel. In Romans 11:26, after saying that all Israel would be saved, Paul immediately quoted Isaiah 59:20–21, part of which reads: "'A Redeemer will come to Zion, and to those who turn from transgression in Jacob,' declares the LORD." The section of Isaiah's prophecy that Paul used speaks of: (1) the return of Jesus; (2) the subsequent deliverance of Israel from both their enemies; (3) the deliverance of Israel from their sins; and most important, (4) God making a covenant with Israel, promising that His Spirit will rest on them, never to depart. This covenant, of course, is the new covenant, whereby God will give the whole house of Israel a new heart and new spirit. No wonder Paul quoted this passage!

THE RESTORED KINGDOM OF ISRAEL

The prophecy, however, does not end there. In chapter 60, which immediately follows, the prophecy continues to flow directly into a description of *the future restoration of the kingdom of Israel!* That's right. Immediately following the Messiah-Deliverer coming to Zion,

Isaiah describes a restored and glorified kingdom of Israel as the center of global rule, with other nations being drawn to her leadership: "Nations will come to your light, and kings to the brightness of your rising" (v. 3). The Gentile nations throughout the earth are described as coming to pay tribute, to show honor, and to bring gifts to the kingdom of Israel: "Then you will see and be radiant, and your heart will thrill and rejoice; because the abundance of the sea will be turned to you, the wealth of the nations will come to you" (v. 5). The Gentiles are even described as helping to restore the kingdom itself, offering themselves as workers for its restoration and glorification: "Foreigners will build up your walls, and their kings will minister to you . . . Your gates will be open continually; they will not be closed day or night, so that men may bring to you the wealth of the nations, with their kings led in procession. For the nation and the kingdom which will not serve you will perish, and the nations will be utterly ruined" (vv. 10–12).

The surrounding nations will even help to rebuild the Jewish Temple, where the Lord is portrayed as being physically present: "The glory of Lebanon will come to you, the juniper, the box tree and the cypress together, to beautify the place of My sanctuary; and I shall make the place of My feet glorious" (v. 13). Israel's former enemies will come and prostrate themselves, acknowledging that Israel indeed is the Lord's chosen people: "The sons of those who afflicted you will come bowing to you, and all those who despised you will bow themselves at the soles of your feet; and they will call you the city of the LORD, the Zion of the Holy One of Israel" (v. 14).

When Paul brought his case for the future salvation of all Israel to its dramatic conclusion, he tied the future lifting of Israel's temporary hardening and their future salvation with Isaiah's descriptions concerning the following things:

- the return of Jesus

- the deliverance of Israel from their enemies and God's

- the deliverance of Israel from their sins

- the Spirit of God resting on them forever

- the salvation of all Israel

- God's restoration of the kingdom of Israel to the Jewish people

All of these events will take place within the same time period. Paul could not have been more emphatic in making this point. Any Old Testament–literate Jew from that time would have fully understood the point Paul was making.

THEY WILL LOOK UPON HIM WHOM THEY HAVE PIERCED

Another key reason we know Paul was placing the salvation of all Israel in the future is because the eschatological, corporate salvation of the Jews had already been declared by the prophet Zechariah and by Jesus Himself! In other words, even if Romans 11 didn't exist, the teaching that all Israel will be saved when Jesus returns is clearly established in other portions of the Bible.

Let us begin with the prophecy of Zechariah. In the first passage, Zechariah speaks of "the Branch," which virtually all Christian commentators acknowledge to be a reference to Jesus the Messiah. Zechariah then declares that this Branch will cause the sins of the land of Israel to be purged and atoned for in a single day, after which we are immediately told that that day, that particular time period, coincides with the millennial era of peace in Israel: "'Behold, I am going to bring in My servant the Branch. For behold, the stone that I have set before Joshua; on one stone are seven eyes. Behold, I will engrave an inscription on it,' declares the LORD of hosts, 'and I will remove the iniquity of that land in one day. In that day,' declares the LORD of hosts, 'every one of you will invite his neighbor to sit under his vine and under his fig tree'" (Zech. 3:8–10).

Later in Zechariah's prophecy, the prophet detailed the repentance that will take place among the inhabitants of Jerusalem and the "house of David" as they recognize the One they have pierced: "'I will pour out on the house of David and on the inhabitants of Jerusalem, the Spirit of grace and of supplication, so that they will look on Me whom they have pierced; and they will mourn for Him, as one mourns for an only son, and they will weep bitterly over Him like the bitter weeping over a firstborn. In that day there will be great mourning in Jerusalem'" (Zech. 12:10–11).

Zechariah's prophecy continues to describe a corporate repentance that spreads across the nation of Israel, to every clan and family. Then, in the same stream of thought, chapter 13 describes the Lord removing the sins of Israel: "In that day a fountain will be opened for the house of David and for the inhabitants of Jerusalem, for sin and for impurity" (v. 1). This is a profound passage. The people of Israel will look upon the Lord whom they (and we all) have pierced, and as a result, they will mourn, resulting in the spirit of grace being poured out upon them and a fountain being opened for the forgiveness of sins! Even if Paul had never written Romans 9–11, Zechariah would have already established the fact that, specifically at the time of the return of Jesus, the floodgates of repentance, forgiveness, and grace will be poured out upon Israel!

Yet if any would be so disposed to claim that Zechariah was not speaking of these things, then the interpretation of this passage by Jesus Himself should settle the matter. He expanded upon Zechariah's prophecy in His Olivet Discourse and then again in the book of Revelation, leaving absolutely no doubt as to its timing. First, Jesus said, "And then the sign of the Son of Man will appear in the sky, and then *all the tribes of the earth will mourn,* and they will see the Son of Man coming on the clouds of the sky with power and great glory. And He will send forth His angels with a great trumpet and they will gather together His elect from the four winds, from one end of the sky to the other" (Matt. 24:30–31; emphasis added).

Notice that when Jesus spoke of His return, He quoted from a portion of Zechariah 12 speaking of all the tribes of the earth, or land, mourning when they see His return in the sky coming on the clouds. Note that Jesus spoke these words before His crucifixion. Yet even before He was arrested, He knew that He was the One described in Zechariah's prophecy as the One "whom they have pierced."

The words of Jesus in the book of Revelation further ties in Zechariah's prophecy to the return of Jesus: "Behold, He is coming with the clouds, and every eye will see Him, even those who pierced Him; and all the tribes of the earth will mourn over Him. So it is to be. Amen" (Rev. 1:7). Considered together, these three passages reveal that the following events are all integrally linked:

- the return of Jesus on the clouds (Matt. 24:30; Mark 13:26; Luke 21:27; Acts 1:9–11)

- all the tribes of Israel looking upon Him as He returns in glory

- the tribes of Israel acknowledging Jesus as the one whom they (and we all) pierced

- the tribes of Israel repenting and mourning

- the spirit of grace being poured out upon them

- the Lord's purging of the sins of that nation "in one day"

Paul the apostle knew the prophecies of Zechariah and that Jesus had linked them to His return. He also knew that Christ's return would result in the spirit of repentance and grace being poured out on all the tribes of Israel and the national cleansing of sins in a single day (Isa. 27:9). There is no doubt that Paul in Romans 11 was simply expounding these previously established scriptural truths!

What is so disappointing is that in all of Storms's discussion of this issue and of Romans 11, not once does he reference Zechariah 12, Matthew 24:30, or Revelation 1:7. Are not these texts all supremely relevant to the discussion?

THE FLAWED LOGIC OF N. T. WRIGHT

Within the evangelical world, British scholar Tom "N. T." Wright is a veritable rock star. There is no question that he is a profoundly eloquent, gifted, and innovative thinker. But even the most brilliant mind is at a profound disadvantage when defending something that is not true. Unfortunately, Wright is a staunch supersessionist, though he has strangely denied such a label on various occasions; on other occasions he has vigorously defended this position. Upon being challenged concerning his supersessionism, Wright turned to Philippians 3:3, wherein Paul stated, "We are the true circumcision, who worship in the Spirit of God and glory in Christ Jesus and put no confidence in the flesh." To this statement Wright triumphantly declared: "Paul, breathtakingly, snatches the phrase 'the circumcision' away from ethnic Israel and claims it for those in Messiah. . . . This, by the way, is at the heart of the correct answer to those who suggest that I and others are guilty of imposing something called 'supersessionism' on Paul. If such critics would show that they had read Philippians 3.3 . . . they might deserve to be taken more seriously."[3]

After you get past Wright's belittling of any who would dare challenge his perspective, having just reviewed Paul's position as expressed in Romans 11, what would you say is the glaring problem with his logic here? The answer is simple. Wright has applied Paul's rebuke of a particular group of Jews in his day to all of "ethnic Israel." Paul himself called any such claim "arrogance," a boasting of the wild olive branches (Gentiles) that had been graciously grafted in against the natural, cultivated branches that had been cut off (ethnic Israel). He warned that such condescension could potentially result in one actually being cut off from God. Why does the Church continue to so adamantly and persistently refuse to heed Paul's warning? While it is true that many, but not all, of the Jews of Paul's day rejected Jesus, that corporate hardening of the Jewish heart to the truth, as we have seen, was only *partial* and *temporary*. Wright has manipulated Paul's rebuke of *some* Jews in his own day to mean that *all* of "ethnic Israel," to the very last day, has been forever rejected, their very *identity* having been "snatched" away. As offensive and transparently unbiblical as this is, with a twist, a spin, and a little sleight of hand, many fall for Satan's truly vile lie known as supersessionism.

GOD'S BELOVED ENEMIES AND THEIR IRREVOCABLE CALLING

Let us reiterate once again, first, that no one will be saved apart from faith in Jesus. And second, the Lord makes no distinction between Jew or Gentile in terms of His offer of salvation. It is open and freely available to all: "For the Scripture says, 'Whoever believes in Him will not be disappointed.' For there is no distinction between Jew and Greek; for the same Lord is Lord of all, abounding in riches for all who call on Him; for 'Whoever will call upon the name of the Lord will be saved' (Rom. 10:11–13). But Paul also informs us that although a majority of Jews today are "enemies" of the Gospel, *because of God's faithfulness to His covenant promises,* "they are beloved." There yet remains a special, unique, and irrevocable calling upon Israel as a corporate people: "From the standpoint of the gospel they are enemies for your sake, but from the standpoint of God's choice they are beloved for the sake of the fathers; for the gifts and the calling of God are irrevocable" (Rom. 11:28–29).

Paul could not have been more clear. He specifically stated that Israel's calling is "irrevocable." Make no mistake: in brazen and direct conflict with the words of Paul, supersessionists argue that God has indeed revoked His calling and election of corporate ethnic Israel. In fact, yet another term that would be entirely fair to use to refer to supersessionism or replacement theology could be "revocation theology," for that is precisely what it is.

Restorationists affirm the emphatic words of the apostle Paul in acknowledging a future restoration of Israel. We deny that Israel's calling had been revoked. Several times in Romans 11 he reiterated that God has not dismissed corporate Israel: "God has not rejected His people, has He? May it never be! . . . God has not rejected His people whom He foreknew. . . . I say then, they did not stumble so as to fall, did they? May it never be!" (Rom. 11:1, 2, 11).

When Paul twice wrote, "May it never be!" (*mē ginomai*), he was actually using the strongest possible construction in the Greek language to confront the absolute ludicrousness of the supersessionist claim that the Jewish people as a whole, as a nation, have been rejected. In Paul's mind, the notion that *the God of Israel*, has forever rejected *Israel* was a complete absurdity.

THE SEED OF ABRAHAM

Supersessionists repeatedly object that the promises were not even made to Israel, but exclusively to Jesus. To argue this point, they will nearly always cite Galatians 3:16: "Now the promises were spoken to Abraham and to his seed. He does not say, 'And to seeds,' as referring to many, but rather to one, 'And to your seed,' that is, Christ."

Before explaining what Paul was really saying, it is important to first explain what he was not saying. Paul was absolutely not saying that we should look to every occasion throughout the Old Testament where God's promises were expressed to Abraham's "descendants" and read it as singular "descendant," or "seed," referring only to Jesus. I actually met a man who argued that based on Paul's words here, we could simply go back to the many accounts in the Old Testament where God made the promises to the patriarchs, and wherever we find the word "seed," or "descendant," we could simply insert the name Jesus there. Consider how absurd this would be if we actually did this.

As the Abrahamic covenant was being made, God prophesied concerning a future time when Abraham's "descendants" through

Isaac and Jacob would become slaves in Egypt: "Know for certain that your *descendants* [seed] will be strangers in a land that is not theirs, where they will be enslaved and oppressed four hundred years. But I will also judge the nation whom they will serve, and afterward they will come out with many possessions" (Gen. 15:13–14; emphasis added). What would happen if we simply inserted the name "Jesus" in the place of "seed"? This would be silly. It was not Jesus who was a slave in Egypt, but the ancient sons of Israel. Or when the Lord said to Abraham, "Look toward the heavens, and count the stars, if you are able to count them. So shall your descendants [seed] be" (Gen. 15:5), was he speaking only of Jesus, or of Abraham's descendants collectively? The answer is obvious. Countless other examples could be cited.

In no way was Paul saying that the Lord never made a promise to Abraham, Isaac, and Jacob's numerous physical descendants—that is, national, corporate Israel. It is abundantly clear that He did precisely this many times. We have cited several examples. As a thoroughly Old Testament–literate Jew, the apostle Paul was well aware of this fact.

So what *was* Paul saying?

First, Paul was identifying which specific descendants of Abraham were recipients of the promise and which were not. Scholars agree that Paul was interpreting the Hebrew word *zera* ("descendant" or "seed") as a *collective singular*. What this means is that although Abraham had eight sons altogether (Gen. 25), God's promise was only to the descendants of his one son Isaac (Gen. 17:15–21; 21:9–13), and then to the descendants of Isaac's son Jacob, that is to say, Israel. Thus, when Paul said that the promises were spoken to Abraham's "seed" and not "seeds," first, he was specifically ruling out Abraham's other descendants, such as his son Ishmael, or Esau his grandson, and reminding his readers who the promises were made to, namely, "the house of Israel."

Second, Paul expanded on this limitation of the promises by highlighting the fact that the promises to Israel will only ultimately be received by those who have faith in Jesus (a descendant of Abraham, Isaac, and Jacob), who will rule as the Jewish King over the Jewish people when they finally inherit the land that God repeatedly promised to them. So it is through Jesus, the ultimate "seed," that Abraham's descendants will inherit the land promises.

Finally, Paul was making the point that anyone can come to enjoy the blessings of the coming Jewish kingdom if they show the same kind of faith that Abraham showed, believing in Jesus, the promised Seed.

THE SUPERSESSIONIST STORY VERSUS THE RESTORATIONIST STORY

As we continue to consider the stark differences between the supersessionist narrative and the restorationists' narrative, we must ask ourselves which story best testifies to the character of God. Which better conveys the faithfulness, perseverance, and mercy of God?

If there is one thing that the book of Acts makes clear, it is that the new covenant has flung wide the doors of the kingdom of God and made its future inheritance freely and widely available to all people. Both supersessionists and restorationists agree on this. Restorationism affirms, however, that while the Lord has indeed opened His promises and blessings up to all people, He has done so without rejecting the Jewish people corporately. After all, they are the ones to whom the promises were originally made.

Restorationism affirms that the new covenant represents an expansion and blossoming of the Lord's original plans to include the Gentiles. The promises are far greater than we could have ever imagined! In no way, however, does the new covenant represent an abrogation or a change in His original plans to corporate Israel. Unfortunately, supersessionism, while acknowledging the universalization of the blessings, also views the new covenant as bringing a radical abrogation of the promises of the Abrahamic covenant to Israel. Let us honestly ask ourselves which view better represents the God who refers to Himself as the God of Israel more than two hundred times throughout the Scriptures and which position portrays a God who is faithful and reliable? As I have already said, by claiming that God has rejected Israel as a nation, supersessionists unintentionally cast God as an unfaithful, fickle, mind-changing promise-breaker. If you are reading this and presently hold to some form of supersessionism, I appeal to you with all sincerity to truly consider just what is being conveyed about God's character when you espouse the view that God didn't really mean what He said and that His words must be fundamentally reinterpreted or read figuratively to be understood properly. Try to imagine how such claims would make you feel if you were Jewish. I urge you to consider the simple and straightforward position of restorationism, with its message concerning a faithful God who says what He means and can be absolutely trusted to accomplish all that He has promised.

Supersessionists must not only reinterpret the words of the Old Testament, but they must also minimize or even negate Paul's words concerning the salvation of all Israel to mean nothing more than the historical trickle of Jewish believers that have come into the Church. For them, this alone is enough to entail the full meaning of "all Israel." What a vapid and hollow reflection of the glories that Isaiah described! How sad the supersessionist interpretation would have been to anyone whose expectations and vision of redemption were formed by the profoundly powerful words of the prophets that spoke of such a glorious restoration of the Jewish kingdom. The contrast between the magnificent vision of restorationism and the sad satisfaction with the status quo of supersessionism is nowhere more glaring than in their respective interpretations of this chapter. On one hand, after taking a whole chapter to argue that the present remnant of Jews is most likely all we will ever see come in, as Storms concludes his arguments, the best he can muster is this:

> Romans 11 does not provide explicit support for the expectation that the mass of ethnic Jews still alive at the second coming of Christ will be brought forth ravingly into the kingdom of God . . .

Romans 11, as I understand the chapter, is simply silent on whether or not such a mass turning of Jews to faith in Christ will occur in conjunction with the return of Christ at the close of history. One may, indeed *should* certainly pray for this to happen (as one should also pray for the conversion of all people groups throughout the world). But I do not believe Romans 11 gives us biblical warrant for declaring that it assuredly *will* come to pass.[4]

What an enormous wet blanket this is! What a tremendous let-down. Nowhere in Paul's words will one find Storms's pessimism and resignation. Instead, after announcing the good news that, indeed, "all Israel will be saved," Paul broke out into jubilant rejoicing: "Oh, the depth of the riches both of the wisdom and knowledge of God! How unsearchable are His judgments and unfathomable His ways! For who has known the mind of the Lord, or who became His counselor? Or who has first given that it might be paid back to Him again? For from Him and through Him and to Him are all things. To Him be the glory forever. Amen" (Rom. 11:33–36).

With Paul, every believer should shout aloud, "Amen and amen!"

CONCLUSION

Today God is calling all people to repent through Jesus Christ, whether Jew or Gentile. Even more wonderful, however, is the fact that in the days ahead, when Jesus returns, He will fulfill His promises to the Jewish people and they will "all" be saved, *exactly as He said they would be.* The Lord will take those who throughout history have in so many ways been His "mission impossible," His "beloved enemies" and through them, He will display His faithfulness before all the nations. In fact, Paul informs us that the Jews' coming to faith will result in a global, millennial revival: "Now if their transgression is riches for the world and their failure is riches for the Gentiles, how much more will their fulfillment be! . . . For if their rejection is the reconciliation of the world, what will their acceptance be but life from the dead?" (Rom. 11:12, 15).

This will be the pattern: We will first see the full number of Gentiles in this present age come in, followed by the return of Jesus, then the salvation of all Israel, after which will come the redemption of the whole earth. Behold the beauty, the magnificence, and the wisdom of the Lord's plans! While it may presently seem like a somewhat drawn-out and even confusing dance that the Lord has ordained, in the end, not only will Israel, His firstborn, His chosen people, all be serving Him, but so also will an uncountable number of Gentiles join the Jewish people in serving the Lord together. *Oh, how I long for that day!*

HOW SHOULD GENTILE BELIEVERS RELATE
TO UNBELIEVING JEWS?

Before we continue, it is so important that we stop to ponder and discuss the crucial issue of how Gentile Christians are to relate to Jewish people today, particularly those who do not believe in Jesus. Paul took great pains to both exhort and warn Gentile believers concerning how they should relate to the Jewish people, whether believers or unbelievers. To summarize his counsel, he wanted Gentiles to be humble, to be informed, and to show honor where honor is due.

In Ephesians, Paul warned Gentile believers to always remember and acknowledge where they came from. Before any Christian can truly appreciate what he now has in Christ, he must first grasp where he has come from, as well as the sacrifices that were made to open the way for his entrance into the kingdom. Paul captured this quite profoundly in his letter to the Ephesians, where he wrote that Christian Gentiles were formerly "separate from Christ, excluded from the commonwealth of Israel, and strangers to the covenants of promise, having no hope and without God in the world" (Eph. 2:12). I think that very few Christians today fully grasp that before the coming of Christ, unless a Gentile had joined himself to the God of Israel, he had "no hope" of salvation and was "without God." Through understanding this background, we can fully appreciate the free gift of salvation and eternal life that we now possess.

In Romans 11, Paul warned Gentiles to show honor to the

Jewish people, who, although the majority were (and continue to be) "enemies" of the Gospel within God's sovereign plan, were hardened by God specifically so that the Gentiles could come in. Gentiles should thus show honor where honor is due and not look down upon those Jews who were "broken off." To not do so is to be "arrogant," "conceited," and ungrateful for the undeserved grace that has come to them. It puts one at risk of being "cut off" from Christ. Showing honor where honor is due is an issue that the Lord takes very seriously.

During a recent visit to Israel, I attended a Pentecost celebration (*Shavuot* in Hebrew) just outside of Jerusalem. This national gathering is held each year with messianic believers from all over the land gathering to worship and celebrate together. In the midst of the festivities, I had the opportunity to sit down with Avner Boskey. Avner is a highly respected Messianic Jewish leader from Israel who possesses not only profound theological clarity, insight, and intellect, but also a sense of humor and a sharp wit like few others I've ever known. Avner is also a former teacher of mine, and more than anyone else, I credit him with first opening my eyes to the thoroughly Israel-centered emphasis of the Scriptures. In the midst of our conversation, we turned to the subject of how Gentile believers should relate to the Jewish people. Avner's comments captured the simplicity of the matter quite well: "The issue of God's choosing of the Jewish people, and how Gentiles are to relate to the Jewish people, really is an issue of what I call 'court etiquette,'" he told me. "This is the way that we're supposed to behave in the courts of the king. So when we give honor to the things that God gives honor to, we are lining up with Him; we are coming into alignment in terms of kingdom realities."

Is this not what we should all desire? Shouldn't it be everyone's goal to align themselves with the Lord, to embrace the things that please Him, and to give honor to those things which He Himself honors?

To further communicate the present situation concerning Israel and the Church in perspective, I would like to share a parable. I made an effort to fashion it after the model of many of the parables of Jesus in the New Testament. I hope it will help some to better understand what I believe Paul was communicating and what so many Christians continue to miss today.

A TALE OF TWO SONS

Once upon a time, there was a father who had one son. The father had raised his only son from a very young age in the ways of the Lord. He would pray over his child as a baby and sing him to sleep with spiritual songs from the Scriptures. As the boy grew, the father read his son Bible stories and taught him the Scriptures. He instructed him to distinguish right from wrong. The son become a proficient student of the Word of God even at a young age.

As the boy reached the age of sixteen, the father heard about another young man who was in desperate need of a home and a family. Although he knew that this boy had had a very difficult life and continued to have many problems, after prayerfully weighing his decision, he felt it was right to adopt this young man into his family. But it was not until the boy had lived for some time with the family that the father learned the full extent of his new son's past. He discovered that by the age of eleven, his adopted son was already immersed in the drug culture. By thirteen, he was getting high every day. By fifteen he was using *and selling* virtually any drug available. And of course there was the theft, the vandalism, the violence, and so much more. Before he even came into the home, by age eighteen the boy had been arrested several times.

But then the unexpected happened. After hearing the Word of God for the first time, the adopted son repented of his sins, of his former life, and believing in Jesus Christ, he fully dedicated his life to the Lord. The transformation was wondrous to behold, and it surely made the father's heart rejoice beyond expression. But this was not the only unexpected thing that happened.

At the same time that the adopted son came to faith, the natural son, who had been raised in the ways of the Lord, suddenly left home. He began drinking and doing drugs, and soon it was as if he had fully taken on the former life of his adoptive brother. It was not long before he had even surpassed his brother's depravity. He became reckless in his sins and actually began to prostitute himself. When the father learned of all this, he was heartbroken beyond expression. When the newly converted adoptive son learned of the wickedness of his brother, he sought him out, berated him for his sins, and lectured him concerning his behavior. But when he refused to repent, in fit of self-righteous rage, the adoptive brother beat the naturally born son to death.

The father was grieved in his heart. First there was the unspeakable pain of watching his son, in whom he had poured his very heart and soul, as he turned to the ways of the world and gave himself over to complete reprobation, ultimately dying in a profoundly depraved state. Likewise, he was devastated for his adoptive son. For though he had greatly rejoiced when his son repented of his sins, his heart was doubly grieved that after receiving such forgiveness, mercy, and grace, the boy had become so self-righteous and arrogant that he had actually murdered his own brother. The father had the adoptive son arrested, and he was sentenced to life in prison. He remained there for the rest of his life, consumed with the most bitter regret.

Of course, this parable is merely my best effort to create a story that reflects the relationship between God the Father, Israel, and the Gentile-majority Church throughout the past two thousand years. With regard to Israel, the Bible refers to them as the Lord's firstborn (see Exodus 4:22; Jeremiah 31:9). They were the people whom the Lord had raised up and to whom He had given the covenant promises, His Law, the Temple, and their own land. They had the miracles, the history, the instruction, even the Messiah Himself! If you understand the background and history of the Lord's dealings with Israel, then you can see how profoundly shocking, scandalous, and painful is the fact that a majority of the Jewish people have rejected Jesus and chosen not to follow their own King. Avner Boskey expressed it to me this way: "So, if Queen Elizabeth were rejected in her own country, it would be a tragedy. Even if she is accepted in America, it would still cause great pain to her. The same thing is true with Yeshua, with Jesus. Jesus is the Messiah of the Jewish people. The term *Messiah* is a Hebrew term, *Mashiach*. Only when you translate it into Greek do you get the word *Christos*, or *Christ*. But it is actually a title; it means a descendant of the family of David. And David is our royal dynasty."

This is precisely why Paul was so deeply grieved over the situation that he expressed his desire that he could be cut off instead of Israel: "For I could wish that I myself were accursed, separated from Christ for the sake of my brethren, my kinsmen according to the flesh, who are Israelites, to whom belongs the adoption as sons, and the glory and the covenants and the giving of the Law and the temple service and the promises, whose are the fathers, and from whom is the Christ according to the flesh, who is over all, God blessed forever. Amen" (Rom. 9:3–5).

We can also understand why Paul rebuked any Gentiles who look down upon unbelieving Israel, even warning them that harboring such an ungrateful and arrogant heart places them in great risk of being cut off God:

> But if some of the branches were broken off, and you, being a wild olive, were grafted in among them and became partaker with them of the rich root of the olive tree, do not be arrogant toward the branches; but if you are arrogant, remember that it is not you who supports the root, but the root supports you. You will say then, "Branches were broken off so that I might be grafted in." Quite right, they were broken off for their unbelief, but you stand by your faith. Do not be conceited, but fear; for if God did not spare the natural branches, He will not spare you, either. Behold then the kindness and severity of God; to those who fell, severity, but to you, God's kindness, if you continue in His kindness; otherwise you also will be cut off. (Rom. 11:17–22)

But instead of heeding Paul's warnings, the majority or the Christian Church throughout history has embraced supersessionism and has indeed looked down upon the Jewish people, far too many times even becoming violent and murderous toward them. The long history of Christian anti-Semitism is the great stain on Christendom that cannot be erased. But while Christians today cannot change the past, we can pay heed to Paul's warnings, repent of all forms of supersessionism, and relate to the Jews in a way that the Lord expects: by showing mercy, love, and honor. This will be quite natural if we acknowledge where we came from.

I should mention that in many ways, I am the adoptive son in the parable. As a result of divorce and minimal oversight, by age eleven I was already using drugs. The entirety of my preteen and teenage years was a downhill slide toward destruction. I was arrested seven times by age nineteen. I cannot count how many times I mixed multiple drugs, alcohol, and even inhalants together in my body, or how many times I was so drunk that I couldn't remember driving home or getting in a fight the night before. I won't belabor all of the details. I know many others reading this have their own dark backstories, and some are *far* worse than mine. My point, however, is that when I look back at just the beginning of my life, even these twenty-plus years after becoming a believer, I am still deeply in touch with the fact that I genuinely should have died at a very young age. If I had truly reaped the fruit of my own early choices, I would either be in prison or in hell right now. But instead of meeting an early death, at age nineteen I met the Lord. But it was not because I was searching for Him. Instead, He chose to reveal Himself to me. I am the embodiment of the passage from Isaiah (quoted by Paul in Romans 10:20) wherein the Lord said, "I permitted Myself to be found by those who did not seek Me" (Isa. 65:1). At the very moment when I should have been sent directly to jail, to the grave, or to hell, almost out of nowhere, the Lord intervened, invited me to be His follower, and offered me eternal life. And I accepted the offer. *Since that time, He has continued to show me such tremendous mercy.*

How does this all relate to the Jewish people? Very simple. When

I look at the vast majority of Jewish people today who do not know Him, I cannot help but feel grateful and deeply indebted to them, knowing that apart from their history, apart from their God, their Messiah, and even apart from their hardening, from their tremendous sacrifices and unfathomable loss, I myself would never have been able to come into the blessings I now enjoy. And so of course I yearn that they would know their God even as I have come to know Him. No doubt, the fact that they are not all serving Him pains the Lord's heart beyond what we could ever begin to fathom. And so I pray to receive just a drop of that pain from the Lord's heart to drive me to my knees in prayer for their protection and salvation. I ask for the Lord's heart to motivate me to proper action and to fill my mouth with the words necessary to perhaps awaken some before the day when they will all come to Him. This isn't just a personal revelation for me, however. I believe this is just a very small part of how the Lord wants all Gentile Christians to relate to the Jewish people. The Father desires that we would all remain humble, that we would all be properly informed concerning these matters, and that we would show proper honor where honor is due. I think this is all quite reasonable, and I trust that you do as well.

SUPPORTING MESSIANIC JEWS

I think it is also necessary to say that it is the duty of Gentile believers to show particular support for Messianic Jews. If the apostle Paul is right that Gentile believers should honor unbelieving Jews (those branches that have been broken off), then how much more should they honor the believing Jews (the natural olive branches)? Gentile believers must understand what a profound minority Jewish believers are within the larger, global body of Messiah. There are roughly 2 billion Christians globally, and only 1 million of those are Messianic Jewish believers.[1] Of the 6 million Jews in Israel, there are only around 20,000 Messianic Jews.[2] No matter where they are, Messianic Jews are a minority. Jewish believers are often persecuted by Jews and misunderstood by many Gentile Christians. Many Jews don't even consider Messianic Jews to be "real Jews." Many Orthodox Jews would even go so far as to say that the very term "Messianic Jew" is an oxymoron, as Jews are only those who practice Judaism.[3] They very much need the understanding and support of the larger Gentile Christian community.

Believing Jews have a unique role in the body of Messiah that no one else can fill. Jewish believers are uniquely qualified, among other things, to help Gentile believers better understand the Jewish roots of their faith, to practice a more biblically rooted faith, and to understand the nature of the coming messianic kingdom. Additionally, they serve as indigenous ambassadors to the Jewish community and are able to fulfill the call to preach the Gospel to Jews much better than most Gentiles. I am absolutely convinced that every congregation should adopt at least one Messianic Jewish ministry or congregation to support through prayer, finances, and encouragement.

At the conclusion of the prophecy of Malachi, in the final two verses of the Old Testament, the Lord made the following promise, "Behold, I am going to send you Elijah the prophet before the coming of the great and terrible day of the LORD. He will restore the hearts of the fathers to their children and the hearts of the children to their fathers, so that I will not come and smite the land with a curse" (Mal. 4:5–6). Although there are various suggestions as to what was being prophesied here, I believe that one of the primary intentions of the Lord's heart is that a healthy balance and relationship between the "fathers," those believing Jews sprinkled throughout the body of Messiah, and the "children," that vast number of Gentile believers throughout the earth, will be fully restored. Let us absolutely look forward to the days of Elijah when the full restoration takes place, but at the same time, let's not wait until those days to show the proper honor to the fathers (and mothers) that has been lacking in the Church for far too long.

1

THE COMING KINGDOM OF GOD

As Jesus began His public ministry, He went "throughout all Galilee, teaching in their synagogues and proclaiming the gospel of the kingdom" (Matt. 4:23; 9:35). Later, in His final sermon before His crucifixion and death, He prophesied "this gospel of the kingdom shall be preached in the whole world as a testimony to all the nations, and then the end will come" (Matt. 24:14). The word "gospel" is the Greek *euaggelion* and is also frequently translated simply as "good news" or "glad tidings." What exactly is this good news concerning the kingdom that Jesus was proclaiming? What exactly is the "gospel of the kingdom"? I would suggest that many in the Church today actually wouldn't know how to answer this properly. For far too many Christians, the Gospel is essentially this: *Jesus Christ died for your sins so that when you die, you can go to heaven.* But this is not what the Bible actually teaches. While it is certainly true that if any believer were to die today, his or her spirit would go on to be with Jesus (see 2 Corinthians 5:8 and Revelation 20:4), the true "hope" of all Christians is not to eternally exist in a disembodied state in heaven. The hope of every believer is to experience the resurrection of the body and to participate in a yet-to-come, physical, and earthly kingdom that is spoken of throughout the Bible. In this chapter, we will turn to the Scriptures to examine exactly what the Bible says concerning this coming, earthly, physical kingdom. Let us examine exactly what Jesus meant when He proclaimed to the people *the Gospel of the kingdom.*

THE KINGDOM OF JUSTICE

Hands down, one of the premier issues that continually burns on God's heart is the issue of justice. While there are more than enough great injustices throughout the earth, let us just touch on a couple of the more egregious examples. According to the World Health Organization, every single day, approximately 125,000 of the most innocent little lambs that this world has to offer, the very definition of "the defenseless," are slaughtered before ever taking their first breath.[1] That equates to 40 to 50 million abortions every year. Today there are close to 30 million, mostly very young women and children, who are prisoners in the sex slave trade. Every day, these girls are subjected to the most unimaginable abuse: sexually, physically, and psychologically. As a father of four daughters, I cannot imagine the fury that burns within God the Father's heart over this unrelenting evil. Every sob, every wail, every cry, the Lord hears. The Scriptures testify to the fact that the Lord is filled with compassion for the enslaved, the violated, the broken, the suffering, the oppressed, the depressed, the outcast, the rejected, the afflicted, the forgotten, the sick, the poor, and the weak. These are the things that the Lord repeatedly speaks about healing and utterly bringing to a decisive end when He returns. Let's consider a very small sampling of passages that speak of the justice the Lord will carry out specifically when He returns—on the Day of the Lord:

- "Behold, My Servant, whom I uphold; My chosen one in whom My soul delights. I have put My Spirit upon Him; He will bring forth justice to the nations." (Isa. 42:1)

- "But with righteousness He will judge the poor, and decide with fairness for the afflicted of the earth." (Isa. 11:4)

- "'In that day,' declares the LORD, 'I will assemble the lame and gather the outcasts.'" (Micah 4:6)

- "The afflicted also will increase their gladness in the LORD, and the needy of mankind will rejoice in the Holy One of Israel." (Isa. 29:19)

- "Then the eyes of the blind be opened and the ears of the deaf unstopped. Then will the lame leap like a deer, and the mute tongue shout for joy." (Isa. 35:5–6)

- "I will save the lame, and gather those who were driven out; I will appoint them for praise and fame in every land where they were put to shame" (Zeph. 3:19 NKJV)

- "He will have compassion on the poor and needy, and the lives of the needy he will save." (Ps. 72:13)

- "I will seek the lost, bring back the scattered, bind up the broken and strengthen the sick." (Ezek. 34:16)

Needless to say, the list could go on and on. The Day of the Lord is the Day of Justice! I think of the massive number of young Christians today who are so passionate about the issue of justice, but who have absolutely no interest in the subject of the end times. Yet the focal point of the end times is the Day of the Lord, and the very essence of that day is the issue of justice! Not only will that day be about justice, but it will also be the very essence of the kingdom that He will establish when He returns. There will be no more weeping, no more mourning, no more oppression, no more slavery, no more human trafficking, no more abortion, no more exploitation, no more war. This is the good news that Jesus spoke of when He went about Galilee proclaiming "the gospel of the kingdom."

A NEW GLOBAL GOVERNMENT

Not only will Jesus lift up from the ashes those whose lives have been trodden underfoot, but He will also take those who have unjustly oppressed others, those who have exalted themselves, and those who have used others as stepping-stones to force their way to the top, *and He will thrust them down*. According to the Scriptures, when Jesus returns, He will humble those who are proud and tear down those who have exalted themselves: "The eyes of the arrogant man will be humbled and the pride of men brought low, the LORD alone will be exalted in that day. The LORD Almighty has a day in store for all the proud and lofty, for all that is exalted (and they will be humbled)" (Isa. 2:11–12 NIV).

The primary purpose of any position of leadership, particularly within government or the Church, is to serve. Yet today I think it is fair to say that many, if not most, politicians and leaders within the churches seek and maintain positions of authority not primarily for the purpose of truly serving others, but to secure greater wealth, power, and control. Not all, but certainly a majority. This is true virtually no matter where one looks. But there are certainly extreme cases. I think of the fabulous wealth and gaudy excess of the leaders of the Kingdom of Saudi Arabia. I think of the equally gaudy and outright gross exaltation of Kim Jung-un, the present dictator of North Korea, who is treated like a god as His people languish in conditions that are beyond appalling. Even in the United States, rising to the office of president has become a guarantee of profound, lifelong wealth. The abuse of power for selfish gain at the expense, and often on the backs, of the people is a problem that is common throughout the world in virtually every sphere of society. How will Jesus respond to this when He returns? Many are familiar with Psalm 110 because of the profound messianic prophecy it contains: "The LORD says to my Lord: 'Sit at My right hand until I make Your enemies a footstool for Your feet'" (Ps. 110:1). But rarely is the final portion of the prophecy discussed from the pulpits, which says that when the Messiah returns, He will kill unrighteous rulers and politicians throughout the earth: "The Lord is at Your right hand; He will shatter kings in the day of His wrath. He will judge among the nations, He will fill them with corpses, He will shatter the chief men over a broad country" (vv. 5–6).

That's right! When Jesus returns, He will actually kill a host of unrighteous, self-serving politicians, dictators, and leaders throughout the earth. And not only will He cleanse the earth of oppressive and self-serving leaders, but He will also replace them with those who have proved themselves faithful and humble in the small things of their lives. "Well done, my good servant! Because you have been trustworthy in a very small matter, take charge of ten cities," He will declare (Luke 19:17 NIV). This is yet another part of the message that Jesus was proclaiming when He went about Galilee and preached the "gospel of the kingdom."

THE GREAT REVERSAL

Because the coming of the kingdom of God entails this exaltation of the humble and the humbling of the exalted, I refer to the Day of the Lord as "the great reversal." The earth today is so fundamentally unjust that only through such a great reversal can the earth be made just. So the Day of the Lord will be the day when all wrongs are made right, and much of this present system will be fundamentally turned upside down. This is why every sincere Christian must take to heart the exhortation of Paul the apostle, who said:

> Do nothing from selfishness or empty conceit, but with humility of mind regard one another as more important than yourselves; do not merely look out for your own personal interests, but also for the interests of others. Have this attitude in yourselves which was also in Christ Jesus, who, although He existed in the form of God, did not regard equality with God a thing to be grasped, but emptied Himself, taking the form of a bond-servant, and being made in the likeness of men. Being found in appearance as a man, He humbled Himself by becoming obedient to the point of death, even death on a cross. (Phil. 2:3–8)

For those who took Paul's advice in this age and, in the imitation of Christ, chose to serve, they will be exalted. For those who reject Paul's advice and exalt themselves, they will be humbled and possibly even cast into the lake of fire. The kingdom that will be established when Jesus returns will be built upon a foundation of justice. The message that Jesus proclaimed was a message of severe warning to the proud, to the self-confident, and to the oppressor. But to the humble, the broken, and the oppressed who placed their hope in God alone, the message was purely *good news*.

REBUILDING THE EARTH

During the time of the Great Tribulation, the Bible speaks of tremendous natural disasters, including multiple great earthquakes, which will result in entire cities collapsing and tremendous topographical changes across the globe:

> And there were flashes of lightning and sounds and peals of thunder; and there was a great earthquake, such as there had not been since man came to be upon the earth, so great an earthquake was it, and so mighty. The great city was split into three parts, and the cities of the nations fell. Babylon the great was remembered before God, to give her the cup of the wine of His fierce wrath. And every island fled away, and the mountains were not found. And huge hailstones, about one hundred pounds each, came down from heaven upon men; and men blasphemed God because of the plague of the hail, because its plague was extremely severe. (Rev. 16:18–21)

So it is in this context that after Jesus returns the righteous will begin the renovation of the earth: "Then they will rebuild the ancient ruins, they will raise up the former devastations; and they will repair the ruined cities, the desolations of many generations" (Isa. 61:4). Now, perhaps you are saying to yourself, "What? We have to rebuild the earth? That seems like *a lot* of work!" But stop and consider the wonder of what is being conveyed here. How many reading this would jump at the opportunity to be part of Jesus's official kingdom architectural and engineering team, or His official Global garden-planning committee? What primary architectural style will be used during this time? Will Jesus direct us to simply build traditional Middle Eastern–style concrete-block homes, or will He enjoy building ornately detailed Victorian mansions, or Gothic castles, or Hobbit-style homes with an organic Art Nouveau flair? Or, will an entirely new form of architecture be used, one that humankind has never seen before? This may all sound a bit silly in its speculation, but I actually believe we should get lost in such dreaming as we meditate upon the nature of the age to come. For in truth, this reality, that of our participation in renovation of the earth in partnership with the King of kings, is as real as our present day-to-day drudgery. This kind of dreaming is very much the hope of the Gospel.

But how often are these substantial and physical realities of the age to come ever discussed in churches when the Gospel is preached? At least in my experience, almost never. Yet the truth is that when we hear these things, something in our hearts leaps and rejoices. Being free to utilize our full potential as our Creator made us, to create the most dazzling and regal gardens and homes and landscapes, makes us far more excited than the idea of eternally floating around a cloudy, celestial realm that we cannot truly relate to. We cannot truly relate to a disembodied state precisely because we were created to have immortal and glorified bodies and to live on a glorified and liberated earth! Thus it is such substantial, physical, and real descriptions that profoundly resonate within us. This is what we were created for. And if we turn to Jesus for the cleansing of our sins and remain firm in our faith, this is exactly what we will inherit. When Jesus preached the good news of the kingdom to the people of Galilee, this is what He was talking about!

THERE WILL BE GARDENING

If you asked just about anyone you know what they would prefer—

to go to their daily jobs or to work out in their gardens—a vast majority would prefer to simply "play" in their gardens. There's something profoundly soothing about the work one does in a garden. There is a primal, deep satisfaction that comes from enjoying the fruit of one's own labors and partnering with nature to produce beauty and sweetness.

A few years ago, I took several wooden poles, each about twenty feet long, and made a massive tepee about a stone's throw outside my back window. I planted a mixture of morning glory and pole beans all around the tepee except the front, to allow for a clear doorway. The plan was that by the end of the summer, we would have a towering pyramid of flowers that would also serve as a fort for my kids. And while they hid inside, they could eat all the green beans they wanted. It was, I thought, the perfect plan. The problem was, that year, for some reason nothing grew well, so my "bean pyramid of glory" was only a partial success at best. Such is life in this present age. Perhaps I'll try it again sometime with better success. But in the age to come, the prophet Amos informs us that all of our gardening adventures will be pure success:

> "Behold, days are coming," declares the LORD, "when the plowman will overtake the reaper and the treader of grapes him who sows seed; when the mountains will drip sweet wine and all the hills will be dissolved. Also I will restore the captivity of My people Israel, and they will rebuild the ruined cities and live in them; They will also plant vineyards and drink their wine, and make gardens and eat their fruit. I will also plant them on their land, and they will not again be rooted out from their land which I have given them," says the LORD your God. (Amos 9:13–15)

The imagery of the plowman overtaking the reaper simply means that there will be such an abundance of fruits and vegetables to harvest that the one picking the fruit will still be reaping when it is time to plow the fields for next year's crops. There will never be an off year when the heat or the rain or the humidity or anything will be too much or not enough. The Lord will breathe upon and bless every step of the process. The inhabitants of the land are portrayed as planting vineyards and enjoying the wine, as planting gardens and enjoying the fruit. "'In that day,' declares the LORD of hosts, 'every one of you will invite his neighbor to sit under his vine and under his fig tree'" (Zech. 3:10). When Jesus preached the good news, He was simply expositing what had already been proclaimed through the writings of the Jewish prophets. He was explaining all of the good things that the Lord has in store for everyone who repents of sin and turns to Him. These are the things Jesus spoke of when He proclaimed *the Gospel of the kingdom!*

NO MORE WAR

I am not a pacifist. I believe that in a world filled with evil, unfortunately, there is a time when wars and a violent response are necessary. But I also know that war is never something to be yearned for or that anyone should rejoice in. When I consider the number of American veterans who are now suffering with post-traumatic stress disorder or are committing suicide on a daily basis, I hate war. When I look at the ongoing carnage and death unfolding in the nations of Iraq and Syria, I hate it. This is why everyone, soldier and pacifist alike, would agree that we can all rejoice in the age to come, when "[Christ] will judge between many peoples and render decisions for mighty, distant nations. Then they will hammer their swords into plowshares and their spears into pruning hooks; nation will not lift up sword against nation, and never again will they train for war" (Micah 4:3).

Jesus Himself will be the King of the earth. He will settle disputes among nations, and there will no longer be any wars. Instead of manufacturing missiles, the people of the earth will be assembling farming instruments. Never again will a child lie in bed trembling through the night as the ground rumbles beneath her bed from the shelling of a nearby target. Never again will a father or mother go off to war and not come home. No more prosthetic limbs or traumatic brain injuries. There will be no more "improvised explosive devices." All of the horrors of war will forever be a thing of the past. This is the nature of the age to come. When Jesus proclaimed the Gospel of the kingdom to the people, this was an integral part of His message.

THE RESURRECTION OF THE BODY

For many, the idea of a physical, earthly eternity is an entirely new concept. Yet the resurrection of the body and the redemption of the earth are both taught throughout the Bible. An afterlife that includes perpetually floating around in the spirit realm is what was taught by Greek philosophy. Though this belief has in many ways become a dominant way of thinking in the Church, it is actually a corruption of the true biblical hope. While a future physical resurrection is different from what many have always been taught, there is something nonetheless that deeply resonates within all of us when we talk about things like gardening in a glorified, redeemed, restored creation. Something in us leaps with eager expectation when we talk of these things far more than when we talk about floating around forever in a disembodied state in the clouds. Randy Alcorn, author of the book *Heaven*, accurately explains this dynamic:

> I've never met anyone who wants to be a ghost. The resurrected Jesus reassured his fearful disciples, "Touch me, I'm not a ghost." Yet we picture an afterlife in which we become ghosts—the very things his disciples were afraid of and Jesus promised he wasn't.
>
> Our bodies and our God-given appetites and taste buds don't permit us to desire to eat gravel. Why? Because we were not made to eat gravel. Trying to develop an appetite for a disembodied existence in a non-physical Heaven is like trying to develop an appetite for gravel. It's not going to work. Nor should it.
>
> What God made us to desire, and therefore what we do desire, is exactly what God promises to those who follow Jesus: the resurrected life in a resurrected body, with the resurrected Christ on a resurrected earth. Our desires correspond precisely

to God's plans. It's not that we want something, then engage in wishful thinking that what we want exists. It's the opposite—the reason we want it is precisely because it does or will exist. Resurrected people in a resurrected universe isn't our idea—it's God's.[2]

When Jesus proclaimed the Gospel of the kingdom, this is precisely what He was proclaiming. Jesus was calling everyone to repent in light of the Day of Judgment, when we will all either inherit the resurrection of the righteous to life or the resurrection of the unrighteous to eternal condemnation.

THE AMILLENNIALIST CORRUPTION OF THE BIBLICAL TESTIMONY

Throughout the majority of Church history, Christians were taught two things about the age to come. First, they were taught that the hope and destiny of Christians is in a heavenly, disembodied state and not on the earth. Second, Christians were taught that because God is done with the Jews, the coming kingdom of God would have no distinctly Jewish characteristics whatsoever. This belief is what is called *amillennialism*. This was the predominant belief of most Christians throughout much of Church history. Ever since the work of scholar Anthony Hoekema (d. 1988), however, many Christian theologians have begun to see the error of their ways and now acknowledge that the kingdom of God will in fact be on the earth. This is good! It is a wonderful thing to see Christian theologians casting off the Greek corruption of Christian theology and returning to the testimony of Scripture. But it is not enough. For despite acknowledging the error of their ways concerning the earthly, material nature of the coming kingdom, amillennialists continue to argue that in no way will the coming kingdom of God be a Jewish kingdom. In the next chapter, we will discuss what the Bible says concerning the *very* Jewish nature of the coming kingdom.

THE RESTORATION OF THE JEWISH

KINGDOM

As wonderful and glorious as all of the various descriptions of the coming kingdom are that we reviewed in the last chapter, they are only a small part of the picture that the Bible describes. Beyond being a restored Eden, a glorified agrarian utopia, it is also absolutely essential that we recognize that the Bible also describes a glorified Jewish kingdom. As we will see, the scriptural testimony is thorough, consistent, and clear that after Jesus returns, Israel will exist as a national kingdom, with many other distinct nations throughout the world rallying to her as the global leader. At the heart of the nation of Israel will be Jerusalem and the Temple, from which Jesus the Jewish King will reign over His people. While the Gentile nations will receive and fully benefit from all the blessings of that age, numerous passages describing this time portray a thoroughly distinct Jewish nation at the center of the world. The following diagram portrays the global order during the millennium as it is described throughout the Scriptures.

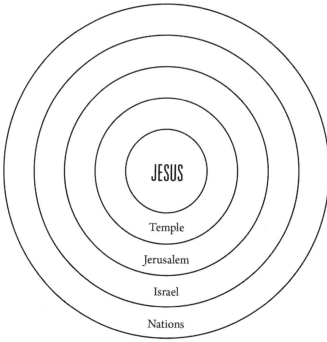

Structure of the Millennial Kingdom

Although the following survey is far from comprehensive, let us consider just some of the more prominent passages that speak of the distinctly Jewish nature of the age to come.

THE THRONE OF DAVID

The first feature of the age to come that we should highlight, a theme that is repeated throughout the Scriptures, is Jesus the Messiah sitting on "the throne of David," which is located on Mount Zion in Jerusalem. Of course, throughout the Scriptures, the term "the throne of David" is an obvious reference to the seat of authority over the Jewish royal dynasty. The word *Zion*, originally referring to the hill on the southeastern edge of Jerusalem where "the city of David" was located (see 2 Samuel 5:7–9), eventually came to be used as a synonym alternately for the Temple, all of Jerusalem, or even all of Israel.

Any effort to understand these terms as referring to anything apart from the Davidic (Jewish) royal dynasty is to miss its clear meaning as it is conveyed throughout the Scriptures. We have already reviewed the Davidic covenant, wherein God promised to King David that his throne would be established as eternal, with the promised "descendant" of David forever ruling from it:

> "The LORD also declares to you that the LORD will make a house for you. When your days are complete and you lie down with your fathers, I will raise up your descendant after you, who will come forth from you, and I will establish his kingdom. He shall build a house for My name, and I will establish the throne of his kingdom forever . . . Your house and your kingdom shall endure before Me forever; your throne shall be established forever." (2 Sam. 7:11–16)

The Davidic covenant, the promise of a restored Jewish kingdom, is reiterated many times throughout the Scriptures. In Psalm 110, God says to the Messiah, "'Sit at My right hand until I make Your enemies a footstool for Your feet.' The LORD will stretch forth your strong scepter from Zion, saying, 'Rule in the midst of Your enemies'" (vv. 1–2).

Another famous messianic prophecy in Isaiah informs that a promised child would be born to rule on David's throne forever:

> For a child will be born to us, a son will be given to us; and the government will rest on His shoulders; and His name will be called Wonderful Counselor, Mighty God, Eternal Father, Prince of Peace. There will be no end to the increase of His government or of peace, *on the throne of David* and over his kingdom, to establish it and to uphold it with justice and righteousness *from then on and forevermore.* The zeal of the LORD of hosts will accomplish this. (Isa. 9:6–7; emphasis added)

Later, Isaiah also states that "a throne will even be established in lovingkindness, and a judge will sit on it in faithfulness in the tent of David" (Isa. 16:5).

Another profound reiteration of the promises made to Israel and David are found in the prophecies of Jeremiah:

> "Behold, days are coming," declares the LORD, "when I will fulfill the good word which I have spoken concerning the house of Israel and the house of Judah. In those days and at that time I will cause a righteous Branch of David to spring forth; and He shall execute justice and righteousness on the earth. In those days Judah will be saved and Jerusalem will dwell in safety; and this is the name by which she will be called: the LORD is our righteousness." (Jer. 33:14–16)

This passage contains important elements from both the Abrahamic and the Davidic covenants. First, the reference to the "house of Israel and the house of Judah" is attributable to both covenants. And second, the phrase "Branch of David" is another clear reference to the promised descendant of King David who will specifically rule over and protect all Israel and Judah. We must take note of the references to both the northern and the southern kingdoms. Jesus will not merely rule over "the house of Israel," but also "the house of Judah," being together the fully restored and unified "whole house of Israel."

AMILLENNIALISM AND THE DAVIDIC COVENANT

Amillennialism, we must understand, interprets all of these prophecies concerning a future restored Jewish kingdom in an allegorical or non-literal manner. For example, according to N. T Wright, the city of Jerusalem, "had been simply an advance metaphor."[1] Whether we are speaking of Israel, the land, the Temple, Jerusalem, or the Jewish kingdom, according to the amillennialist view, none of these things are to be taken literally. They are nearly all interpreted as metaphors pointing to something much better yes, but quite different from their historical counterparts. While it is true of course that the things to come will be much better than, for example, the historical Jewish Temple or the ancient Jewish kingdom, to say that they will be something entirely different than what God has promised, quite frankly, is to accuse Him of being dishonest. What God has promised, He will deliver on. This isn't to say that the Bible does not use metaphors or symbolic language. But when one examines just how far amillennialists must go to reinterpret such common biblical themes in a symbolic manner, absent of any distinctly Jewish characteristics, it can truly begin to border on absurd. Let us take seriously the comments of David Baron, the eighteenth-century Messianic Jewish exegete who warned against going too far in "spiritualizing the prophecies—making Israel and Zion to mean the Church":

> I confess this system of interpretation has no consistency about it, and makes the Word of God the most meaningless and unintelligible book in the world. For instance, we read here, "I will bring again the captivity of My people Israel and Judah . . . and I will cause them to return to the land that I gave to their fathers." (Jer. 30:3 KJV) If Israel be the Church, who is Judah? If Judah be the Church, who is Israel? What is the "captivity" the Church has endured? And where is "the land" from which the Church has been driven out, and to which it will return?[2]

Hundreds of other such examples could be considered, some of which we will examine as we move on. Simply stated, the amillennialist perspective simply cannot be reconciled with any straightforward reading of the Scriptures, which repeatedly affirm a future restoration of the Jewish kingdom. Nowhere within the New Testament is there ever even the slightest hint of the new covenant superseding or doing away with the promises made to King David concerning a future restoration of his kingdom.

By accepting in a literal sense these prophecies that speak of the Messiah who will one day rule as the Jewish king on the throne of David, the Magis from the East came and asked, "Where is He who has been born *King of the Jews? For we saw His star in the east and have come to worship Him*" (Matt. 2:2; emphasis added). Of course, the Magi were correct. The King of the Jews had been born! Later, just before His crucifixion, "Jesus stood before the governor, and the governor questioned Him, saying, 'Are You the King of the Jews?' And Jesus said to him, 'It is as you say'" (Matt. 27:11). Yes, Jesus fully understood and affirmed that He was the King of the Jewish people who would someday rule as king over a restored Jewish kingdom—one that would last *"from then on and forevermore."* We cannot claim to affirm the Gospel as it was understood and proclaimed by the apostles unless we proclaim the future coming of the Jewish King who will rule the world from Jerusalem. To proclaim anything less is to diminish and distort the message of the Gospel.

ISRAEL WILL BE EXALTED AS THE CHIEF AMONG THE NATIONS

Not only will a Jewish man return to rule the world, but as the King of the Jewish people, He will rule over a restored Jewish kingdom that will in turn be exalted above all other nations. Within the prophecy of Isaiah, we find at least two of the most significant and substantial prophecies that describe the coming Jewish kingdom. The first is found in chapter 2, beginning with, "The word which Isaiah the son of Amoz saw concerning Judah and Jerusalem." The substance of the prophecy begins:

> Now it will come about that in the last days the mountain of the house of the LORD will be established as the chief of the mountains, and will be raised above the hills; and all the nations will stream to it. And many peoples will come and say, "Come, let us go up to the mountain of the LORD, to the house of the God of Jacob; that He may teach us concerning His ways and that we may walk in His paths." For the law will go forth from Zion and the word of the LORD from Jerusalem. And He will

judge between the nations, and will render decisions for many peoples; and they will hammer their swords into plowshares and their spears into pruning hooks. Nation will not lift up sword against nation, and never again will they learn war. (Isa. 2:1–4)

The key phrase that we must zero in on is, "In the last days the mountain of the house of the LORD will be established as the chief of the mountains." Throughout the Scriptures, "mountain" is used to refer to a kingdom or a nation (see Jeremiah 51:25; Daniel 2:35; Obadiah; Psalms 30:7; 72:3; and Revelation 17:9–11). So the kingdom of the House of YHVH God (which was previously identified with Judah and Jerusalem) will be the leader among all the other nations of the earth, which will come "streaming" to Jerusalem. The law for the whole earth will go forth from Israel. What this passage makes quite clear is that during the coming Millennium, distinct nations will continue to exist, and Israel will be their exalted leader.

The prophet Amos also described the future restoration of the Jewish (Davidic) kingdom, which would "possess" many other nations: "'In that day I will raise up the fallen booth of David, and wall up its breaches; I will also raise up its ruins and rebuild it as in the days of old; that they may possess the remnant of Edom and all the nations who are called by My name,' declares the LORD who does this" (Amos 9:11–12). ("Possessing" other nations here is simply a reference to their leadership over these nations.)

The final seven chapters of Isaiah's prophecy also have much to say about the age to come. Chapter 60, speaking of the coming Jewish kingdom, begins with a hearty call for rejoicing: "Arise, shine; for your light has come, and the glory of the LORD has risen upon you. For behold, darkness will cover the earth and deep darkness the peoples; but the LORD will rise upon you and His glory will appear upon you" (vv. 1–2). And once more, Israel is described as the center of the earth, with other nations being drawn to her leadership: "Nations will come to your light, and kings to the brightness of your rising" (v. 3). After this, foreigners are pictured as bringing

Jews from among the nations to their home in Israel: "Lift up your eyes round about and see; they all gather together, they come to you. Your sons will come from afar, and your daughters will be carried in the arms" (v. 4). Then comes a glorious picture of Gentiles from throughout the region and throughout all the earth coming to pay tribute, to show honor, and to bring gifts to the kingdom of Israel:

> Then you will see and be radiant, and your heart will thrill and rejoice; because the abundance of the sea will be turned to you, the wealth of the nations will come to you. A multitude of camels will cover you, the young camels of Midian and Ephah; all those from Sheba will come; they will bring gold and frankincense, and will bear good news of the praises of the LORD. All the flocks of Kedar will be gathered together to you, the rams of Nebaioth will minister to you; they will go up with acceptance on My altar, and I shall glorify My glorious house. Who are these who fly like a cloud and like the doves to their lattices? Surely the coastlands will wait for Me; and the ships of Tarshish will come first, to bring your sons from afar, their silver and their gold with them, for the name of the LORD your God, and for the Holy One of Israel because He has glorified you. (vv. 5–9)

But beyond bringing Jews from among the nations back to their homeland, along with tremendous wealth and gifts, the Gentiles will also help build the kingdom itself, offering themselves as workers for its glorification:

> Foreigners will build up your walls, and their kings will minister to you; for in My wrath I struck you, and in My favor I have had compassion on you. Your gates will be open continually; they will not be closed day or night, so that men may bring to you the wealth of the nations, with their kings led in procession. For the nation and the kingdom which will not serve you will perish, and the nations will be utterly ruined. The glory of Lebanon will come to you, the juniper, the box tree and the cypress together, to beautify the place of My sanctuary; and I shall make the place of My feet glorious. (vv. 10–13)

Even those who were Israel's greatest enemies will come and prostrate themselves before Israel, acknowledging that they indeed are the people that the Lord has chosen, through which He will glorify His name. Imagine a sea of representatives coming from Lebanon, Saudi Arabia, Syria, Jordan, Iran, and other nations throughout the region, coming and "bowing" down to Israel, declaring that Jerusalem is indeed the city of YHVH God Almighty: "The sons of those who afflicted you will come bowing to you, and all those who despised you will bow themselves at the soles of your feet; and they will call you the city of the LORD, the Zion of the Holy One of Israel. Whereas you have been forsaken and hated with no one passing through, I will make you an everlasting pride, a joy from generation to generation" (vv. 14–15).

I was recently talking to two Muslims whose children attend a class with one of my daughters. I was sitting there reading a book by British Bible teacher David Pawson, titled *Defending Christian Zionism*. This caught the attention of these two Muslims, and a friendly, though slightly awkward conversation began. They both expressed that for Muslims, the word *Zion* is filled with immense negative connotations. In fact, it is actually the worst word they know. Now, of course, I tried to explain the actual biblical meaning of the term *Zion* to alleviate their irrational fears and to share the Gospel a bit in the process, but it did little to assuage their angst over the word *Zionism* splashed across the cover of my book. As we talked, I could see the hatred that this word conjured up, and I thought of this passage in Isaiah and how truly profound it really is. Imagine a cloud of repentant (former) Muslims, coming to Israel, to the Jewish people, and declaring that Jerusalem is "the city of the LORD, the Zion of the Holy One of Israel." This is truly profound! It will be a miracle of miracles, a profound moment of reconciliation! Yet this is precisely what Isaiah says will take place in the age to come after Jesus returns. *Come, Lord Jesus!*

Finally, in Isaiah 61, we are again told that during this period, the Jews, together with those who have come from the surrounding nations, will rebuild Israel, much of which will have been destroyed or greatly damaged during the final three and a half years of the tribulation (we will discuss this in much more detail later):

> Then they will rebuild the ancient ruins, they will raise up the former devastations; and they will repair the ruined cities, the desolations of many generations. Strangers will stand and pasture your flocks, and foreigners will be your farmers and your vine-dressers. But you will be called the priests of the LORD; you will be spoken of as ministers of our God. You will eat the wealth of nations, and in their riches you will boast. (Isa. 61:4–6)

As you can see, "strangers" (a biblical term used for foreigners) will assist Israel in the reconstruction of the kingdom. Israel is portrayed as enjoying an exalted state, receiving from and enjoying the wealth of the nations.

THE MILLENNIAL PILGRIMAGE

Zechariah the prophet, after describing the military gathering of the nations against Jerusalem in the last days followed by the return of Jesus on the Mount of Olives, then continued his prophecy by detailing the magnificent pilgrimage that will take place each year when many nations will travel to Jerusalem to worship Jesus and celebrate the Feast of Tabernacles, or Booths (Hebrew: *Sukkot*). Every year, multitudes of people from throughout the nations will go up to Jerusalem for this purpose. Consider this profoundly powerful picture of the coming Jewish kingdom:

> Then it will come about that any who are left of all the nations that went against Jerusalem will go up from year to year to worship the King, the LORD of hosts, and to celebrate the Feast of Booths. And it will be that whichever of the families of the earth does not go up to Jerusalem to worship the King, the LORD of hosts, there will be no rain on them. If the family of Egypt does not go up or enter, then no rain will fall on them; it will be the

plague with which the LORD smites the nations who do not go up to celebrate the Feast of Booths. (Zech. 14:16–18)

Isaiah also touches on this theme, speaking of the glory of the nations flowing to Jerusalem like a stream: "Behold, I extend peace to her like a river, and the glory of the nations like an overflowing stream" (Isa. 66:12). During this time, "many peoples will come and say, 'Come, let us go up to the mountain of the LORD, to the house of the God of Jacob. He will teach us his ways, so that we may walk in his paths'" (Isa. 2:3). Among all of the wonderful things that Jesus likely spoke of when He declared the *Gospel of the kingdom*, the coming annual pilgrimage to Jerusalem, "the city of the great King," was one of them (Matt. 5:35).

THE GREAT ISLAMIC COUNTERFEIT

Of course, it is difficult for me to consider this picture of the nations streaming to Jerusalem each year to worship Jesus without my mind turning to that which in so many ways is the great counterfeit of this present age: the Islamic hajj to Mecca. One of the five foundational "pillars" of Islam is that every Muslim believer who is able to raise the necessary funds should at least once in their lifetime make a religious pilgrimage to Mecca. As a result of the colossal number of Muslims making hajj each year, the Grand Mosque in the city of Mecca is the most visited site on earth.

There is a series of traditions (Arabic: *ahadeeth*) that involves traveling to Mecca to kiss a black stone embedded on the corner of the shrine known as the Kaaba ("the cube"). Muslim tradition holds that this black stone fell from heaven: "The Messenger of Allah (peace and blessings of Allah be upon him) said: 'The Black Stone came down from Paradise.'"[3] This is strikingly similar to the tradition that existed in Ephesus during the first century regarding the image of Artemis: "After quieting the crowd, the town clerk said, 'Men of Ephesus, what man is there after all who does not know that the city of the Ephesians is guardian of the temple of the great

Artemis and of the image which fell down from heaven?" (Acts 19:35). Not surprisingly the head of the Artemis statue was also made of a carved black meteorite, just like the black rock embedded into a corner of the Kaaba.

Muslims believe that the stone has the ability to absorb and absolve the sins of those who kiss or touch it: "When the Black Stone came down from Paradise, it was whiter than milk, but the sins of the sons of Adam made it black."[4]

And so, according to these sacred traditions, when a Muslim comes to touch the black stone during their pilgrimage, all of their sins committed until that point in their lives are believed to be wiped clean: "the Messenger of Allah . . . said: 'Touching [the Black Stone] is an expiation for sins.'"[5]

Strangely, it is said that the Black Stone will become animated, possessing eyes and a mouth, and actually stand as a witness on the Day of Resurrection and judgment, either condemning or acquitting those whose sins it had absorbed: "The Messenger of Allah . . . said concerning the Stone: 'By Allah, Allah will bring it forth on the Day of Resurrection, and it will have two eyes with which it will see and a tongue with which it will speak, and it will testify in favor of those who touched it in sincerity.'"[6]

So on one side, the Bible says that the day is coming when all people will make an annual pilgrimage to Jerusalem to worship Jesus, who will sit in the center of the Temple in the midst of Jerusalem. And on the other side, here today, Muslims from every nation come to Mecca each year to kiss the Black Stone, which sits at the center of Al-Masjid Al-Haram, the Grand or Sacred Mosque. This, of course, is pure idolatry and a clear remnant of the pagan roots of Islam. The Islamic hajj is no doubt the great Satanic counterfeit of the true pilgrimage that God has ordained for all the nations who will stream to Jerusalem each year to worship Jesus the King!

THE JEWISH TEMPLE WILL BE REBUILT

Perhaps one of the most detailed and amazing portions of scripture that describes the future, messianic, millennial kingdom of Israel—specifically, a rebuilt Jewish Temple—is found in Ezekiel 40–48. This text, one continuous prophecy, is also one of the most glaringly difficult for amillennialists who deny there will be a literal, future, messianic, millennial kingdom in Israel. Because these nine chapters contain such a tremendous amount of meticulous detail, any effort to interpret them symbolically or metaphorically will inevitably result in a circus of bizarre interpretations and speculation that would make even Origen blush.

The first segment of the vision begins in chapters 40–43, wherein Ezekiel is given an angelically guided tour of a future Jewish Temple in Jerusalem. Consider just the following brief sample:

> And behold, there was a wall on the outside of the temple all around, and in the man's hand was a measuring rod of six cubits, each of which was a cubit and a handbreadth. So he measured the thickness of the wall, one rod; and the height, one rod. Then he went to the gate which faced east, went up its steps and measured the threshold of the gate, one rod in width; and the other threshold was one rod in width. The guardroom was one rod long and one rod wide; and there were five cubits between the guardrooms. And the threshold of the gate by the porch of the gate facing inward was one rod. (Eze. 40:5–7)

Here we have an amazingly detailed floor plan for a temple, the divinely designed contours of which will someday rise above the millennial city of Jerusalem. But if this small description does not yet sufficiently inspire, I trust the beauty of the following descriptions will.

In chapter 44 there is a reference that many might easily pass over. Speaking of the duties of those who are called to be priests from the tribe of Levi, verse 11 says, "They shall slaughter the burnt offering and the sacrifice for the people, and they shall stand before them to minister to them." I understand that this might not appeal to everyone reading this, but in my case, the aroma of a good barbecue is something truly glorious. One of my neighbors has what is called a Big Green Egg—essentially a large, green, porcelain cooker that can be used as a grill, an oven, or a smoker. Sometimes he slow-smokes meats from morning till night. The blessed aroma blankets the neighborhood—a small reminder of the aroma that will emanate day and night from the future Jewish Temple. Let all the vegetarians shout, "Hallelujah!"

But beyond the aroma of the grilled meat, there will also be the wafting fragrance of incense. The specific recipe for the incense to be offered on the altar is described in Exodus: "Then the LORD said to Moses, 'Take for yourself spices, stacte and onycha and galbanum, spices with pure frankincense; there shall be an equal part of each. With it you shall make incense, a perfume, the work of a perfumer, salted, pure, and holy'" (Ex. 30:34–35).

I've always had a fondness for the authentic resin incenses used by the monks and priests in Catholic or Orthodox churches and monasteries. While frankincense is the most common and dominant resin used in most mixtures, there are in fact dozens of delicate and complex resins and spices used. No matter how men may try, with all of their advancements in the knowledge of chemical composition, artificial flavorings, and synthetic fragrances, they simply cannot match the delicacy, complexity, and variety of flavors and fragrances that the Lord causes to spring forth from the earth. Who can replicate the unique flavor of garlic, ginger, galanga, or Jamaican cinnamon, or the fragrance of a jasmine flower or a gardenia? Of course, we tend to think of sight and sound as the most powerful of the senses. We all know that a photograph, no matter how wonderfully composed, can never fully capture the power of seeing a gloriously colorful sunset in the desert. Neither can an audio recording ever truly capture the vibrantly layered resonation of your favorite music played or sung live. There is as much evocative power to stir one's memories, emotions, and imagination in fragrances and aromas as there is in any of these other things. I love to imagine and ponder the glory of the coming city, where the very real aroma of grilled meats and the fragrance of divinely formulated incense will continually fill the air around the vicinity of the Temple, all intermingled with the worship songs of the mass choirs as they sing the melodies of heaven, perpetually glorifying the Lord. *All of these things should make our hearts rejoice!* In passages such as these, not only do we have a description of the coming kingdom that we can all appreciate and get excited about, but we also clearly have a description of a thoroughly Jewish kingdom. When Jesus preached *the Gospel of the kingdom*, this was a fundamental part of what He proclaimed.

THE JERUSALEM RIVER

In Ezekiel 47 we again find a description of something that many might think very little of, but which I find deeply moving on a personal level. A little bit of background is necessary. I grew up about twenty-five miles south of Boston, only fourteen miles from the Atlantic Ocean. All my life, my father has been a commercial rod-and-reel fisherman. As far back as I can remember, I was on the water with my dad. Together we've fished all over Cape Cod Bay, Buzzard's Bay, Nantucket Sound, and out as far as Stellwagen Bank.

As I mentioned earlier, I was an extremely difficult teenager. When I came to faith at age nineteen, the dramatic and sudden transformation in my life was one of the more significant contributing factors to my dad coming to the Lord at age fifty-two. The Lord has been so merciful and gracious to my family. A year and a half after I came to faith, I moved to the Midwest to attend Bible school. But what was intended to be a temporary move has now grown to well over twenty years. Though I've returned several times to visit since I first left, I've never been able to go fishing with my father.

Several years ago, my dad announced that he was in the advanced stages of macular degeneration and is losing his sight. His fishing days are quickly drawing to a close. With a large family (my wife and I have five kids) and an extremely busy schedule, I'm doubtful that I will ever be able to get out there again on the water with my dad. Just the thought breaks my heart. But having said all of this, when I read the following portion of Ezekiel's prophecy that speaks of the coming messianic kingdom in which a river will run out of Jerusalem southward, turning the Dead Sea into a freshwater lake filled with fish, my heart leaps. I've been blessed to share with my father that in the age to come, *there be will be fishing!*

On a recent trip to Jordan, visiting some missionary friends, we took a trip to the eastern shores of the Dead Sea. As I stood there in that hot, salty, and oily brine, looking out over this vast lake that doesn't contain a single fish, I pondered Ezekiel's prophecy. *Someday my dad and I are going to go fishing there together*, I thought. I challenge anyone who loves fishing to read the following passage without becoming thoroughly excited about the nature of the coming messianic kingdom:

> [The] waters go out toward the eastern region and go down into the Arabah; then they go toward the sea, being made to flow into the sea, and the waters of the sea become fresh. It will come about that every living creature which swarms in every place where the river goes, will live. And there will be very many fish, for these waters go there and the others become fresh; so everything will live where the river goes. And it will come about that fishermen will stand beside it; from Engedi to Eneglaim there will be a place for the spreading of nets. Their fish will be according to their kinds, like the fish of the Great Sea, very many. (Ezek. 47:8–10)

Needless to say, this good news ministers to my heart in a powerful way, edifying my spirit, building up my hope in the age to come. When I think about *the Gospel—the good news—*of the kingdom, this passage is always at the forefront of my mind. This was the Gospel of the kingdom that Jesus preached.

THE MESSIANIC KINGDOM IN THE NEW TESTAMENT

Although supersessionists claim that the New Testament "reinterprets" (read: *changes*) common concepts found throughout the Old Testament, the truth is that every time the coming kingdom of God is referenced through the New Testament, it thoroughly reflects and carries on the theme of the Old Testament.

At the every onset of the Gospel account in Luke, we find the angel Gabriel announcing to Mary the son she would carry and bear. And in doing so, he used exclusively Jewish terms and descriptions: "And behold, you will conceive in your womb and bear a son, and you shall name Him Jesus. He will be great and will be called the Son of the Most High; and the Lord God will give Him the throne of His father David; and He will reign over the house of Jacob forever, and His kingdom will have no end" (Luke 1:31–33). Notice that Gabriel told young Mary that her son would receive the "throne of his father David" and would "reign over the house of Jacob forever."

Much later, as Jesus spoke to His disciples of the time of His return and His enthronement as King, He also used profoundly Jewish descriptions. In Matthew 19 we see a perfect example of Jesus proclaiming the *Gospel of the kingdom*:

> Jesus said to them, "Truly I say to you, that you who have followed Me, in the regeneration when the Son of Man will sit on His glorious throne, you also shall sit upon twelve thrones, judging the twelve tribes of Israel. And everyone who has left houses or brothers or sisters or father or mother or children or farms for My name's sake, will receive many times as much, and will inherit eternal life. (vv. 28–29)

This passage implies that each of the twelve disciples will represent one of the twelve tribes. How much more Jewish can you get? The fact that Jesus spoke of the restoration of all twelve tribes in the age to come shows that He was indeed looking forward to a fully restored Jewish kingdom.

THE RESTORATION OF THE KINGDOM TO ISRAEL

Finally, we come to one more passage that truly proves that Jesus's Gospel centered around the coming Jewish kingdom. After Jesus returned from the dead and was dwelling among his disciples in His immortal, resurrected body, His disciples asked Him, "'Lord, is it at this time You are restoring the kingdom to Israel?' He said to them, 'It is not for you to know times or epochs which the Father has fixed by His own authority'" (Acts 1:6–7).

Notice that Jesus did not rebuke His disciples for their question (something He had done several other times when they'd asked bad questions). Instead, while refusing to address the timing, He assured His disciples that at the proper time, set by the Father, He Himself would return and restore the kingdom of Israel. Jesus did not reimagine the kingdom. He did not reinterpret the kingdom. He came to bring about its future restoration.

A short time later, after Pentecost, when Peter preached the Gospel to the Jewish people, he specifically harkened back to Jesus's words and spoke of "the period of restoration of all things about which God spoke by the mouth of His holy prophets from ancient time" (Acts 3:21). The word "restoration" in Greek is *apokatastasis*, which, according to *Thayer's Greek Lexicon*, means "restoration not only of the true theocracy, but also of the more perfect state which existed before the fall."[7] The very word "restore" infers a return to something that previously existed. A coming kingdom that would be utterly void of any Jewish characteristics is not a restoration. In fact, nowhere is the distinction between restorationism and replacement theology more pronounced than in the interpretation of these passages in Acts. If we read the commentaries on Acts 1:6–7 written by replacement theologians, we find much mocking of the disciples for being so "clueless," "oblivious," and "out of touch," for having such a fundamentally wrong perspective. As Gary Burge says, "[The disciples] have it exactly wrong."[8] Even John Calvin, in his commentary on this passage, intimates that Jesus must have looked at the disciples and thought, *How dumb can you be?!*[9] Why, then, was Peter, just two chapters later, under the anointing of the Holy Spirit, still preaching of a restoration of the Davidic theocracy? If you simply approach these passages from the perspective of one who is informed by the many clear promises of God made throughout the Old Testament, as Jesus's disciples indeed were, then the passage is very straightforward and easy to understand. When Jesus returns, at the time appointed by the Father, He will restore the Davidic kingdom of Israel in accordance with the unchanging and ever-reliable promises of God. When Jesus went about Galilee and proclaimed the good news concerning the coming kingdom, the restoration of the Jewish kingdom was precisely what He was preaching!

"Hosanna! Blessed is He who comes in the name of the Lord! The king of Israel!" (John 12:13 NKJV)

PART 2

TWO THOUSAND YEARS OF
SUPERSESSIONISM AND JEW-HATRED

CHRISTIAN JEW-HATRED: FROM INCEPTION
TO THE FOURTH CENTURY

E very Christian who studies Church history quickly becomes
aware that from very early on, something went profoundly
wrong. What began as a Jewish sect that welcomed in the Gentiles, soon became a Gentile-dominated group that looked down
with tremendous disdain upon any Jews who didn't convert to
the Christian faith, fully leaving their Jewish identity behind.
The purpose of this chapter is to demonstrate the clear relationship
and connection of supersessionism to the long historical continuum
of hatred, persecution, and suffering of Israel, God's covenant people.

ANTI-SEMITISM OR JEW-HATRED?

Today, when people speak of hatred toward the Jewish people, they
use the term "anti-Semitism," with someone who hates Jews being
described as an "anti-Semite." This term was first popularized in
1881 by Wilhelm Marr, a German radical, nationalist, and self-
described Jew-hater. Since that time, this term has all but replaced
the German word *Judenhass*, which simply means "Jew-hatred."
Although *anti-Semitism* may connote a more scientific reference,
technically, it might also infer a hatred of all Semitic peoples, of
which Arabs would by necessity be included. I've witnessed Arab
Muslims on several occasions make the claim that it is impossible
for them to be anti-Semitic because they themselves are Semites.
To avoid any such nonsense, and to use terms that are much more

forthright, I've chosen to use the terms "Jew-hatred," "anti-Jewish," or something similar.

DOES THE NEW TESTAMENT PROMOTE HATRED OF THE JEWS?

When studying the subject of Christian hatred of the Jewish people, one will find the common assertion among non-Christian writers that this hatred finds it roots in the New Testament. Within secular literature, it is all but a foregone conclusion that the New Testament actually promotes Jew-hatred. There is a glaring problem with this claim, however. Within the New Testament, what we have is essentially an interfamily dispute. No doubt, there are some passages that contain some very strong charges and harsh words. But in all such cases, these are examples of one Jewish individual, sect, school, or group leveling charges against or rebuking other Jews. One can just as easily find similar charges leveled by the Hebrew prophets throughout the Old Testament, yet these are never interpreted as promoting a hatred of Jews. Family disputes are just that, family disputes. But it is another thing entirely when Gentile Christians later began using these passages or very similar language for their own pro–Gentile Christian, anti-Jewish agendas. The writings of the early Christians employ not only the New Testament but also the Old for the purpose of anti-Jewish polemics and accusations. In either case, this must be acknowledged to be a fundamental abuse of the Scriptures by Gentiles to promote an anti-Jewish agenda. The problem is not with the New Testament (or the Old), but with the misuse and abuse of it by those who fell into arrogance of the worst order, utterly failing to heed the warnings contained within those very Scriptures (Rom. 11:20–25).

SUPERSESSIONISM AS THE FOUNDATION FOR JEW-HATRED

None of the historical abuse of Jews would have been possible if the Church had not rejected Paul's warnings. As we will see, supersessionism is the very foundation and the driving idea behind the vast majority of the hatred and persecution of the Jewish people throughout the earth for the past two thousand years. Following are the primary ideas that define Christian theological supersessionism. Although various teachers will often seek to express these ideas in different ways, these basic concepts are essentially shared by all supersessionists:

- The Church is the new and true Israel.

- Israel is no longer the people of God.

- The destruction of the Temple and Jerusalem in AD 70 was God's public demonstration of His rejection of Israel as His people.

- Israel's national rejection is permanent.

- Israel has rightly suffered, and continues to suffer, the curses of disobedience.

- The suffering of the Jews since AD 70 is the result of God's righteous judgment due to their collective guilt for their unbelief in rejecting and killing Jesus.

- The Jews are under God's divine curses for their disobedience.

- The suffering of the Jews is thus self-inflicted.

- The people who call themselves Jews today are the enemies of the Gospel and the Church.

Once one begins with these theological ideas, then the dangerous logic of supersessionism is fairly straightforward. While not every supersessionist necessarily carries these beliefs through to their logical conclusions, as we will see, a vast number of confessing Christians down through history, once they have embraced supersessionism, have gone on to carry out the most profoundly un-Christlike behavior imaginable toward the Jewish people. As we survey the many comments expressed by prominent leaders and theologians down through Church history, we will see all of these ideas expressed quite directly, multiple times, often in the vilest, most adversarial manner. The reality is that the step from claiming that an entire people has been forever rejected and cursed by God to actually hating and carrying out acts of hatred or violence is a small one. Most often, all that is necessary is some measure of political power in the hands of those who believe or espouse these things, and soon the most heinous acts follow. Let us consider the following partial, but altogether damning list of evidences.

TIME LINE OF CHRISTIAN SUPERSESSIONISM AND JEW-HATRED

AD 115 – In his Epistle to the Magnesians, Ignatius, bishop of Antioch, argued that any form of Judaism is incompatible with belief in Jesus as Messiah. "For if even unto this day we live after the manner of Judaism, we avow that we have not received grace."[1]

One can imagine just how shocked and grieved Paul the apostle, who continued to openly practice pharisaical Judaism throughout his life and ministry (cf. Acts 18:18; 21:26; 23:6; Phil. 3:6), would have felt upon reading such condemnations of any form of Jewish expression.

Paul made it quite clear that before Gentiles repented of their sins and put their faith in God and Jesus His Messiah, they were "separate from Christ, excluded from the commonwealth of Israel, and strangers to the covenants of promise, having no hope and without God in the world" (Eph. 2:12). He also presented the beginnings of the Church as a story of repentant Gentiles, former pagans, coming into the commonwealth of Israel and being grafted into a very Jewish olive tree (Rom. 11:17–19). Using this olive tree analogy, Paul reminded Gentiles that "it is not you who supports the root, but the root *supports* you" (Rom. 11:18; emphasis added). Yet according to Ignatius, it was the Jews who came to the Christian Church. Ignatius fundamentally reversed the equation: "It is monstrous to talk of Jesus Christ and to practice Judaism. For Christianity did not believe in Judaism, but Judaism in Christianity."[2]

"OUR COVENANT"

AD 120 – In the Epistle of Barnabas, we already find strong supersessionist sentiment expressed. There are repeated references to Christians as "the new" people, and the Jews as those who had been forever rejected. One passage actually states that the new covenant is "our covenant" that was not even given to the Jews. As we saw in a previous chapter, however, through the prophet Jeremiah, God said, "I will make a new covenant with *the house of Israel and with the house of Judah*" (Jer. 31:31; emphasis added). But Barnabas claimed that not only was the new covenant not made with Israel but that at the moment when Moses descended from Mount Sinai and broke the two tablets, the Jews "lost it . . . for ever":

> [C]ertain persons who pile up sin upon sin, saying that our covenant remains to them also. Ours it is; but they lost it in this way for ever, when Moses had just received it. For the scripture saith; And Moses was in the mountain fasting forty days and forty nights, and he received the covenant from the Lord, even tablets of stone written with the finger of the hand of the Lord. But they lost it by turning unto idols. For thus saith the Lord; Moses, Moses, come down quickly; for thy people whom thou broughtest out of the land of Egypt hath done unlawfully. And Moses understood, and threw the two tables from his hands; and their covenant was broken in pieces, that the covenant of the beloved Jesus might be sealed unto our hearts in the hope which springeth from faith in Him.[3]

"WE ARE THE TRUE ISRAELITIC RACE"

AD 150 – In Justin Martyr's "Dialogue with Trypho the Jew," we begin to find a much more well-developed supersessionist theology.

Speaking to Trypho, Justin said: "Since then God blesses this people [the Church], and calls them Israel, and declares them to be His inheritance, how is it that you repent not of the deception you practice on yourselves, as if you alone were the Israel, and speaking ill of the people whom God has blessed?"[4]

Bewildered by Justin's suggestion, Trypho then asks, "What, then? Are you Israel? And speaks He such things of you?" to which Justin later responded, "Christ is the Israel and the Jacob, even so we, who have been quarried out from the bowels of Christ, are the true Israelitic race."[5]

In just over one hundred years after the ministry of Jesus, the Gentile Christians had already begun to view themselves as the "true Israelitic race." This is profoundly dangerous thinking. Please think thorough this with me. If the Church is "the true Israelitic race," then are the Jews a false Israelitic race? Or are they simply no race at all? If the Jews are no longer Israel, then who are they? Once any group has been stripped of their identity and existence *in theory*, it is only a matter of time before someone will seek to strip them of their very existence *literally*. As tragic as it is, for the next two thousand years the belief that the Gentile-majority Christian Church is the new or true Israel has dominated the thinking of so much of the Church, even to this present day. The ramifications of the doctrine of supersessionism has for more than eighteen hundred years consistently produced the worst form of hatred and abuse imaginable.

"YOU NOW SUFFER JUSTLY"

Not only did Justin claim that the Jews had been replaced by the Church; he also offered a radical reinterpretation of the sign of the Abrahamic covenant. Circumcision, of course, was a sign that God had given to the sons of Israel to indicate their having been set apart through His covenant with them. Justin negatively reinterpreted this sign along with the Sabbath not as signs of God's promises to Israel but in order that they could perpetually be singled out to "justly suffer":

For the circumcision according to the flesh, which is from Abraham, was given for a sign; that you may be separated from other nations, and from us; and that you alone may suffer that which you now justly suffer; and that your land may be desolate, and your cities burned with fire; and that strangers may eat your fruit in your presence, and not one of you may go up to Jerusalem. For you are not recognized among the rest of men by any other mark than your fleshly circumcision . . . As I stated before it was by reason of your sins and the sins of your fathers that, among other precepts, God imposed upon you the observance of the sabbath as a mark.[6]

This is where the dangerous logic of supersessionism is manifest. Once the Jews are viewed as being both rejected by God and justly punished then virtually any form of abuse becomes acceptable. After all, the abusers are simply reinforcing the very will of God. Very quickly did such abuse become a normal part of how Christians related to the Jewish people.

THE PEOPLE MADE VOID

AD 165 – Melito of Sardis, the bishop of Sardis near Smyrna in the region of modern-day Turkey, wrote a sermon titled "On the Pascha" (Easter). In this sermon, Melito perfectly articulated the theology of the divine rejection of the Jewish people: "The people Israel was precious before the Church arose, and the law was marvelous before the gospel was elucidated. But when the Church arose and the gospel took precedence, the model was made void, conceding its power to the reality . . . the people was made void when the church arose."[7]

It is critical to note Melito's articulation of supersessionism. If God Himself has rendered the Temple of Israel, the law, and the nation of Israel to be things of the past, then it logically follows that God Himself has made that people who are defined by those very things "void"—a nothingness, an empty space. Soon, the idea of Israel no longer being a people, and worse yet, *the effort to realize that idea* became a normal component of the mission of the Church.

ETERNALLY REJECTED BY GOD

AD 210 – Hippolytus of Rome, often referred to as the most important theologian of the third century, wrote his polemical "Expository Treatise against the Jews." Hippolytus developed the theme that because the Jews are collectively guilty for killing Jesus (deicide), they have corporately been eternally and forever cut off from God, both in this age and the next:

> Now, then, incline your ear to me, and hear my words, and give heed, you Jew. Many a time do you boast yourself, in that you condemned Jesus of Nazareth to death, and gave Him vinegar and gall to drink; and you vaunt yourself because of this. Come therefore, and let us consider together whether perchance you do not boast unrighteously, O Israel, (and) whether that small portion of vinegar and gall has not brought down this fearful threatening upon you, (and) whether this is not the cause of your present condition involved in these myriad troubles . . . And then hear what follows: "Let their eyes be darkened, that they see not." And surely you have been darkened in the eyes of your soul with a darkness utter and everlasting. . . . I produce now the prophecy of Solomon, which speaks of Christ, and announces clearly and perspicuously things concerning the Jews; and those which not only are befalling them at the present time, but those, too, which shall befall them in the future age, on account of the contumacy and audacity which they exhibited toward the Prince of Life.[8]

Not only did Hippolytus cast the Jews' alleged rejection by God as "everlasting," but he also claimed their suffering and collective punishment to be perpetual.

How soon the Church had forgotten the words of Paul, who said that though, yes, they had rejected their Messiah and "stumbled," their fallen state was not at all permanent: "I say then, God has not rejected His people, has He? May it never be! . . . God has not rejected His people whom He foreknew . . . I say then, they did not stumble so as to [permanently] fall, did they? May it never be!" (Rom. 11:1, 2, 11).

According to Paul, the Jews were *partially and temporarily* hardened, but at the proper time, they all would be fully restored to their God (vv. 25–26). The result of their restoration would be "riches for the world" and "life from the dead" (vv. 12, 15). Yet the Church quickly began to claim that the Jews were permanently rejected by God. And if one surveys the writings of supersessionists today, it is easy to find this error repeated a thousand times over.

"THEY KILLED THE SON"

What horrific sin could an entire race commit that would condemn them to perpetual suffering? The answer, of course, was that such great suffering could only come from the ultimate and unforgivable sin of killing Jesus. Hippolytus expressed it this way:

> But why, O prophet, tell us, and for what reason, was the temple made desolate? Was it on account of that ancient fabrication of the calf? Was it on account of the idolatry of the people? Was it for the blood of the prophets? Was it for the adultery and fornication of Israel? By no means, he says; for in all these transgressions they always found pardon open to them, and benignity; but it was because they killed the Son . . . [9]

The idea that all Jewish people are collectively guilty for the crime of killing Jesus and that the guilt is genetically passed on has been widely held within the Church throughout much of its history. Multiple examples of various leaders, theologians, and "saints" of the Church follow in this time line. The idea may be partially rooted in the misapplication of a passage found in the gospel of Matthew, where we read of the Jews of Jesus's day calling down the blood of Jesus on themselves and their children:

> When Pilate saw that he was accomplishing nothing, but rather that a riot was starting, he took water and washed his hands in front of the crowd, saying, "I am innocent of this Man's blood;

see to that yourselves." And all the people said, "His blood shall be on us and on our children!" Then he released Barabbas for them; but after having Jesus scourged, he handed Him over to be crucified. (Matt. 27:24–26)

The problem, of course, with seeking to place the guilt for Jesus's death on any particular race is twofold. First, Jesus said of His own life, "No one has taken it away from Me, but I lay it down on My own initiative. I have authority to lay it down, and I have authority to take it up again" (John 10:18). In other words, although it was a joint effort on the part the Jews *and the Romans* to carry out His crucifixion, it was all ultimately His decision and His own plan. The second obvious problem in blaming the Jewish people for the death of Jesus lies in the collective guilt of all humanity.

WHO REALLY KILLED JESUS?

According to the prophet Isaiah, it was the sins not merely of the Jewish people but of all of us that specifically required Jesus to lay His life down: "All of us like sheep have gone astray, each of us has turned to his own way; but the LORD has caused the iniquity of us all to fall on Him" (Isa. 53:6). The long history of Christian accusation and condemnation toward the Jewish people for their alleged collective guilt in the death of Jesus is a demonstration of the Church's fundamental lack of understanding concerning its own sins and its own guilt. It betrays a complete of lack of awareness of the mercy it claims for itself. In the ultimate prophetic irony, by persecuting God's covenant people, the Church has essentially crucified the Jew and brought the bloodguilt for an unfathomable measure of suffering and death onto itself. No doubt, in God's eyes, Christians have been pointing the finger of accusation at themselves all along. Today, the Church must fall to its knees and cry out for mercy for its past sins. Even if we ourselves have not participated in these sins, we must all pray to avoid walking in the shameful manner of our forefathers.

"OUR JESUS"

AD 220 – The next shameful example of supersessionism producing disdain for the Jews can be found in the writings of Origen, who in the third century wrote of his "utter confidence" that the Jews were forever rejected by God: "We may thus assert in utter confidence that the Jews will not return to their earlier situation, for they have committed the most abominable of crimes, in forming this conspiracy against the Savior of the human race."[10] Origen continued: "Hence the city where Jesus suffered was necessarily destroyed, the Jewish nation was driven from its country, and another people [the Church] was called by God to the blessed election."[11]

We will repeatedly find the theme of God having destroyed Jerusalem, the Jewish Temple, and the entire nation as evidence of God's permanent rejection of the Jews as His people. So often will one find it claimed that such circumstances will remain forever. But if the destruction of the Nation and the Temple were evidence of God's rejection of the Jewish people, then would not the rebirth of the State of Israel indicate that God is not done with the Jewish people? This is precisely why supersessionists in modern times have either sought to diminish the many evidences of the miraculous and sovereign reestablishment of the State of Israel or have gone so far as to work diligently to delegitimize it.

Origen went on to use his supersessionist framework as the basis to issue abusive and condemning remarks about the Jews as a corporate people, all of which came as a result of their sins against not their Jesus, but *ours*: "And these wicked calamities, they have suffered, because they were a most wicked nation, which, although guilty of many other sins, yet has been punished so severely for none, as for those committed against *our Jesus*."[12]

Again, we can only imagine the grief of the apostle Paul at such comments. Not to mention the grief of Jesus Himself as Origen sought to strip the Jews of any claim to their own Messiah, though Jesus self-identified as "the King of the Jews" (Matt. 27:11).

LEGAL RESTRICTIONS

By the beginning of the fourth century, the separation between the Church and the Jewish community had become so wide that the Church began issuing restrictions on various forms of social interaction between the two groups. In time, the restrictions and decrees would become far more prohibitive.

AD 306 – The Church Synod of Elvira placed restrictions on various forms of community or social interaction between Christian and Jews. On threat of the loss of communion, canon 16 prohibited Christians from marrying Jews. Canon 48 made it a sinful act to bless a Jew's crops, and canon 50 forbade Christians to eat with Jews.[13] It had now become forbidden by Church law to even sit down and share a meal with a Jew!

No sooner were such Church restrictions issued than actual legal restrictions were added. Once Christians began to assume political power, it would become commonplace for the legal authorities to issue decrees rooted in their supersessionist prejudice toward the Jews.

AD 315 – Emperor Constantine published the Edict of Milan, and Jews could no longer live in Jerusalem. Although the Lord Himself had given the city of Jerusalem to the Jewish people (see Deuteronomy 1:8), now the Church had forbidden them from even living there. Jews were also forbidden to seek to dissuade any who left Judaism, at the threat of being burned alive. Any Christian who converted to Judaism was threatened with severe punishment:

> We wish to make it known to the Jews and their elders and their patriarchs that if, after the enactment of this law, any one of them dares to attack with stones or some other manifestation of anger another who has fled their dangerous sect and attached himself to the worship of God [Christianity], he must speedily be given to the flames and burned together with all his accomplices. Moreover, if any one of the population should join their

abominable sect and attend their meetings, he will bear with them the deserved penalties.[14]

AD 325 – The Council of Nicaea determined to forever separate the Christian celebration of Easter from its Jewish roots in the Passover. Seemingly forgetting that Jesus and the disciples all celebrated the Passover, the Council stated:

> Iit is unbecoming beyond measure that on this holiest of festivals we should follow the customs of the Jews. Henceforth let us have nothing in common with this odious people . . . We ought not, therefore, to have anything in common with the Jews . . . Our worship follows a . . . more convenient course . . . We desire, dearest brethren, to separate ourselves from the detestable company of the Jews . . . How, then, could we follow these Jews, who are almost certainly blinded."[15]

AD 330 – In this year, Tertullian, an early church theologian, wrote his treatise *Adversus Judaeos* (Against the Jews), which is a well-developed argument from the Bible for the rejection of the Jews and their replacement by the Church. Among his general claims, he argued at length that the Church is now the heir to the promises made to the Jewish people in the Abrahamic, Davidic, and new covenants. Using Daniel 9 as his basis, Tertullian contended that the destruction of the Temple and Jerusalem in AD 70 was God's prophesied stamp of rejection over the Jewish people. Today, this is a foundational belief among supersessionists. Rather than seeing AD 70 as yet another *temporary expulsion* of the Jews from the land and *a short-term chastisement* of the Lord on His covenant people, in direct accordance with the curses found in the Mosaic covenant, virtually all supersessionists see this as a defining event whereby the Jews were *permanently* cast off by God, losing any claim to a future reclamation of the covenant promises.

HEAVEN IS FOR US, NOT FOR YOU!

AD 320 – Cyprian, the Bishop of Carthage, wrote *Three Books of Testimonies against the Jews*. In these books, all of the arguments that had now become widely accepted in the Church are reiterated. Specifically, Cyprian states that Gentiles, and not Jews, would inherit "the kingdom of heaven":

> The Jews have fallen under the heavy wrath of God because they have forsaken the Lord, and have followed idols . . . It was previously foretold that they would neither know the Lord, nor understand, nor receive Him . . . The Jews would not understand the Holy Scriptures, but that they would be intelligible in the last times, after that Christ had come . . . The Jews should lose Jerusalem, and should leave the land which they had received. Also that they should lose the light of the Lord. Two peoples were foretold, the elder and the younger; that is, the old people of the Jews, and the new one which should consist of us. The Gentiles rather than the Jews attain to the kingdom of heaven.[16]

AD 341 – The Council of Antioch forbade Christians from celebrating Passover with the Jews.[17]

AD 350 – Christian Emperor Constantius forbade marriage between Jewish men and Christian women. Even existing marriages were to be dissolved. Christian men who married Jewish women were actually threatened with the penalty of death.[18]

AD 343-381 – The Laodicean Synod approved canon 38, which stated: "It is not lawful [for Christians] to receive unleavened bread from the Jews, nor to be partakers of their impiety."[19]

"A GREAT RUBBISH HEAP OF HARLOTS"

AD 380 – The vilest, most inflammatory, and venomous of the anti-Jewish polemics of the early centuries were a series of discourses known as Homilies against the Jews by John Chrysostom. Chrysostom, perhaps better than most other Christian leaders, grasped the logic of supersessionism, claiming that because God so hates the Jews, Christians are "to hate them and long for their blood."[20] While much has been written about Chrysostom's hateful rhetoric toward God's covenant people, I will simply cite a small sampling of it here:

> Jews are gathering choruses of effeminates and a great rubbish heap of harlots.[21]
>
> They [Jews] live for their bellies, they gape for the things of this world, their condition is not better than that of pigs or goats because of their wanton ways and excessive gluttony. They know but one thing: to fill their bellies and be drunk.[22]
>
> What is this disease? The festivals of the pitiful and miserable Jews are soon to march upon us one after the other and in quick succession: the feast of Trumpets, the feast of Tabernacles, the fasts. There are many in our ranks who say they think as we do. Yet some of these are going to watch the festivals and others will join the Jews in keeping their feasts and observing their fasts. I wish to drive this perverse custom from the Church right now.[23]
>
> But do not be surprised that I called the Jews pitiable. They really are pitiable and miserable . . . Although those Jews had been called to the adoption of sons, they fell to kinship with dogs.[24]
>
> The Jews are more savage than any highwaymen and do greater harm to those who have fallen among them. They do not simply strip off their victim's clothes nor inflict wounds on his body as did those robbers on the road to Jericho. Rather, the Jews mortally hurt their victim's soul, inflicting ten thousand wounds, and leave it lying in a pit of ungodliness.[25]

Finally, it is important to note that this man who has become known as a "saint" by the traditional churches literally demonized the Jewish people:

The synagogue is not only a brothel and a theater; it also is a den of robbers and a lodging for wild beasts . . . But when God forsakes a people, what hope of salvation is left? When God forsakes a place, that place becomes the dwelling of demons.[26]

Indeed the synagogue is less deserving of honor than any inn. It is not merely a lodging place for robbers and cheats but also for demons. This is true not only of the synagogues but also of the souls of the Jews, as I shall try to prove at the end of my homily.[27]

Little needs to be said about what happens when one dehumanizes an entire race, casting them all as demonized beasts. While John Chrysostom calls the Jews harlots, goats, pigs, and demonized dogs, Hitler referred to them as vermin. One man was crowned by the Christian Church as a saint, while the name of the other rightly will forever live in infamy. Author Steven Katz refers to John Chrysostom's polemic against the Jews as "the decisive turn in the history of Christian anti-Judaism, a turn whose ultimate disfiguring consequence was enacted in the political antisemitism of Adolf Hitler"[28]

CHRISTIAN STATE TERROR BEGINS

AD 379-395 – In the history of Christian Jew-hatred, this period was a profound turning point, as Emperor Theodosius made Christianity the official state religion of the Roman Empire. The marriage between Church and state was complete, and the full power of the state now belonged to the supersessionists.

AD 388 – In this year, Christians burned down a synagogue in the city of Callincum on the Euphrates River near the modern-day city of Ar-Raqqah in north central Syria. The local bishop encouraged the burning. When the local civic ruler sent a letter to Emperor Theodosius I to ask that he issue a decree that the bishop make restitution and rebuild the synagogue, Archbishop Ambrose of Milan, often known as Saint Ambrose, intervened and sent his own letter to the emperor, arguing that the order of restitution should be rescinded. He contended that if the bishop obeyed the emperor and gave the Jews the justice they sought, he would become an apostate. He also argued that if the synagogue was rebuilt, it would mean that the Jews had triumphed over the local Christians, which was entirely unacceptable. Ambrose's letter reads as follows:

> Ambrose, Bishop, to the Most Clement Prince, and Blessed Emperor, Theodosius the Augustus. A report was made by the military Count of the East that a synagogue had been burnt and that this was done by the authority of the Bishop. You gave command that the perpetrators should be punished and the synagogue be rebuilt by the Bishop himself. . . . Are you not afraid, O Emperor, that he may comply with your sentence; do you not fear that he may fail in his faith? . . . Which, then, is of greater importance, the show of legal discipline or the cause of religion? It is needful that legal censure should yield to religion. There is, then, no adequate cause for such a commotion, that the people should be punished so severely for the burning of a building; and much less since it is the burning of a synagogue, a home of unbelief, a house of impiety, a receptacle of folly which God himself has condemned. . . . Will you give this triumph over the Church of God to the Jews? This victory over Christ's people? This exultation, O Emperor, to the unbelievers? This rejoicing to the Synagogue, this sorrow to the Church?

Ambrose finished his declaration by stating that "God forbids intercession to be made for those [Jews]."[29]

As stated earlier, no sooner had the authority of the Church become infused with the power of the state, than open violation and abuse of the Jews became normalized. The hatred and maltreatment that were previously expressed primarily through theological declarations and insults quickly became outwardly violent and militant. For at least the next thousand years, Christianity was the sponsor of state terror and the greatest source of global persecution for the Jewish people.

AD 410 – Theodosius II passed the Third New Law, which prohibited Jews from holding any honorific office or position within the Roman state. Jews were compelled, however, to assume or remain within those public offices which would result in a financial loss to them. The Third New Law also forbade the building of new synagogues. This prohibition would later be mimicked and implemented by Muslim governments and, ironically, was often carried out with regard to Christian churches as well. Today the remnants of these laws are still seen in nations such as Saudi Arabia, which forbids any churches from being built. Here's a portion of the Third New Law of Theodosius:

> . . . we ordain by this law to be valid for all time: No Jew . . . shall obtain offices and dignities; to none shall the administration of city service be permitted; nor shall any one exercise the office of a defender of the city. Indeed, we believe it sinful that the enemies of the heavenly majesty and of the Roman laws should become the executors of our laws—the administration of which they have slyly obtained and that they, fortified by the authority of the acquired rank, should have the power to judge or decide as they wish against Christians, yes, frequently even over bishops of our holy religion themselves, and thus, as it were, insult our faith. Moreover, for the same reason, we forbid that any synagogue shall rise as a new building. However, the propping up of old synagogues which are now threatened with imminent ruin is permitted.[30]

AD 415 – Cyril, the Patriarch of Alexandria, immediately after assuming office, initiated a series of measures leading to the expulsion of every Jew in Alexandria. All of the city's synagogues were torn down, and Jewish homes and businesses were burned to the ground. Edward Gibbon, author of *The Decline and Fall of the Roman Empire*, described it this way:

Without any legal sentence, without any royal mandate, the patriarch, at the dawn of day, led a seditious multitude to the attack of the synagogues. Unarmed and unprepared, the Jews were incapable of resistance; their houses of prayer were leveled with the ground, and the Episcopal warrior, after-rewarding his troops with the plunder of their goods, expelled from the city the remnant of the unbelieving nation . . . In this promiscuous outrage, the innocent were confounded with the guilty, and Alexandria was impoverished by the loss of a wealthy and industrious colony.[31]

AD 415 — Augustine of Hippo, perhaps the most important theologian in all of Church history, strongly articulated supersessionism while casting insults upon the Jewish people: "The Christian people then is rather Israel . . . But that multitude of Jews, which was deservedly reprobated for its perfidy, for the pleasures of the flesh sold their birthright, so that they belonged not to Jacob, but rather to Esau. For ye know that it was said with this hidden meaning, 'That the elder shall serve the younger.'"[32]

It is important to note that when Augustine said that the Jews had been "reprobated," he was speaking of his doctrine of unconditional election, which holds that some people (the elect) are predestined by God for salvation while others are chosen for damnation. The obvious problem, of course, with Augustine's position is that he applied this reprobation not to any particular individual but to the entire race. Worse yet, he applied the term *reprobated* specifically to the Jewish people, of whom Paul the apostle stated quite clearly that though *some* will be cut off for their unbelief, their corporate election for salvation remains forever (see Rom. 9-11).

Picking up on this theme, in his commentary on the Psalms, Augustine repeatedly compared the Jewish people to Judas Iscariot, who remains forever guilty for the death of Jesus:

Judas doth represent those Jews who were enemies of Christ, who both then hated Christ, and now, in their line of succession, this species of wickedness continuing, hate Him. Of these men, and of this people, not only may what we read more openly discovered in this Psalm be conveniently understood, but also those things which are more expressly stated concerning Judas himself.

The Psalm [109] then continueth: "His delight was in cursing, and it shall happen to him" (ver. 17). Although Judas loved cursing, both in stealing from the money bag, and selling and betraying the Lord: nevertheless, that people more openly loved cursing, when they said, "His blood be on us, and on our children . . . He loved not blessing, therefore it shall be far from him." Such was Judas indeed, since he loved not Christ, in whom is everlasting blessing; but the Jewish people still more decidedly refused blessing.[33]

Augustine specifically spoke of the Day of Judgment as the time when eternal damnation would be meted out to the Jewish people: "'When the Son of man shall come in His glory, and all the holy angels with Him, and before Him shall be gathered all nations'; and the rest that is foretold of the future judgment in that place even to the last sentence. And the Jews, inasmuch as they will be punished in that judgment for persisting in their wickedness, as it is elsewhere written, 'shall look upon Him whom they have pierced.'"[34]

The problem once more is that Augustine fundamentally twisted Zechariah's words to support precisely the opposite of what the prophet was actually saying. Augustine only quoted a portion of Zechariah 12:10, using it to argue that the Jewish people corporately will be damned at the Day of Judgment. The full verse actually says that when the Jewish people look upon the one whom they have pierced, they will repent and receive "the Spirit of grace." Augustine also ignored Paul's explicit reference to the fact that when Christ returns, "all Israel will be saved" (Rom. 11:26). It is clear that Augustine's supersessionism and prejudice toward the Jewish people blinded him in his ability to responsibly and honestly exposit these texts. How many other otherwise excellent teachers and theologians today are under the same spell of supersessionism, crippled in their ability to properly interpret so many critical portions of Scripture?

THE SYNAGOGUE IS "THE DEVIL'S REFUGE, SATAN'S FORTRESS"

AD 418 – Jerome, the Latin Church Father, in speaking of the Jewish synagogues, used the most inflammatory descriptions imaginable: "If you call it a brothel, a den of vice, the Devil's refuge, Satan's fortress, a place to deprave the soul, an abyss of every conceivable disaster or whatever you will, you are still saying less than it deserves."[35] Elsewhere, he extolled his own visceral hatred of the Jews: "If it is expedient to hate any men and to loathe any race I have a strange dislike for those of the circumcision. For up to the present day, they persecute our Lord Jesus Christ in the synagogues of Satan."[36]

In the eyes of the Church, the Jews had now become thoroughly demonized as a people, and their synagogues had become the gathering halls for the work of Satan in the earth. How distant from Jerome's words was the pain-filled cry of Paul the apostle for the salvation of the Jews when he declared, "For I could wish that I myself were accursed, separated from Christ for the sake of my brethren, my kinsmen according to the flesh" (Rom. 9:3).

AD 489–519 – During this period, Christian mobs destroyed numerous synagogues in the cities of Antioch, Daphne, and Ravenna.[37]

AD 531 – Emperor Justinian passed the Justinian Code, prohibiting Jews from building synagogues, reading the Bible in Hebrew, assembling in public, celebrating Passover before Easter, or testifying against Christians in court: "We . . . ordain that no heretic, nor even they who cherish the Jewish superstition, may offer testimony against orthodox Christians who are engaged in litigation, whether one or the other of the parties is an orthodox Christian."[38]

AD 535 – The Synod of Claremont decreed that Jews could not hold public office or have any form of authority over Christians.[39]

AD 538 – The Third and Fourth Councils of Orleans prohibited Jews from appearing in public during the Easter season. Canon 30 decreed that "from the Thursday before Easter for four days, Jews may not appear in the company of Christians." Marriages between Christians and Jews were forbidden and Christians were prohibited from converting to Judaism.[40]

CONCLUSION

In the period from the beginning of the second century to the late fourth century, we saw the development of supersessionist thought and its firm establishment within the Church. Then, as the authority of the Church became infused with the power of the state, the Jewish people were consistently subjected to an ongoing series of abuses, persecutions, and at times, the wholesale expulsion of entire communities. It is easy to directly connect supersessionism with the actual effort to divest the Jewish people of their property, livelihoods, happiness, peace, dignity, and ultimately, their very identities and right to live.

Oh Lord, may we who seek to follow you learn from the sins of those who came before us. May we repent of every form of prejudice, either attitudinally or theologically toward the sons of Israel. As we proclaim your gospel, may we truly show the love of Jesus the Messiah to your covenant people.

10

CHRISTIAN JEW-HATRED: FROM THE FOURTH CENTURY TO THE HOLOCAUST

n the previous chapter, we traced the inception of supersessionism in the early church to the widespread hatred, abuse, and persecution of the Jewish people, all of which increased exponentially once the authority of the Church became infused with the power of the state. After that point, throughout Christendom, the Jewish people were subjected to almost three hundred years of consistent persecution. After the fifth century, anti-Semitism became fundamentally ingrained into the very fabric of European Christian culture. This period was marked by sporadic persecutions, the kidnapping of Jewish children, forced baptisms and conversions, harsh economic pressures, the seizure of property, expulsions, forced enslavement, and even multiple massacres of entire communities of Jews.

Before further considering the damning record, I want to caution against reading through this material in a perfunctory manner. I understand that due to its redundancy, it is easy to become desensitized to the gravity of what is being conveyed. Episode after episode, account after account, of Christians persecuting, abusing, betraying, enslaving, murdering, and massacring Jews is not easy reading. It is essential that we do not simply emotionally check out and harden ourselves to this material. I encourage you to take a moment to pause and ask the Lord to convey His heart to you concerning these horrors and to allow His passion for His people to well up within your heart. I encourage the reader to allow a genuine and heartfelt revulsion and repentance for the horror of what confessing Christians for the past two thousand years have willingly allowed to flourish in the name of Jesus. It is only through such repentance that the Church will be able to avoid making precisely the same mistakes should such evil days befall us once again.

AD 558 – Ferréol the Bishop of Uzès, in France, gathered all of the Jews in his diocese to the Church of St Theodoric to hear a baptismal sermon. Any Jews who did not convert were expelled from his district.[1]

AD 613 – Very serious persecution broke out in Spain. Jews were given the option of converting to Christianity or being expelled from the country. Many Jewish children over six years of age were taken from their parents and reeducated as Christians.[2]

692 AD – A Church council held in 692 under Justinian II at Constantinople, known as the Quinisext Council or the Council in Trullo, sought to break all social interaction between Christians and Jews: "Let no one . . . eat the unleavened bread of the Jews, nor have any familiar intercourse with them, nor summon them in illness, nor receive medicines from them, nor bathe with them . . . Whoever even calls Jews in as physicians or bathes with them is to be deposed."[3] According to *The Catholic Encyclopedia*, "The council was attended by hundreds of bishops from both the east and the west."[4]

AD 694 – The Seventeenth Church Council of Toledo, issued by King Egica of Spain, in its eighth canon, stated in part: "The Jews . . . shall be deprived of their property for the benefit of the exchequer, and shall be made slaves forever. Those to whom the King sends them as slaves must watch that they may no longer practise Jewish usages, and their children must be separated from them, when they are seven years of age, and subsequently married with Christians."[5]

Of course, this enslavement of the Jewish people no doubt

found its support in the writings of the various renowned Christians, such as Chrysostom, Origen, and Jerome, all of whom argued that God had consigned the Jews to a life of perpetual slavery because of their collective guilt for killing Jesus.

AD 722 – Leo III outlawed Judaism. Many Jews throughout Europe were forcibly baptized against their will.[6]

AD 1078 – Pope Gregory VII decreed that Jews could not hold office or be superiors to Christians.[7]

THE FIRST HOLOCAUST

AD 1096 – In this year, the First Crusade was launched. This was the first of eight crusades, lasting more than two hundred years. Although the primary goal of the crusades was to liberate Jerusalem from Muslim control, Jews also became a significant secondary target. As the soldiers passed through Europe on the way to the Holy Land, large numbers of Jews in Germany, France, and England were killed, leading some historians to refer to this period as "the first Holocaust."[8] In the First Crusade, twelve thousand Jews were massacred in the Rhine Valley alone.

AD 1099 – In Jerusalem, the Crusaders forced all of the Jews of the city into a central synagogue and set it on fire. Those who tried to escape were forced back into the burning building.[9]

INHUMAN, WILD BEASTS

AD 1120 – Peter the Venerable, a powerful French abbot, in his treatise *Against the Inveterate Obduracy of Jews*, created one of the more extreme examples of Christian abuse of the Jewish people in Church history. The prologue to his rather lengthy supersessionist diatribe begins: "I approach you, O Jews—you. I say, who even till this day deny the Son of God. How long, wretches, will ye fail to believe the truth?"[10]

Peter cast Jews as inhuman beasts, whose only purpose was to be paraded before the world as examples of spiritual reprobation: ". . . if nonetheless, you are human. In fact, I do not dare avow that you are human, lest perhaps I lie, because I recognize that that rational faculty that separates a human from the other animals or wild beasts . . . is extinct, or rather, buried in you. . . . I lead, then, the monstrous beast out from its lair, and push it laughing onto the stage of the whole world, in the view of all peoples . . . O Jews, O wild beasts . . ."[11]

AD 1121 – Jews were driven out of Flanders, a region now part of Belgium. They were not to return nor to be tolerated until they repented of killing Jesus Christ.[12]

AD 1146 – The Second Crusade began. Radulphe, a French monk, through his preaching and condemnation of the Jews, inspired several massacres in the Rhineland, Cologne, Mainz, Worms, and Speyer. He openly called for the massacre of Jews, stating, "The Jews should be slain as the enemies of the Christian religion."[13] From Germany, Radulphe's idea of "beginning the Crusades at home" reached France, resulting in Jews being massacred in Carentan, Rameru, Sully, and Bohemia.[14]

AD 1180–1181 – The French king Philip Augustus seized all Jewish property and expelled the Jews from the country. All of their homes became the property of the king.[15] A monk named Rigord, left us with the following account:

> [Philip heard] that the Jews who dwelt in Paris were wont every year on Easter day, or during the sacred week of our Lord's Passion, to go down secretly into underground vaults and kill a Christian as a sort of sacrifice in contempt of the Christian religion. For a long time they had persisted in this wickedness, inspired by the devil, and in Philip's father's time,

many of them had been seized and burned with fire. . . . in the same year in which he was invested at Rheims with the holy governance of the kingdom of the French, upon a Sabbath, the sixteenth of February [1180], by his command, the Jews throughout all France were seized in their synagogues and then bespoiled of their gold and silver and garments . . . This was a harbinger of their expulsion, which by God's will soon followed.[16]

AD 1182 – King Philip published the following edict of expulsion: "Immovable property, however, such as houses, fields, vineyards, barns, and wine-presses, he confiscated . . . In July they were compelled to leave France and all of their synagogues were converted into churches."[17]

AD 1189 – At the coronation of King Richard the Lionheart, although Jews were banned from the ceremony, some Jewish leaders arrived to present gifts to the new king. Richard's courtiers stripped and flogged them. This resulted in a rumor that Richard had ordered all Jews to be killed, resulting in a massacre of Jews throughout London. Many Jews were beaten to death, robbed, and burned alive. Many Jewish homes were burned down, and Jews were forcibly baptized.[18]

SLAVES REJECTED BY GOD

AD 1205 – "By their own guilt," wrote Pope Innocent III to two of his archbishops, "the Jews are consigned to perpetual servitude because they crucified the Lord . . . As slaves rejected by God, in whose death they wickedly conspire, they shall by the effect of this very action, recognize themselves as the slaves of those whom Christ's death set free."[19]

It is important to truly stop and consider the effects that such statements would have had on the general culture of Europe. The pope himself, the most authoritative spiritual leader in all of Christendom, the so-called *vicar* of Christ, declaring that all Jews, through their own guilt, are irretrievably wicked and have been divinely assigned forever the role of slaves to Christians. Not only had Paul's warnings been long forgotten by this point, but they had been thoroughly trampled upon, as Christianity itself had nearly become synonymous with hatred for and humiliation, deprivation, and subjugation of the Jewish people. *How far the Church had fallen.*

THE BADGE

Few are aware that the infamous Jewish badge of Nazi Germany had been a long established practice throughout Christian Europe. According to *The Jewish Encyclopedia,* "The idea of such a discrimination seems to have been derived from Islam, in which the dress of the Jews was distinguished by a different color from that of the true believer as early as the Pact of Omar (640), by which Jews were ordered to wear a yellow seam on their upper garments. This was a distinct anticipation of the Badge."[20]

According to Bernard Lewis, a scholar of Islamic history, both Christians and Jews under Islamic rule were forced to wear distinct emblems on their clothes. The yellow badge specifically seems to have been first introduced by a caliph in Baghdad in the ninth century, and spread to the West in medieval times.[21]

Although this practice began under Islam, it was alternately used by both Muslims and Christians and soon became a common practice throughout Europe. In 1269, Louis IX of France imposed a fine on any Jew caught in public not wearing the badge. Enforcement was repeated by various local councils in the French cities of Arles in 1234 and 1260, Béziers in 1246, Albi in 1254, Nîmes in 1284 and 1365, Avignon in 1326 and 1337, Rodez in 1336, and Vanves in 1368.[22] It was used in England (in the shape of two tablets), in France (in the form of a cloth ring), as well as Spain, Italy, and throughout Europe. This dishonoring sign was used intermittently in various locations for six centuries, exposing the Jews to public contempt everywhere they went throughout Europe. When Hitler came into power, he simply adopted a long-held Christian practice, changing what was a yellow oval badge to the Star of David.

AD 1215 – The Fourth Lateran Council approved canon laws requiring that "[Jews], whether men or women, must in all Christian countries distinguish themselves from the rest of the population in public places by a special kind of clothing." They also had to wear the badge or special clothing to distinguish them from Christians.[23]

AD 1218 – Pope Honorius III issued a papal bull demanding the enforcement of the Fourth Lateran Council that Jews wear clothing to distinguish themselves and that they be made to pay a tithe of all their income to local churches.[24] Both items were frequently repeated by later popes.

AD 1227 – The Synod of Narbonne, canon 3, ruled: "That Jews may be distinguished from others, we decree and emphatically command that in the center of the breast (of their garments) they shall wear an oval badge, the measure of one finger in width and one half a palm in height."[25]

AD 1239 – Pope Gregory IX ordered that Church leaders in England, France, Portugal, and Spain confiscate Jewish books on the first Saturday of Lent. The Talmud and all other Jewish books suspected of blasphemies against Jesus and Christianity were burned. The burning of Jewish books was ordered several times from the thirteenth to the sixteenth centuries.[26]

AD 1259 – A synod of the archdiocese in Mainz, Germany, ordered all Jews within its borders to wear yellow badges.[27]

AD 1285 – The entire Jewish community of Munich, some 180 individuals, were burned alive due to blood libel.[28]

AD 1288-1293 – Most of the Jewish communities in the Kingdom of Naples, the cradle of European Jewish culture at the time, were destroyed. Elsewhere in Italy, Jews were expelled or forced to convert to Christianity.[29]

AD 1290 – On July 18, King Edward I issued commands to the sheriffs of all the English counties, ordering them to forcibly remove all Jews who did not willingly leave England before All Saints' Day of that year. They were allowed to carry their portable possessions; the remainder became the property of the king. Sixteen thousand Jews were expelled. Many were robbed by the local authorities, and others drowned on their way to France. The Jews did not formally return to England until 1655—nearly four hundred years later.[30]

AD 1298 – Jews were persecuted in Austria, Bavaria, and Franconia. One hundred forty Jewish communities were destroyed, killing more than one hundred thousand Jews over a six-month period.[31]

AD 1306 – One hundred thousand Jews were exiled from France, with only the clothes on their backs.[32]

AD 1337 – Jews in Belgium were wiped out in a series of massacres. According to the *Jewish Encyclopedia*:

> The Jews of Belgium at this time were, like their brethren all over Europe, persecuted on charges of having desecrated the host, of having killed infants, and of having poisoned wells. The storm that swept over the Jews of Belgium annihilated them; and so completely was the work of destruction done that scarcely a trace of their existence has remained. A series of massacres appears to have taken place during a period of twenty years, which finally culminated in the Brussels massacre of 1370.[33]

AD 1338 – The councilors of Freiburg banned the performance of anti-Jewish scenes from the town's passion play because of the bloody and lethal reactions by Christians against Jews which would frequently follow the performances.[34]

AD 1347 – After being blamed for the Black Death, Jews were murdered en masse. In Bavaria, 12,000 were massacred; in the small town of Erfurt, 3,000; near Tours, an immense trench was dug, filled with blazing wood, and 160 Jews were burned alive. In Strausberg 2,000 Jews were burned. In Maintz, 6,000; in Worms, 400.[35]

AD 1366 – Great persecution broke out in Spain: "When Henry de Trastámara ascended the throne as Henry II there began for the Castilian Jews an era of suffering and intolerance, culminating in their expulsion." Henry "demanded that the Jews . . . should not be allowed to hold public office, should live apart from the Christians, should not wear costly garments nor ride on mules, should wear the badge, and should not be allowed to bear Christian names."[36]

AD 1394 – Jews were exiled, for the second time, from France.

AD 1431 – The Council of Basel forbade Jews to go to universities, prohibited them from acting as legal agents in contracts that involved Christians, and required that they attend church to hear Christian sermons.[37]

AD 1434 – Jewish men in Augsburg had to sew yellow buttons to their clothes. Across Europe, Jews were forced to wear a long undergarment, an overcoat with a yellow patch, bells, and tall pointed yellow hats with a large button on them.

AD 1453 – The Franciscan monk Capistrano persuaded the King of Poland to terminate all Jewish civil rights.

AD 1478 – Spanish Jews had been heavily persecuted from the fourteenth century. Many had outwardly converted to Christianity. The Spanish Inquisition was set up by the Church in order to detect insincere conversions. Laws were passed that prohibited the descendants of Jews or Muslims from attending university, joining religious orders, holding public office, or entering any of a long list of professions.

AD 1490 – In the middle of winter, all the Jews in the city of Geneva were forced to leave the city and the surrounding region.[38]

AD 1492 – In Spain, Ferdinand and Isabella issued the Edict of Expulsion. It ordered all Jews of whatever age to leave the kingdom by the last day of July (one day before Tisha B'Av). Jews were given the choice of being baptized as Christians or banished from Spain. Estimates of Jews exiled during this time range between 165,000 to as many as 800,000.[39]

AD 1497 – In Portugal, Manuel the Great "issued the inhuman decree that on a certain day all Jewish children, irrespective of sex, who should have reached their fourth year and should not have passed their twentieth should be torn from their parents and brought up in the Christian faith at the expense of the king."[40]

Upon hearing of this plan, approximately twenty thousand Jews fled the country rather than be baptized as Christians. Many others committed suicide or suffered martyrdom for their faith:

> Many parents smothered their children in the last farewell embrace or threw them into wells and rivers and then killed themselves. "I have seen with my own eyes," writes the noble Coutinho, "how a father, his head covered, with pain and grief accompanied his son to the baptismal font and called on the Allknowing as witness that they, father and son, wished to die together as confessors of the Mosaic faith. I have seen many more

terrible things that were done to them." Isaac ibn Zachin, the son of an Abraham ibn Zachin, killed himself and his children because he wished to see them die as Jews.[41]

THE BIRTH OF THE JEWISH GHETTO

AD 1516 – The governor of the Republic of Venice decided that Jews would be permitted to live only in one area of the city. This was the first ghetto in Europe.

The Roman ghetto was later established by Pope Paul IV. Jews were forcibly sent to live there on July 26, 1556. The Roman ghetto consisted of a few narrow, dirty streets, which quickly became thoroughly overcrowded. This section of the city was annually flooded by the Tiber River. Each year the Jews had to go through a humiliating ceremony that included the Jews publicly pleading for the right to continue living there during the ensuing year. After this, they paid an exorbitant tax. This ceremony was observed as late as 1850. The entire degrading event is strikingly similar to the Islamic practice of exacting the *jizya* (tax) upon Jews and Christians living under Muslim rule known as *dhimmis*, or subjected peoples. It is truly sad that such purposeful humiliation and degradation was carried out by confessing Christians. Later, the use of the Jewish ghetto was adopted by Adolf Hitler.[42]

AD 1540–50 – Jews were banished from Naples, Genoa, and Venice.[43]

MARTIN LUTHER

AD 1543 – It was out of this atmosphere of a thousand years of widespread, culturally ingrained hatred and regular persecution of the Jews that Martin Luther, the great Protestant Reformer, emerged onto the world scene. Initially, after his transformation from a Catholic monk to a Protestant Reformer, he made efforts to convert Jews to Christianity. When his efforts failed, his attitude quickly changed and he became enraged at the Jewish people, composing one of the worst examples of anti-Jewish hate literature in all of history.

In this year, Luther wrote a treatise titled *The Jews and Their Lies*. In this book, among many other insults, Luther described Jews as a "base, whoring people, that is, no people of God, and their boast of lineage, circumcision, and law must be accounted as filth." He also wrote that "the blind Jews are truly stupid fools," "lazy rogues," "nothing but thieves and robbers," "miserable and accursed," and, "rejected and condemned people." Their synagogues, he said, were "a den of devils in which sheer selfglory, conceit, lies, blasphemy, and defaming of God [occur]."[44]

Luther went on reduce the Jewish people to the level of a pandemic: "Such a desperate, thoroughly evil, poisonous, and devilish lot are these Jews, who for these fourteen hundred years have been and still are our plague, our pestilence, and our misfortune."[45]

Consider the depths into which Luther allowed himself to sink in dehumanizing and demonizing God's beloved and chosen people: "They are venomous, bitter, vindictive, tricky serpents, assassins, and children of the devil, who sting and work harm stealthily wherever they cannot do it openly . . . These venomous serpents and young devils . . . next to the devil, a Christian has no more bitter and galling foe than a Jew."

Beyond utterly devaluing the entire Jewish race, Luther then went on to conclude his treatise with his own version of "the final solution." As you read the following excerpts, take note of the well-developed theological supersessionism that runs throughout his comments. Every Christian alive today should familiarize him- or herself with this profound stain on the testimony of the Christian Church:

What then shall we Christians do with this *damned, rejected race of Jews?* Since they live among us and we know about their lying and blasphemy and cursing, we can not tolerate them if we do not wish to share in their lies, curses, and blasphemy. In this way *we cannot quench the inextinguishable fire of divine rage* nor convert the Jews. We must prayerfully and reverentially practice a merciful severity. Perhaps we may save a few from the fire and flames [of hell]. We must not seek vengeance. *They are surely being punished a thousand times more than we might wish them.* Let me give you my honest advice.

First, their synagogues should be set on fire, and whatever does not burn up should be covered or spread over with dirt so that no one may ever be able to see a cinder or stone of it. And this ought to be done for the honor of God and of Christianity in order that God may see that we are Christians, and that we have not wittingly tolerated or approved of such public lying, cursing, and blaspheming of His Son and His Christians.

Secondly, their homes should likewise be broken down and destroyed. For they perpetrate the same things there that they do in their synagogues. For this reason they ought to be put under one roof or in a stable, like gypsies, in order that they may realize that they are not masters in our land, as they boast, *but miserable captives*, as they complain of incessantly before God with bitter wailing.

Thirdly, they should be deprived of their prayer-books and Talmuds in which such idolatry, lies, cursing, and blasphemy are taught.

Fourthly, their rabbis must be forbidden under threat of death to teach any more . . .

Fifthly, passport and traveling privileges should be absolutely forbidden to the Jews. For they have no business in the rural districts since they are not nobles, nor officials, nor merchants, nor the like. Let them stay at home . . . If you princes and nobles do not close the road legally to such exploiters, then some troop ought to ride against them, for they will learn from this pamphlet what the Jews are and how to handle them and that they ought not to be protected. You ought not, you cannot protect them, unless in the eyes of God you want to share all their abomination . . .

To sum up, dear princes and nobles who have Jews in your domains, if this advice of mine does not suit you, then find a better one so that you and we may all be free of this insufferable devilish burden—the Jews.[46]

Luther's plans were more than mere threats. On a few occasions, he succeeded in having the Jews expelled from various regions. This took place under his instigation in Saxony in 1537, and in the 1540s his followers drove the Jews from several German towns. After an unsuccessful attempt to get the Jews of Brandenburg expelled, his followers there sacked the Berlin synagogue in 1572. The next year, the Jews were banned from the entire country.[47]

JOHN CALVIN

AD 1560 – John Calvin, the only other Reformer whose influence is comparable to Luther's, is frequently portrayed as being far more tolerant and even friendly toward the Jewish people. In truth, however, Calvin wrote very little about his Jewish contemporaries because he had likely not known any Jews. He lived in Geneva, which today sits within Switzerland, near the borders of France and Italy, and the Jews had all been forced from his city seventy years earlier. Nevertheless, like so many of his predecessors and contemporaries, Calvin did write concerning the Jews in a typically vile, hateful, and shameful manner. In his work "A Response to Questions and Objections of a Certain Jew," he wrote, "Their [the Jews'] rotten and unbending stiffneckedness deserves that they be oppressed unendingly and without measure or end and that they die in their misery without the pity of anyone."[48]

After the Reformation the same general pattern continued in many circles. As much as Protestants would like to say that with a rejection of the authority of the Catholic Church there suddenly developed an immediate rise in love among the Christians of Europe for the Jews, this is only true in a limited sense. While there were various groups that did awaken to recognize the ongoing calling and election of the Jewish people in Scripture, groups such as the Moravians, the Puritans, and various Luthern Pietists, unfortunately it would take a couple hundred years before such ideas began to truly prevail throughout the Church. This recognition of Israel's ongoing calling and election became most pronounced in the nineteenth century, in England, in a movement known as the Plymouth Brethren. This group more than any others before them returned to the eschatology of the earliest Church—restorationism, futurism, and premillennialism. In this movement, not only was there a more correct understanding of the last days, but there also arose a widespread tenderness and humility toward the Jewish people. In chapter 13, we will discuss several of the men who arose out of this movement and how their theology changed the way the Church began to relate to the Jewish people.

THE JEWISH QUESTION

AD 1750 – After fifteen hundred years of persistent European persecution of the Jews, the controversy raged as to what was the proper response or "solution" to the Jewish presence in European Christian society. It was in 1750 that we first find the term "the Jewish Question" being discussed in Great Britain. Soon thereafter it was debated in France ("*la question juive*") and Germany ("*die Judenfrage*"). Of course, the question was not a new one. As we saw, Luther had already offered his own "solution" to the Jewish question.

After the idea of the Jewish question was officially introduced into European Christian society, hundreds of pamphlets, newspaper articles, and books were written on the subject, with everyone weighing in and offering their "solutions." Most often this included the deportation of the Jewish community. On the other side, many hundreds of pamphlets and articles were written opposing these "solutions." These offered ideas such as simple acceptance and integration. Unfortunately, the more humane response did not prevail, and by the mid-nineteenth century in Germany, several scholars and philosophers were making the case for, and even demanding, the "de-Jewifying" of everything from the press, education, the state, economy, and culture. The condemnation of intermarriage between Jews and non-Jews was also a prominent theme during this period.

As Gerhard Falk, author of *The Jew in Christian Theology*, so accurately states, "There is of course no Jewish question. The proposition that Jewish existence ought to be questioned is ipso facto the problem for which the solution can only be an attitude of change on the part of the Christians."[49]

RUSSIAN POGROMS

After such a long history of violent Jew-hatred throughout Europe, many Jews had resettled in Russia. But history shows that hatred would also seek them out there. Beginning in the late nineteenth century, Jews living in Russia were increasingly subjected to what history has come to call "pogroms," which were little more than anti-Jewish riots that often led to the forced expulsion or massacre of Jewish communities throughout the region. In 1905 a pogrom against the Jews of Odessa, in modern-day Ukraine, was the most serious of that period, with reports of up to twenty-five hundred Jews killed.[50] The *New York Times* described one pogrom that took place on Easter in 1903:

> The anti-Jewish riots . . . are worse than the censor will permit to publish. There was a well laid-out plan for the general massacre of Jews on the day following the Orthodox Easter. The mob was led by priests, and the general cry, "Kill the Jews," was taken up all over the city. The Jews were taken wholly unaware and were slaughtered like sheep. The dead number 120 and the injured about 500. The scenes of horror attending this massacre are beyond description. Babies were literally torn to pieces by the frenzied and bloodthirsty mob. The local police made no attempt to check the reign of terror. At sunset the streets were piled with corpses and wounded. Those who could make their escape fled in terror, and the city is now practically deserted of Jews.[51]

Such "pogroms" were repeated in multiple Russian cities for a period of some years.

THE HOLOCAUST

After reviewing what was truly only a very partial survey of the history and development of Christian hatred and persecution of the Jewish people, we can better understand how Hitler was able to execute what he did. Through the majority of Church history, because of the Church's early embrace of a theology of rejection of the Jewish people, hatred of the Jew and Christianity had become virtually synonymous. Hitler did not burst onto the world scene with a new or unique hatred of the Jewish people. What very few Christians today truly understand is that Hitler's Jew-hatred was actually a very typical Christian attitude. There is much debate as to what the Nazi philosophy or inspiration truly was. Was Hitler a Christian or a pagan? There are numerous statements that one can produce to support either position. But for the Christian to cast Hitler's actions as completely foreign to the historical Christian faith, whether Roman Catholic, Eastern Orthodox, or Protestant, is to ignore our collective history and failure to acknowledge the thoroughly "Christian" ideas that inspired Hitler to carry out his plan with the willing assistance of a thoroughly Christian nation.

Though Heinrich Himmler was the chief architect of the plan, it was Hitler himself who referred to it as "the final solution of the Jewish question" (*die endlösung der Judenfrage*). Christian European Jew-hatred, which for fifteen hundred years had consistently borne horrifically bad fruit, had now forever revealed the ultimate results of a supersessionist divestment theology. When all was said and done, the fruit of seventeen hundred years of consistent, wide-scale Christian hatred of the Jewish people resulted in the death of six million Jews throughout Nazi-occupied Europe—two-thirds of the total European Jewish population at that time.

At the time of this writing, we are now only seventy-some years past the Holocaust. There are still many alive today who lived through those evil days. Their numbers, of course, are quickly decreasing. For the average Millennial who is in his or her twenties or early thirties, seventy years ago may seem like ancient history, but in the larger picture, this all took place only yesterday.

THE CHRISTIAN FOUNDATION OF NAZISM AND THE HOLOCAUST

CHURCH LAW OR DECREE	NAZI LAW OR MEASURE [52]
Forbid marriage of Christians with Jews. (Synod of Elvira, canon 15, 306)	"Marriages between Jews and citizens of German or kindred blood are forbidden. Marriages concluded in defiance of this law are void." (Law for the Protection of German Blood and Honor, Section 1, September 15, 1935)
Jews and Christians forbidden to dine together. (Synod of Elvira, canon 50, 306)	Jews barred from dining cars. (December 30, 1939)
Jews were forbidden to hold public office. (Council of Clermont, 535)	All Jews removed from government service. (Law for the Reestablishment of the Professional Civil Service, April 7, 1933)
Jews were forbidden to employ Christian servants or possess Christian slaves. (Third Council of Orléans, 538)	"Jews will not be permitted to employ female citizens of German or kindred blood as domestic servants." (Law for the Protection of German Blood and Honor, September 15, 1935)
From Maundy Thursday to four days onwards (Easter Week), Jews must not appear among Christians. (Third Council of Orléans, 538)	Decree authorizing local authorities to bar Jews from the streets on certain days. (i.e., Nazi holidays) (December 3, 1933)

CHURCH LAW OR DECREE	NAZI LAW OR MEASURE[52]
"Heretical" Jewish books were ordered to be burned. (Twelfth Council of Toledo, 681) Pope Gregory IX persuaded the French king to order the burning of all Talmuds and Jewish books in Paris. About twelve thousand copies were burned. (1242) Subsequent popes ordered the Talmud to be burned. These included Innocent IV (1243–1254), Clement IV (1256–1268), John XXII (1316–1334), Paul IV (1555–1559), Pius V (1566–1572), and Clement VIII. (1592–1605) Martin Luther wrote, "They should be deprived of their prayer-books and Talmuds in which such idolatry, lies, cursing, and blasphemy are taught." (1543)	The Nazis engaged in wide-scale book burnings. (1933) "The era of extreme Jewish intellectualism is now at an end." (Joseph Goebbels)
Christians forbidden to patronize Jewish doctors. (Trulanic Synod, 692)	Jewish doctors were forbidden to treat non-Jews. (Nuremberg Race Laws 1935, Decree of July 25, 1938)
Christians not permitted to live under the same roof as a Jew. (Synod of Narbonne, 1050)	Directive by Hermann Wilhelm Göring providing for concentration of Jews in their own houses. (December 28, 1938)
Jews obliged to pay tithes to support the Church as much as Christians. (Synod of Gerona, 1078)	The "Sozialausgleichsabgabe," which provided that Jews pay a special income tax in lieu of donations for Party purposes, imposed on Nazis. (December 24, 1940)

CHURCH LAW OR DECREE	NAZI LAW OR MEASURE [52]
Jews forbidden to be plaintiffs or witnesses against Christians in the courts. (Third Council of the Lateran, canon 26, 1179)	Proposal by the Party Chancellery that Jews not be permitted to institute civil suits. (September 9, 1942)
Jews forbidden to withhold inheritance from descendants who converted to Christianity. (Third Council of the Lateran, canon 26, 1179)	Justice Ministry voided any wills which offended the "sound judgment of the people." (July 31, 1938)
The Jewish Badge was implemented. (Fourth Council of the Lateran, canon 68, 1215)	That Jews should wear the Yellow Star of David patch. (Decree of September 1, 1941)
Construction of new synagogues prohibited. (Council of Oxford, 1222)	Destruction of synagogues throughout Nazi-occupied territories. (November 10, 1938)
Christians forbidden to attend any Jewish ceremonies. (Synod of Vienna, 1267)	Friendly relations with Jews became forbidden. (October 24, 1941)
"Safe passage on the highways [should] be completely abolished for the Jews." (Martin Luther, 1543)	Nazis forbid the Jews to have a driver's license, but require them to have a Jew identification card. (Judenkennkarte) (1935)
Jew were compelled to live in ghettoes. (Synod of Breslau, 1267)	Jews were forced to live in ghettoes. (September 21, 1939)
Christians were forbidden to sell or rent any kind of real estate to Jews. (Synod of Ofen, 1279)	Decree providing for compulsory sale of Jewish real estate. (December 3, 1938)
Adoption by a Christian of the Jewish religion or return by a baptized Jew to the Jewish religion defined as a heresy. (Synod of Mainz, 1310)	Adoption by a Christian of the Jewish religion places him in jeopardy of being treated as a Jew. Decision by Oberlandesgericht Königsberg, Fourth Zivilsenat. (June 26, 1942)

CHURCH LAW OR DECREE	NAZI LAW OR MEASURE [52]
Jews forbidden to act as agents in the conclusion of contracts between Christians, especially marriage contracts. (Council of Basel, session 19, 1434)	Liquidation of Jewish real estate agencies, brokerage agencies, and marriage agencies catering to non-Jews. (Decree of July 6, 1938)
Jews forbidden to obtain academic degrees. (Council of Basel, session 19, 1434)	Law against Overcrowding of German Schools and Universities. (April 25, 1933)
"Their synagogues should be set on fire . . . their homes should likewise be broken Down and destroyed." (Martin Luther, 1543)	119 synagogues and innumerable Jewish shops and homes burned to the ground. (Kristalnacht, November 9–10, 1938) Synagogues in Riga, Lathvia, were burned. Many Jews confined in the synagogues died in the fires. (1941)
"Let them be driven like mad dogs out of the land." (Martin Luther, 1543)	When a Jewish mother being transported via wagon threw her small child wrapped in a pillow and some money to a nearby gawker, an SS man immediately "unwrapped the pillow, seized the child by the feet, and smashed its head against the wheel of the wagon" in full view of the mother.[53]
"They ought to be put under one roof or in a stable, like gypsies, in order that they may realize that they are not masters in our land, as they boast, but miserable captives . . . Throw brimstone and pitch upon them; if one could hurl hell fire at them, so much the better . . . and this should be done for God and for Christianity, in order that God may see that we are Christians." (Martin Luther, 1543)	The Nazis created more than three hundred concentration camps, of which Jews were among the highest percentage of peoples imprisoned. Of the 9 million Jews who then lived in Europe, more than 6 million were systematically massacred. (1938–1945)

In 1961, historian Raul Hilberg wrote *The Destruction of the European Jews*, which is acknowledged to be the first comprehensive historical study of the Holocaust. In this massive work, Hilberg produced a chart that compared various Church laws or decrees with similar Nazi laws or decrees. Since this time, this chart has been republished widely in various works and on the Internet. While relying on Hilberg's original work, I have significantly modified and added to the chart to include Martin Luther's "solutions." I encourage the reader to carefully consider how closely Nazi laws and actions compare to the many laws and actions of the Christians of Europe.

CONCLUSION

This survey of Christian hatred and persecution of the Jews represents only a partial record of all that has truly transpired over the past two thousand years. If every example of overt Jew-hatred and persecution that Christians or the Church had committed were included here, this whole book could not contain it. What I have sought to do, however, is show just how widespread and common it was throughout all of Christendom, in nearly all of Church history, to treat the Jewish people far worse than any other people group. This is a key point. This was not a case of equal mistreatment. The Jewish people have been the premier targets of *the most focused hatred ever carried out by Christians*. As painful as it is to admit, throughout the majority of Church history, "hatred and abuse of the Jew" and "Christianity" were virtually synonymous. For nearly eighteen hundred years, Jew-hatred was as much a part of Christian doctrine and culture as was the doctrine of the Trinity or the incarnation of God in Christ. In the next chapter, we will more fully explain why the long and shameful history of Jew-hatred falls squarely at the feet of the doctrine of supersessionism, or replacement theology.

11

SUPERSESSIONISM AND JEW-HATRED

While not every supersessionist in history has had a deep hatred for the Jewish people, the overwhelming majority of Jew-haters have been supersessionists. In fact, I challenge you to go back and scour the writings of all of the great Christian theologians of Church history and see what a dearth of examples there are of Christian love for the Jewish people. While Christian hatred for the Jews is common, love for the Jew is quite rare. Most often the best one we will find are calls to avoid violence and to treat the Jews humanely. This, however, is far from the deep emotional love that the apostle Paul expressed—no doubt as an extension of the very heart of God. While few who embrace or espouse supersessionism will admit it, it is beyond argument that what began as a series of theological propositions concerning the divine rejection of the Jewish people, led directly to their rejection and mistreatment by Christians. The eighteen hundred years of Christian hatred and abuse of the Jewish people ultimately falls squarely onto the doctrine of supersessionism. In this chapter, I would like to further develop the causal relationship of supersessionism to hatred for and persecution of the Jewish people.

DIVESTMENT THEOLOGY
While the history of the Church is rife with a more naked hatred of the Jew, most modern supersessionists seek to disguise the true

nature of their beliefs. As such, instead of referring to their position as "replacement theology," they often use terms like "inclusion theology" or "fulfillment theology." This, however, is largely dissimulation. For the average Christian, who has not invested years into this subject, the use of thoroughly Jesus-saturated language such as, "The promises made by God to the Jewish people have now been spiritually fulfilled in Christ" only further confuses the matter. Such comments have a veneer of Christian piety but mask the dark side of supersessionism. Unfortunately, language such as "inclusion theology," catchphrases like "social justice," and even the name of Jesus have together become the bubble gum flavoring that makes the unbiblical, racist, and bitter medicine of supersessionism and anti-Israel theology more palatable.

In my interview with Israeli scholar Avner Boskey in Jerusalem, our conversation eventually came to this issue. "Replacement theology," Avner began. "You know, some people do not like that term, and so instead they use the terms 'inclusion theology,' 'realized theology' or 'fulfillment theology.'" And then he proceeded to hit the nail directly on the head: "But it's kind of like if I come into your house and I steal your table, and I say, 'Well, that *realizes* my dreams; that *fulfills* my hopes of a beautiful living room.' It's theft regardless. Because what does Paul say? Are the promises given to the Jews? Well, Romans 11:28–29 says the gifts that God gave to the Jewish people and the calling that he gives to the Jewish people are *irrevocable.*"

Avner could not be more correct. Any belief that claims to strip Israel of its ongoing, corporate calling and election or which rejects the notion of a future restoration of the very Jewish kingdom of Israel is indeed theological theft. Regardless of what one calls it, whether "replacement," "fulfillment," or "inclusion" theology, as long as the equation includes taking away either of those two things and replacing it with something different, it is replacement theology, pure and simple.

For a theology to truly be called "inclusion theology," it would have to see a future Jewish kingdom that welcomes and includes anyone who would say yes to the God of Israel. True "fulfillment theology" would argue that God will *fulfill* His promises to the Jewish people. But behind all of the smoke screens, the "inclusion theology" and "fulfillment theology" of today's supersessionists is simply a reworking of the same old replacement theology.

Missionary and author Dalton Thomas has also offered a useful term to describe supersessionism or replacement theology: "In an attempt to circumvent dealing with this long-standing argument over semantics that has the potential to distract us from the heart of the matter, I choose to use the term *Divestment Theology* and encourage others do the same. When all of the definitions are boiled down to their essence we are dealing with a basic argument over the issue of divestment."

Thomas goes on to cite Merriam Webster's definition of "divestment":

- to deprive or dispossess especially of property, authority, or title

- to undress or strip especially of clothing, ornament, or equipment

- to rid or free

- to take away from a person . . .

He concludes:

At the heart of [the supersessionist perspective] is the idea that the long-established national hope of the Jewish people has been abrogated and "redefined" so as to constitute a "different fulfillment." What kind of fulfillment? A fulfillment whereby the "whole creation" is included on the one hand and Israel is *divested* of their national destiny and hope on the other. [1]

Thomas's comments are spot-on. Even if one includes "all of creation" in their equation of who is welcome into the "people of God," if one maintains that God has rejected Israel on a corporate and national basis and will not actually deliver on His promises to restore the Davidic Jewish kingdom, it continues to be a stripping of Jewish hope. In fact, while Thomas highlights the divestment of Israel's national destiny and hope, it is actually much more than that. What supersessionism actually does is divest or strip the Jewish people of their very identity, of their very right to exist as a people. Let us very carefully consider the dangerous logic of supersessionism. According to supersessionists Gary Demar and Peter Leithart, one of the primary purposes for Christ's first coming was to destroy the very state of Israel: "A clear example of Christ's rule over the nations for His church was the destruction of the Jewish state that persecuted the early church (Matt. 24; Luke 21; cf. Acts 6:8–15). *In destroying Israel*, Christ transferred the blessings of the kingdom from Israel to a new people, the church. This is an important theme in the gospels."

Demar and Leithart's persecutive is not a fringe belief but is actually standard supersessionism. Mind you, we are not speaking only of a temporary destruction, but a permanent one. As German scholar Martin Noth explains, by the year AD 70, "Jerusalem had ceased to be the symbol of the homeland, Israel had ceased to exist and the history of Israel came to an end."[2]

Now let us consider the implications of this. If the permanent destruction of Israel was the very will of God, and if the history of Israel has now come to an end, then what is the Christian to think of the State of Israel today? If the history of natural Israel ended in AD 70, and the Church became the new Israel (or as Justin Martyr said, "the true Israelitic race"), then who are the people who call themselves Israel today? Are these people and their state somehow a non-entity? Then what should we do with the eighteen hundred years of Jewish history between then and now? And most important, what are we to make of their future? If one carries the logic of supersessionism forward, by permanently destroying the Temple and the state around which the Jewish people find their very identity, the Lord was in effect destroying the Jewish people. For it is these very things—or at the very least, the hope of their future restoration—that give the Jewish people their identity. This is the conclusion of supersessionist Albertus Pieters:

> God willed that after the institution of the New Covenant there should no longer be any Jewish people in the world—yet here they are! That is a fact—a very sad fact, brought about by their wicked rebellion against God; but is it not monstrous to hold that by reason of this wickedness the said undesired and undesirable group are now heirs to the many and exceedingly precious promises of God? Shall we be accused of anti-Semitism, because we speak thus of the Jews? . . . How is it possible to believe that there are still prophecies of divine grace to be fulfilled in a group upon which the wrath of God has come "to the uttermost"?[3]

While supersessionists are rarely as blunt as Pieters, his comments do in fact very accurately represent the very natural but deadly logic of supersessionism. The simple truth is that theology, doctrines, and beliefs affect one's attitudes and actions. The relationship of belief to action as it concerns supersessionism and the divestment of the Jewish people of their nation, their history, their hope, and their very identity is one that many modern supersessionists do not like to acknowledge. Yet any honest survey of Church history reveals that the long historical embrace of supersessionism far too frequently resulted in brazenly racist attitudes and has many times erupted into violent and murderous action. This is precisely why I find Dalton's use of the term "divestment theology" so accurate. For not only does supersessionism divest Israel of its "national destiny and hope," but it divests them of their very identity, of their very right to exist. If the Jewish people no longer have a national hope, calling, or future, they become a mere ghost of a people who once existed and who are now in the process of being dissolved. Thus, the adamant determination of the Jewish people not only to continue existing, but even worse, to reestablish their own state in the actual promised land—this can only be viewed as the will of ungodly men, or as Pieters portrays it, a wicked and rebellious act, completely outside of the will of God.

Of course, I want to very clearly qualify that I am in no way inferring that every Christian who espouses supersessionism hates Jews. No doubt, few of the teachers who espouse these ideas today actually possess any kind of emotional hatred for the Jewish people. The overwhelming majority of these teachers are very much well-intentioned; they love Jesus, genuinely believe they are conveying truth, and may even have an actual love for the Jewish people. Nevertheless, such good intentions do nothing to diminish the very real law of unintended consequences. The hard genocidal hatred of radical Islam or Nazism and the more subtle but inherently undermining effects of supersessionism indeed all exist on the same spectrum. They all work toward or support precisely the same end, which is the undermining, divestment, and ultimately, destruction of the Jewish state and the Jewish people.

Consider again Pieters's previous comments. First he said that it is a "very sad fact" that there are "any Jewish people in the world." Then he says that it is "monstrous" to hold that the Jews "are now heirs to the many and exceedingly precious promises of God." Now consider the fact that this was all written in 1950, only a few years after the Holocaust! What kind of blindness and insensitivity do such comments require?

Please hear me when I say that ideas have consequences, whether intended or not, particularly when we are dealing with issues of race and identity and especially within the context of this most ancient spiritual battle. Who will deny that believing that it was God's will to permanently destroy Israel both as a state and as a people, to actually wishing that it were so, and finally, to actually assisting God in making this a reality, are not dramatic leaps from one idea to the next? If Christians are to be honest, we must acknowledge that there is a very direct correlation between the Church's historical embrace of these doctrines and its long history of hateful, adversarial, abusive attitudes, or outrightly violent and murderous actions toward the Jewish people.

CONCLUSION

Behind all of the theological talk, ultimately, supersessionism is an unbiblical theology created by Gentile believers who, rather than being content with having been graciously welcomed into the people of God, after freely receiving God's underserved grace, feel the need to turn around and strip and dispossess the Jewish people of everything that has been promised to them by the God of Israel. Again, no matter what one calls it or how one packages it, if the end result is the disenfranchisement and divestment of the Jewish people from their future calling, election, identity, and promises, then it is theological racism. As we stated at the beginning of this chapter, while it is certainly true to say that while not every supersessionist in history has hated the Jewish people at the gut level, it is also quite fair to say that the vast majority of those who have openly hated or persecuted the Jews were supersessionists. While, no doubt, most who embrace or espouse supersessionism will refuse to acknowledge the obvious, the past two thousand years of Christian hatred and persecution of the Jewish people stand as a resounding witness against the doctrine of supersessionism. The bad fruit of supersessionism includes the Holocaust. As Roman Catholic theologian Hans Küng very accurately once said, "Nazi anti-Judaism was the work of godless, anti-Christian criminals. But it would not have been possible without the almost two thousand years' pre-history of 'Christian' anti-Judaism."[4]

Secular historians clearly see this, Jewish historians clearly see this, and today a multitude of Christians clearly see this. The only ones who refuse to see it, or acknowledge it, are those who either determinedly embrace or espouse it. Let us pray for the eyes of Christians everywhere to be opened to this fountain of evil that has flooded the Church for far too long.

ISLAMIC SUPERSESSIONISM

A s we discuss the clear relationship between supersessionism and Jew-hatred, it is important to recognize that beyond Christianity, Islam embraces its own form of supersessionism. As with Christianity, the presence of supersessionism within Islam has led to the frequent abuse and hatred of the Jewish people for the past fourteen hundred years. So harsh has been the mistreatment of Jews by the Muslims that in 1172, Moses Maimonides, the great Jewish sage, very tellingly stated: "The nation of Ishmael . . . persecute us severely and devise ways to harm us and to debase us . . . None has matched it in debasing and humiliating us. None has been able to reduce us as they have."[1]

HOW ISLAM ADOPTED SUPERSESSIONISM FROM CHRISTIANS

The story of how Islam came to embrace supersessionism is actually quite simple. When Muhammad emerged as a fledgling young "prophet" in seventh-century Arabia, all of the Christians he encountered were supersessionists. As the religion of Islam developed, Muhammad simply took the lead of the only Christians he knew, adopting their supersessionism and making it his own. In a tragic, but unsurprising twist, the Christians of Arabia soon found themselves victims of supersessionism. Islamic supersessionism, however, was a stronger strain, a mutated form of Christian supersessionism. Islamic supersessionism is far more than theological replacement;

it is also profoundly militant, seeking to eradicate all non-Muslims. Not only is Islam as a religion intended to replace Christianity, Judaism, and every other religion, but Muslims are intended to replace Christians, Jews, and every other people. Thus, very soon, the Christians were being either subjugated or simply wiped out alongside the Jews of Arabia. During Muhammad's career, one of his most celebrated accomplishments (among Muslims) was literally eliminating every last Jew from the Arabian Peninsula. Christians didn't fare much better.

Almost immediately after Muhammad died in 632, the Muslim conquests began. Under the direction of Caliph Abu Bakr and his general Khaled Ibn Walid, Islamic supersessionism was on the march. It was only a short four years before approximately a third of a million Christians throughout the Middle East—the ancient heartland of the Church—were slaughtered. The earliest Islamic records of these events show that the Muslims would besiege a city, kill all resistors, distribute the booty, and march an average of thirty to fifty thousand women back to Mecca to be married to Muslims or to be used as sex slaves. Within a mere ten years, more than a million Christians were killed. In less than one generation, Islam had crushed the ancient heart of Christendom. Within a hundred years, 50 percent of global Christianity had come under Islamic subjugation and rule.[2] In a tragic but remarkable turnabout, Christianity's supersessionist chickens had come home to roost.

ISLAMIC CULTURAL SUPERSESSIONISM

Of course, the Islamic manifestation of supersessionism was first observed in the earliest days of Islam, when Muhammad went to the pagan shrine of the Kaaba in Mecca and sanitized it of all of its idols, converting it into the center of Muslim worship. Islamic supersessionism continued to play out throughout its history, serving as a catalyst for the literal erasure of previous cultures and religions wherever it spread. With the swell of Islam, a vast number of religious sites were converted into mosques as symbols of Islamic triumph. The once-glorious Hagia Sophia in Constantinople (modern-day Istanbul), originally built in AD 360 and once the largest church in the world, was converted into a mosque by Mehmet the Conqueror in 1453. The cross on the dome, having long been removed, has been replaced by a crescent moon. Towering minarets surround the structure. Throughout the interior, massive, gaudy plaques with the names of Allah, Muhammad, and the first four caliphs (successors) of Islam in Arabic script are haphazardly hung about. Today it is a museum in which Muslims gather for prayer, but Christians are forbidden to even pray individually.

The supersessionist program is also well observed on the Temple Mount in Jerusalem, where Muslims have erected the Dome of the Rock and the Al-Aqsa Mosque and where the Muslim waqf seeks to erase all evidence of a previous Jewish presence there. Islamic supersessionism is observed in the destruction of the ancient Buddha statues of Bamiyan in Afghanistan and of hundreds of churches and monasteries throughout the Middle East, the Balkans, and now even across Europe. Thousands of similar examples could be cited. The supersessionist view that Islam is the final, true religion, divinely ordained to supplant all others, has driven Islamic imperialism for the past fourteen hundred years, and it will continue to do so until Christ returns.

THE THEOLOGICAL BASIS OF ISLAMIC SUPERSESSIONISM

The theological foundation of Islamic supersessionism begins with both the Qur'an and Muhammad himself, for it is in the Qur'an that Muhammad declared himself to be the "Seal of the Prophets" or "the final prophet" (Arabic: *Khātam an-Nabiyyīn*) (Qur'an 33:40). The title "the Seal of the Prophets" is understood to mean that Muhammad is the last in a long line of prophets chosen by God to deliver the message of Islam. Muslims agree that Muhammad received the final revelation from God in the form of the Qur'an, and that it was intended for all mankind, for all time, never to be replaced or improved upon. The idea that the Qur'an is essentially the last and final "Testament" is also inferred in verse 5:3 of the Qur'an: "This day have I perfected your religion for you, completed my favor upon you, and have chosen for you Islam as your religion." These are also supposed to be the last verses revealed to Muhammad before his death in 632. In other Islamic sacred traditions, Muhammad is recorded as having said, "Truly Allah made me the Seal of Prophets while Adam was still between water and clay,"[3] and, "I am the last in line of the Prophets of Allah and my congregation is the last congregation,"[4] and "So I came and in me the line of prophets has ended."[5] All of this is looked to as proof of the finality and supremacy of Islam over all other religions. Among Muslim scholars there is complete consensus that Muhammad is the last of the prophets who gave mankind a new, final, and perfect law (sharia). According to the Muslim worldview, Judaism and Christianity, including their Scriptures, have been corrupted. Islam is viewed as the restoration of the one true religion. A recent Muslim campaign across Australia featured billboards with the slogan declaring, "The Holy Quran: the final testament." Today, a supersessionist, supremacist mentality permeates every aspect of Islamic theology and Muslim identity. Muslims are taught that theirs is the final religion, superior to all others, intended to ultimately replace all others, subsuming and dominating the whole world. What's more, they are taught that Muslims themselves will replace all other peoples and that the day will come when everyone throughout the earth will say, "None has the right to be worshipped but Allah."[6]

ISLAMIC END TIMES: THE TRIUMPH OF ISLAM

Islamic supersessionism is even seen in the Muslim last-days traditions. According to Islamic eschatology—what Islam teaches concerning the end times—when Jesus returns, He comes back as a Muslim to judge according to Islamic law. As the tradition goes, Jesus will return and specifically break crosses and encourage others to do so to indicate His disapproval of this symbol of Christian error. According to the Qur'an, Christians wrongly believe that Jesus died on a cross. Jesus is also said to abolish the jizyah tax, which means that the option of Christians who live under Islamic law to pay a "protection tax" and live as "dhimmis," or subjected peoples, will no longer be an option. In other words, according to Islamic tradition, Jesus returns to abolish Christianity.

THE HADITH OF THE GHARQAD TREE

Even worse than Islam's perspective concerning Jesus's return, however, is the infamous hadith of the gharqad tree, which envisions a final, last-days holocaust carried out by Muslims against the Jewish people in the land of Israel: "Judgment Day will not come before the Muslims fight the Jews, and the Jews will hide behind the rocks and the trees, but the rocks and the trees will say: Oh Muslim, oh servant of Allah, there is a Jew behind me, come and kill him—except for the gharqad tree, which is one of the trees of the Jews."[7]

Consequently, this hadith is the centerpiece of the official charter of Hamas, even guiding the movement. This view, namely, that it is the divine destiny of Muslims to destroy the Jewish people and the State of Israel, is a theme that has been repeated among Palestinian politicians and religious leaders a thousand times over. In May 2011, Hamas MP and cleric Yunis Al Astal, on Al-Aqsa TV, stated:

> The Jews are brought in droves to Palestine so that the Palestinians—and the unified Islamic nations behind them—will have the honor of annihilating the evil of this gang . . . In just a few years, all the Zionists and the settlers will realize that their arrival in Palestine was for the purpose of the great massacre . . . When Palestine is liberated and its people return to it, and the entire region, with the grace of Allah, will have turned into the United States of Islam, the land of Palestine will become the capital of the Islamic Caliphate.[8]

Thus, not only does the Muslim end-time narrative envision Jesus returning as a Muslim prophet to abolish Christianity, but it also envisions Muslims executing a final genocide against the Jewish people. Within Islamic end-time narrative, the last days mark the time when Islamic supersessionism will be most fully implemented, more victorious than any other time in history. Needless to say, we should not take such a vision lightly, as this is precisely the mission the Bible says the Antichrist and his followers will seek to accomplish.

CONCLUSION

None of this should be surprising. After all, when one steps back and looks at the big picture, in truth, it was Satan himself who was the first and ultimate supersessionist, desiring to supersede even God Himself: "But you said in your heart, 'I will ascend to heaven; I will raise my throne above the stars of God . . . I will ascend above the heights of the clouds; I will make myself like the Most High'" (Isa. 14:13–14).

13

THE NEW CHRISTIAN ANTI-SEMITISM

I n the twentieth century, two events have profoundly transformed the Christian expression of anti-Jewish ideas and actions. The first event, of course, was the Holocaust—the systematic murder of two-thirds of the total population of European Jews. The second event was the rebirth of the State of Israel in 1948. Both events have forever altered the way Christian supersessionist belief is expressed. As we have already seen, throughout Church history, numerous Christian leaders and theologians have confidently asserted that the nation of Israel and the Jewish Temple would forever be things of the past. In the words of Origen: "We may thus assert in utter confidence that the Jews will not return to their earlier situation, for they have committed the most abominable of crimes, in forming this conspiracy against the Savior of the human race."[1] From the supersessionist perspective, after AD 70, it was all over; God Himself had forever dissolved that nation and destroyed the Jewish Temple, casting the Jews off into a state of perpetual exile. In all of this, we were told, God Himself was sending the message that the Christian Church is the new Temple, and the promised land is something much greater than a little piece of land in the Middle East. Such was the testimony of Christian supersessionist theologians for eighteen hundred years.

But then, as if overnight, this all changed. The State of Israel— against all odds, a miracle of miracles—was restored. It was both a profound embarrassment and a tremendous challenge to those who claimed that God had decreed that this would never be. If supersessionism is true, then the rebirth of the State of Israel could have only taken place as some sort of fluke, essentially outside the sovereign will of God. The Israel of today, they say, is essentially an aberration, a coincidence, having no relevance to biblical prophecy or the promises of God. Down through history, in Jewish suffering, supersessionists had claimed they were being punished, believing the Jews of their day to be experiencing the just punishment for the sins of the forefathers. With the Jewish people now successful— triumphant, even—in their own nation, suddenly the theology of association has been reversed. No longer is there an effort to connect the Jews of today to the Jews of Jesus's day. After all, how could God bless those guilty of killing His son? Today's Israel is not the Israel of biblical times, they adamantly declare. But why the sudden change of tone? To be blunt, today there is a profound theological and even psychological need within supersessionists to fight against Israel's legitimacy and its very existence. One can hear in the comments of N. T. Wright the psychological fear among supersessionists that arises at the mere possibility that the present State of Israel is indeed the fulfillment of God's sovereign plans: "To suggest, therefore, that as Christians we should support the state of Israel because it is the fulfillment of prophecy is, in a quite radical way, to cut off the branch on which we are sitting."[2] *Precisely.* For Wright, support for Israel equals an admission that supersessionism as a theological system is wrong. To support Israel is to affirm God's hand in establishing it and to undercut the supersessionism which Wright says supports him. The problem, however, is that as we have seen, the branch itself is filled with termites and rot and will fall off on its own soon enough. This is precisely why it is best to get off the branch while there is still time and place one's feet firmly on the unchanging promises of God.

On the other hand, modern Christians after the Holocaust are also now faced with the glaring reality that eighteen hundred years of Christian supersessionism and its resultant Jew-hatred culminated in the unspeakable horror of the deaths of six million Jews. Because of the horrors of the Holocaust, Christian supersessionists today tend to be far more cautious and tactful in how they express their theology of Jewish rejection, rarely expressing it in the overtly racist and hateful manner of so many of their theological forefathers. But this doesn't mean that it is not very much alive and well. British social and political commentator Melanie Phillips has very accurately captured this present reality: "After Auschwitz, this vicious theology unsurprisingly disappeared from view. But it turns out that it only went underground."[3] So on one hand, with the State of Israel such a success, there is a much greater need, an inner drive, to push the theology of Jewish rejection, but on the other hand, it must be done in a much more politically correct manner, in less overtly racial terms. Understanding then, the tensions that supersessionists now face, we can understand why the term *anti-Zionism* has become such a convenient and useful term. Today, supersessionist activism is nearly always expressed behind the fig leaf of "anti-Zionist" political activism. While the true underlying motivation of supersessionism is to prove to the world (and perhaps even more so to supersessionists themselves) that God is done with the Jews and that they have absolutely no *divine covenantal* right to the land, the primary way they wage this war is by arguing that the Jews have no *legal, moral, or political right to the land.* Thus, today it is not at all uncommon to find young evangelical Christians parroting the propaganda of "the Palestinian narrative" or giving support to various movements that seek to undermine the State of Israel, both through violent and nonviolent means. In a world where overt Christian bigotry toward the Jewish people is unacceptable, radical Muslims have become the perfect Christian proxy. In an age when the free flow of information is an all-pervasive reality, trumpeting the idea that God has disinherited the Jews, or that the State of Israel stands against the will of God, unarguably empowers those who hate or wish to kill Jews. There can be no question that the combination of Christian theological supersessionism and political anti-Israelism today absolutely serves to empower the active and violent Jew-hatred of radical Islam and neo-Nazi groups whose numbers are rapidly rising.

SLOUCHING TOWARD SUPERSESSIONISM

Today, the very sad fact is that anti-Israel activism and even outright hatred of Israel is gaining a solid foothold in some of the larger traditional evangelical denominations and is also becoming very popular among a wider range of young evangelicals. What was once the unique purview of leftist activists is now becoming quite fashionable among many otherwise conservative evangelicals. In an article for the *Middle East Quarterly*, author David Brog, executive director of Christians United for Israel, addressed the anti-Israelism rapidly spreading among evangelical millennials: "The days of taking evangelical support for Israel for granted are over. As they are increasingly confronted with an evangelical-friendly, anti-Israel narrative, more and more of these Christians are turning against the Jewish state . . . Questioning Christian support for the Jewish state is fast becoming a key way for millennials to demonstrate Christian compassion and bona fides."[4]

What is so sad is that many young evangelicals today reject Zionism not so much because they have researched the matter from both sides and feel compelled by their consciences to stand against Israel, or because they have searched the Scriptures and concluded that the Abrahamic covenant no longer has any relevance in the matter, but often simply because of the stereotypes they associate with Zionism and Zionists. Supersessionists have done a very good job of casting their restorationist counterparts as less educated, fundamentalist, crass, compassionless, hyper-literalist bumpkins who are unable to recognize either the more subtle and nuanced meanings of Scripture or the complexities of the Middle East conflict. While we would hope that within the Church, various ideas or doctrines would rise or fall based solely on their alignment with

Scripture, unfortunately, the perception of what is hip and what is not will always have a greater sway among the youth.

The result is that today, in some circles of evangelical culture, it is fashionable to espouse the Palestinian narrative, which casts Israel in the most grotesque caricature, essentially as an illegal, apartheid, juggernaut nation that exists only to run roughshod over the poor, oppressed, Palestinian victims. Of course, in swallowing this narrative hook, line, and sinker, they have unwittingly allowed themselves to become pawns in a well-resourced propaganda war funded by Islamic hate groups. The sad irony is that in believing themselves to be standing for the causes of compassion and justice, many Christians have unwittingly placed their canoes into a river of hatred that the Bible says will eventually flood the nation of Israel, leading to yet another unparalleled catastrophe. We will discuss this issue in much more detail as we move on.

King Solomon once famously said, "That which has been is that which will be, and that which has been done is that which will be done. So there is nothing new under the sun" (Eccl. 1:9). Even as so much of the Christian Church throughout history found itself functioning as an instrument of satanic Jew-hatred, it appears that this tragic irony will be repeated in history's final hour. Of course, though we pray that this is not so, the present trending of some evangelicals to take such a harsh posture against Israel is not boding well for that segment of the emerging church. Let's briefly discuss a few of the primary actors in the growing anti-Israel movement.

THE UNITED METHODIST CHURCH OF GREAT BRITAIN

To the sorrow of numerous Jewish leaders and organizations, the Methodist Church of the United Kingdom, at their annual conference in 2010, made it abundantly clear that they are enemies of the State of Israel. At the conference, a vote was taken and passed first to boycott Jewish goods and services produced in Judea and Samaria, and second, to endorse a brazenly anti-Semitic document known as the *Kairos Palestine document.*

The boycott passed by the Methodist Church of Great Britain represents the first time this church has ever boycotted any country. And it's Israel—alone. The boycott stirred to remembrance Hitler's boycott of Jewish-owned businesses in Germany, which began in 1933, as well as the Muslim Arab boycott of all Israeli products from 1922 until the present day. It was six years after the initial boycott that Hitler declared his ultimate purposes: "Today I will once more be a prophet: If the international Jewish financiers in and outside Europe should succeed in plunging the nations once more into a world war, then the result will be . . . the annihilation of the Jewish race in Europe!"[5]

The Kairos Palestine document states, "In this historic document, we Palestinian Christians declare that the military occupation of our land is a sin against God and humanity, and that any theology that legitimizes the occupation is far from Christian teachings."[6] Here is my question: When Christians endorse a document that refers to the Jewish presence of Judea and Samaria as "a sin against God and humanity," will this encourage violence among the radical elements of Palestinian society or discourage it? Not surprisingly, nowhere does the document condemn or call for an end to terrorism, but instead endorses it, referring to brazen terrorist acts in glowing and positive terms. According to the Kairos Palestine document, The Palestinian people have only "engaged in peaceful struggle, especially during the first Intifada." The document is truly a mockery of truth, justifying Palestinian resistance to the State of Israel as fully warranted self-defense. Such was the logic, of course, of Adolf Hitler, who wrote in his book *Mein Kampf,* "Hence today I believe that I am acting in accordance with the will of the Almighty Creator: *by defending myself against the Jew, I am fighting for the work of the Lord.*"[7]

Ironically, the Kairos Palestine document condemns the beliefs of John and Charles Wesley, the spiritual fathers of the Methodist Church, who ardently believed the Scripture's championing of the restoration of the Jewish people to their ancient land. Unfortunately, the United Methodist Church of Great Britain is not the only historical Christian denomination that is abandoning the biblical testimony and embracing the theology of rejectionism.

THE PRESBYTERIAN CHURCH (USA)

Over the past decade, the Presbyterian Church (USA), or PC(USA)—not to be confused with the Presbyterian Church in America (PCA)—has also increasingly taken a harsh anti-Israel position.

In 2012, at its annual General Assembly, it voted on but only narrowly defeated a motion to support the Boycott, Divestment and Sanctions campaign against Israel. The purpose of this movement, as we will discuss shortly, is to wage an economic and ideological war against the State of Israel. Though the vote was shot down, it exposed the growing minority of extremists within the PC(USA).

In 2013, another event exposed the level of growing animus toward the Jewish community within the denomination. This is the story of the Reverend Albert Butzer, a Presbyterian pastor who was forced to resign his role as the moderator of the Committee on Middle East Issues at the denomination's annual General Assembly. His great offense was traveling to Israel in two trips sponsored by a Jewish group as opposed to a Palestinian group. Although Butzer had also toured the land with pro-Palestinian groups, and was even sympathetic to their cause, the simple fact that he had been exposed to the alternative Jewish narrative rendered him a *persona non grata* and led to his forced resignation from any involvement in the discussion.

But the most overt PC(USA) assault against the State of Israel came in February 2014, when the Presbyterians' Israel Palestinian Mission Network (IPMN) released a seventy-four-page illustrated booklet and companion DVD titled *Zionism Unsettled: A Congregational Study Guide*. According to Jonathan S. Tobin, senior online editor of *Commentary* magazine, the booklet is a full-blown attack against the very concept of Zionism and seeks to compare Zionism to the Christian anti-Semitism that led to the Holocaust and other historical atrocities. Its purpose is to brand Israel as an illegitimate entity and to treat its American Jewish supporters as having strayed from the values of their religion . . . It is nothing less than a declaration of war on Israel and American Jewry . . . In *Zionism Unsettled*, the Jews have no right to Israel and no right to defend themselves. On the other hand, it rationalizes and even justifies violence against Israel.[8]

Finally, in June 2014, the PC(USA) passed a resolution to boycott several establishments that do business with Israel. In light of the other profoundly liberal positions this denomination has taken in recent years concerning abortion and homosexual marriage, none of this may come as a huge surprise to some, but no doubt, it will have a profound impact on this once-stalwart denomination's 2.4 million congregants.

THE UNITED CHURCH OF CHRIST

In June 2014, the United Church of Christ, another mainstream Christian denomination, issued a report calling for a boycott of goods produced in Israeli settlements, including eastern Jerusalem, titled "Report of the Working Group on Israel/Palestine Policy." The irony is that this took place at a moment in history when human rights abuses in nations such as Sudan included chaining a pregnant Christian woman in a cell and making her give birth on the floor while she awaited a death sentence for converting to Christianity. But there were no calls for a boycott against Sudan. Only Israel. Israel alone, among all of the nations throughout the world, was singled out for a boycott. The report labels the doctrine of restorationism as "a false doctrine" and depicts Christian support for Israel as a modern form of apostasy and a rejection of God.

The United Church of Christ is the largest denomination in all of Canada. Among notable congregations within the denomination is Trinity United Church of Christ in Chicago, where President Barack Obama worshipped for more than twenty years and where he and his children were baptized.

THE CHURCH OF SCOTLAND

Another church that was once a shining light of truth but has now allowed itself to become a haven for anti-Jewish propaganda is the Church of Scotland. In May 2013, the church released "The Inheritance of Abraham? A Report on the 'Promised Land.'" This document is a combination of the typical Christian theological supersessionism and a harsh indictment of the State of Israel.

On the theological side, the report ironically denies that there even is any such thing anymore as "the Promised Land," which is why "Promised Land" is featured in quotes in the title of the report. To Abraham's great surprise, no doubt, the report makes the ludicrous claim that the "promises about the land of Israel were never intended to be taken literally, or as applying to a defined geographical territory." The document goes on to say, "The 'promised land' in the Bible is not a place, so much as a metaphor of how things ought to be among the people of God. This 'promised land' can be found—or built—anywhere."[9] Please stop and consider what is being stated here. God Himself made a vow unto death to give Abraham's descendants the land that He specified. He repeated His promise hundreds of times in many very literal terms. And yet we are told by the Church of Scotland that these promises were merely metaphors for any piece of land anywhere. One wonders how long it will be until we are told that God Himself is merely a metaphor, not to be taken literally. This report is truly an act of theological vandalism—making an utter mockery of the Bible as a coherent document. Concerning such claims, syndicated Jewish American columnist Dennis Prager makes this very accurate observation: "It would be as if a major post-Christian religious body had announced that 'Jesus,' 'Christ,' 'crucifixion,' and 'resurrection' had never meant what Christians and the New Testament had always understood them to mean. Imagine if a major Muslim body declared that Jesus means Muhammad; Christ means Quran; crucifixion means Islamophobia; and resurrection means the Hajj."[10]

The report then goes on to cast Israel as an unjust, oppressive, racist, military state that cannot be supported by Christians. While making numerous specific charges against Israel, and while only vaguely condemning all violence, no matter who carries it out, it never once actually refers to a single act of Palestinian militaristic aggression, racism, or hatred. Not once. The entire document is a thoroughly anti-Israel diatribe of the worst kind.

After a tremendous amount of international criticism, the Church of Scotland revised the document to include a reference to the fact that Israel has a right to exist. Stop and think about this. We now live in a world where a Christian group needed to be pressured to simply acknowledge that a nation has a right to exist. What other nation in the world is ever even questioned whether or not it has a right to exist? Only Israel. In summary, I find myself in complete agreement with the conclusions of Dennis Prager:

> The Church of Scotland report is not about criticism of Israel; it is about invalidating the Jewish people and invalidating the Jews' historically incontestable claims to the land . . . The Church of Scotland has given voice to the ugliest depiction of Jews since medieval times . . . The report is a combination of medieval Christian anti-Judaism and contemporary leftist anti-Zionism. For Jews and Israel, that's a lethal combination.[11]

BOYCOTTS, DIVESTMENT, SANCTIONS

In 1933, Adolf Hitler and the Nazi Party officially boycotted Jewish businesses. This was just the beginning of a decade of the worst form of Jew-hatred in the history of the world. Today, a new movement to boycott the Jewish state is now under way. This campaign to boycott Israel is called Boycotts, Divestment and Sanctions, or BDS. The BDS is a global campaign that uses economic and political pressure to fundamentally undermine the security, legitimacy, and future of Israel. The organization, although founded by Palestinians, is very active on college campuses across the globe. In this movement, we also find a direct connection between committed leftist organizations, violent radical Islamic groups, and mainstream Christianity.

As'ad AbuKhalil is a Lebanese-American professor of political science at California State University–Stanislaus. He is also a vocal BDS supporter. According to Khalil, "the real aim of BDS is to bring down the state of Israel . . . That should be stated as an unambiguous goal. There should not be any equivocation on the subject. Justice and freedom for the Palestinians are incompatible with the existence of the state of Israel."[12]

Ahmed Moor, another vocal BDS supporter and activist in the United States, has contributed extensively to the *Guardian*, the *Huffington Post*, the *Daily Beast*, *Mondoweiss*, the *Electronic Intifada*, and *Al Jazeera*. According to Moor, "BDS is not another step on the way to the final showdown; BDS is The Final Showdown . . . Ending the occupation doesn't mean anything if it doesn't mean upending the Jewish state itself."[13]

While few congregants or attendees from the Presbyterian Church (USA), the United Church of Christ, or the United Methodist Church of Great Britain today would identify with all of the vile sentiments of the radical Islamic group Hamas, the anti-Israel stance of all of these is causing the gap between Church and terrorist organizations to quickly close. Many believe BDS to simply be a grassroots movement, the purpose of which is to apply pressure on Israel to accede to a Palestinian state. However, this is a complete misrepresentation of what the movement truly is. While many of the Christians who have joined the BDS movement often believe they are supporting a grassroots college movement that stands for equality, justice, and general Christian values, they are in fact supporting a radical and violent movement that ultimately looks for the extermination of the Jewish race. The BDS movement in Europe and the United States is overwhelmingly driven by and directly connected to radical Islamic terror organizations such as Hamas. Both Hamas and the Muslim Brotherhood, most often via the Muslim Students Association, which the FBI has linked directly to the Muslim Brotherhood, provide the primary activists, operatives, and directors for the international BDS and anti-Israel political activities on numerous university campuses across the United States and Europe. Other pro-Palestinian groups associated with the BDS movement, such as American Muslims for Palestine or the Students for Justice in Palestine, have been documented as having channeled hundreds of thousands of dollars to Hamas.[14]

In 2014, during Israel Apartheid Week, BDS groups on US campuses were recorded as chanting, "From the River to the Sea, Palestine will be free." One leading figure of the BDS movement is Azzam Tamimi, a professor of political thought and a leader of the Palestine Solidarity Campaign in London. In a protest in front of the Israeli embassy in London, speaking of the State of Israel and the Jewish people, Tamimi said, "Anybody in the world, with faith or without faith, must come together in order to eradicate this cancer from the body of humanity."[15] In an interview on the BBC, Tamimi claimed that if he were able, he would carry out a suicide bombing in Israel, stating in no unclear terms, "You see, sacrificing myself for Palestine is a noble cause. It is the straight way to pleasing my god and I would do it if I had the opportunity."[16]

Mind you, this is the cause that confessing Christians are now supporting. We are not at all surprised, then, to find that in the literature put out by both the Presbyterian Church (USA) and the United Methodist Church of Great Britain, their language of *indictment* of Israel is virtually identical to Hamas's language of *incitement*.

The anti-Israel activism of BDS on numerous college and university campuses has in many cases created an atmosphere of such strong pressure and intimidation that many Jewish students are now beginning to express that they do not feel safe. In March and April 2014, Jewish students at Northeastern University and New York University received mock eviction notices, which were placed under doors in their dorm. According to Brett Cohen, national campus program director for the pro-Israel group StandWithUs, "The outright harassment and intimidation of pro-Israel students is commonplace wherever BDS rears its hateful head." Cohen listed such intimidating acts as pro-BDS students "violently shouting down opponents and posting actual neo-Nazi anti-Semitic propaganda images to their social media accounts," as well as, "a hostile takeover of the Student Government agenda [with] BDS supporters shouting racial epithets at student senators."[17]

BEN WHITE

One of the most active and outspoken anti-Israel activists is Ben White. White is an Oxford graduate, a longtime anti-Israel blogger, and a sought-after speaker within the anti-Israel speaking circuit. In an article for the online political journal *CounterPunch*, White said, "I do not consider myself an anti-Semite, yet I can also understand why some are. There are, in fact, a number of reasons."[18] Mind you, an anti-Semite is simply someone who hates Jews. White expresses full sympathy for those who hate Jews. It is important to notice that he was not defending anti-Zionism specifically, but anti-Semitism. In other words, the hatred with which he sympathizes is not against Israel as a state, but against Jews as a people. White goes on to list numerous reasons that he feels legitimizes such hatred. This is a prime example of what I mean when I say that modern-day Christian Jew-hatred serves as a support for the rather volcanic hatred of radical Muslims or neo-Nazi groups. Does this kind of language in any way even vaguely resemble the heart of God? I have personally yet to see one of these modern anti-Israel activists express love for the Jewish people.

STEPHEN SIZER

Another of the most inflammatory anti-Israel activists is Stephen Sizer, an Anglican vicar. Sizer is a perfect example of the new anti-Semite. In 2005 he published the book *Christian Zionism: Roadmap to Armageddon?* and in 2008, a simplified version titled *Zion's Christian Soldiers? The Bible, Israel and the Church.* In both books, Sizer argues that those Christians who are not supersessionists are, by simply supporting Israel, fomenting hatred, racism, and injustice and are responsible for creating an atmosphere ripe for war, perhaps even of an apocalyptic level. Sizer is well received within not only those churches that embrace the anti-Israel narrative but also within secular and Muslim anti-Israel circles. Although generally soft-spoken, Sizer is an ideological bomb thrower of the worst variety, frequently letting slip rather incendiary statements concerning Israel and any from that segment of the Church that stand with her. In this sense, although far less witty, Sizer has essentially become the Ann Coulter of the anti-Israel movement. In August 2013, for example, sitting before a crowded church, he made the following statement: "There are certainly churches in Israel and Palestine that side with the occupation, that side with Zionism. One of my burdens is to challenge them theologically and show that they've repudiated Jesus, they've repudiated the Bible, and they are an abomination."[19]

With this comment, Sizer cast the entire Messianic Jewish community in Israel as well as the large evangelical Arab Israeli population as "an abomination" who have "repudiated Jesus." All of this was said with a very large and self-satisfied smile on his face, drawing laughter from many within his audience. Strangely, Sizer later apologized for his words, but later yet, took his apology back, expressing that he was entirely comfortable with his words. On another occasion, Sizer also referred to all Christian or Messianic believers who support Israel as "heretics."[20] On yet another occasion, Sizer again sought to condemn all Christian support for Israel, tweeting that "Christian Zionism prostitutes the Bible. It is an oxymoron."[21] Let the discerning Church ask what spirit is truly driving Sizer to make such over-the-top condemnations and accusations of his fellow Christians and to resort to such inflammatory, divisive, and hateful language?

Nevertheless, Sizer's supersessionism has led him to use much more than just inflammatory rhetoric. It has also led him into profound anti-Israel activities. In 2012, Sizer traveled to Baghdad to the "International Conference in Solidarity with Palestinian and Arab

Prisoners and Detainees in the Prisons of the Israeli Occupation." As a representative of Christ, did Sizer go to make peace and seek reconciliation between Arabs and Jews? Quite the contrary. Instead, he stood before a predominantly Arab body to give an extended and graphic presentation on Israel's torture of Palestinian children. This is no exaggeration. Although Sizer did stop short of accusing the Jews of draining their blood to make matzo, one can see in this a profound echo of the historical blood libel myth used by hysterical Jew-haters of the past to stir up the masses against the Jewish people, often leading to massacres. Let us honestly ask ourselves, does the Muslim world need any more encouragement to hate the Jewish people and the State of Israel? Why do anti-Zionists like Sizer feel it necessary to deliberately pour fuel on the fire of Muslim hatred that is already raging just fine on its own? When we observe this kind of thing, we must ask, what is the real goal, what is the endgame? And what spirit is driving them and the movement they are seeking to create? Don't they recognize that they are in so many ways the modern equivalent of the anti-Jewish theologians and race baiters of the past? Most of all, are these truly the kind of men and movements with which thoughtful Christians of conscience truly wish to associate?

WHO'S HOTWIRING THE APOCALYPSE?

From my perspective, when I observe Stephen Sizer traveling the world to incite the hatred of Israel among Muslims, or when I hear of supersessionists claiming that a rejection of supersessionism is to blame for bloodshed, I can only shake my head. As a teacher who is known for speaking to the subject of Islam's premier role in the last days, I have been accused numerous times of essentially instigating the Battle of Armageddon. In fact, according to many supersessionists, all Christians who support Israel (Christian Zionists) are not only hoping for but furthering the possibility that a real *Armageddon* will take place. Brian McLaren, a well-known supporter of the anti-Zionist movement, actually said that any who take the end-time prophecies about Israel seriously "use a bogus end-of-the-world scenario to create a kind of death wish for World War III, which, unless it is confronted more robustly by the rest of us, could too easily create a self-fulfilling prophecy."[22] Book titles like Sizer's *Christian Zionism: Road-map to Armageddon?*, Hank Hanegraaf's *The Fuse of Armageddon*, or Victoria Clark's *Allies for Armageddon: The Rise of Christian Zionism* are devoted entirely toward arguing that Zionism is a dangerous idea that furthers the potential for a massive regional or even global apocalyptic war. But consider both the layers of irony and hypocrisy here. First, those who argue that Zionists are bringing about the Battle of Armageddon most often deny that the biblical prophecies concerning the Battle of Armageddon should be taken literally or even apply to our day. Yet they accuse any Christian who supports the State of Israel of causing it to happen. *Huh?* But even stranger is the fact that many of these same critics of Zionism, in their opposition to Zionism, are in fact actually encouraging, giving support to, and even nurturing precisely the kind of racial and religious hatred—an "everlasting hatred" (Ezek. 35:5)—that the Bible says will specifically ignite the Battle of Armageddon.

In "An Open Letter to Evangelicals and Other Interested Parties" created by representatives from Knox Theological Seminary, supersessionist authors actually laid all blame for the bloodshed of the Crusades entirely at the feet of those who believed that the land of Israel is in fact the promised land. The document laments, "Bad Christian theology regarding the 'Holy Land' contributed to the tragic cruelty of the Crusades in the Middle Ages."[23] The obvious problem with this statement, however, is that the theology that led to the Crusades was not the view that the land of Israel is the promised land; *rather, it was the supersessionist view that the land specifically belonged to the Christian Church.* The document never once even acknowledged the wholesale slaughter of Jews that took place not only in the land of Israel, but also throughout Europe. The responsibility for this also fell squarely onto supersessionist Jew-hatred. The Crusaders were simply supersessionist-dominionists with swords. Such is the nature of the blindness and the transference of guilt that continue to plague supersessionists to this very day. The hypocrisy is simply beyond the pale.

CONCLUSION

Rabbi Ammiel Hirsch described the growing anti-Israel movement within the Christian Church perfectly when he said, "The world is filled with people who preach love but are full of hate. They project humility but are full of arrogance. They are consumed with passionate intensity—but for the wrong things. They prostitute words and pervert values. They say they are for peace, but their actions promote war."[24]

The growing movement to delegitimize or undermine the State of Israel is not truly about the values of peace, justice, and compassion, as many who champion the movement claim. Under the thin guise of being a political or social justice movement, it is little more than an effort to take down Israel. Samuel Clough, an articulate Bible teacher and friend, perfectly summarized the great danger of the emerging anti-Israel movement within the Church: "These arguments against Israel ultimately are not just intellectual or political arguments. We are dealing with a complete system of thought. In the end, the logical conclusion of that system of thought, is that people die. If WWII taught us nothing else, it taught us that a theology that disenfranchises the Jew, ultimately ends in a concentration camp."[25]

My simple prayer is that the emerging generation of Christian believers would wake up and see the anti-Israel movement for what it truly is, namely, a modern manifestation within the Christian Church of the long historical continuum of hatred directed toward Jews, God's covenant people. It is simply an extension of Christianity's historical effort to put the Jews back in their place as a people rejected by God and destined to remain exiles and slaves. Despite the veneer of social justice with which supporters seek to face their movement, the underlying racism is becoming increasingly visible and brazen. After waking up to this demonstrable reality, I pray that the younger generation of thoughtful and informed believers would reject this movement not only for the bad theology that is behind it but also because of its fundamentally racist agenda. I pray that after rejecting the new Jew-hated, a new generation of Christians would arise to reclaim the hopeful vision of restoration that Jesus and the apostles all proclaimed—a vision where Jesus the Jewish King will reign over both Jew and Gentile, Israeli and Arab alike, who will all serve their Creator together as one diverse, yet fully unified people of God.

PART 3

THE LAST DAYS AND THE JUDGMENT
OF THE NATIONS

THE PROPHESIED JEWISH RETURN
TO THEIR LAND

Bryan Purtle is a pastor who has become a good friend over the past several years. He's a firefighter who comes from a family of firefighters. Bryan is my kind of pastor; he has the mind of a scholar and thoroughly calloused hands. These days he spends a large part of his days in a basement shop, working leather into magnificently crafted fire-helmet shields. He does this on top of raising five kids with his wife and co-pastoring a community of believers. Bryan is also one of the most well-read brothers I know, with one of the most enviable personal theological libraries I've ever seen. He specializes in classics, books that are often hard to find or no longer available. The walls of his library are lined with framed pictures of some of his heroes—venerable pastors, theologians, and missionaries—men such as Charles Spurgeon, R.C. Chapman, Adolph Saphir, Horatius Bonar, A. W. Tozer, and from more modern times, Leonard Ravenhill.

The Purtle family also served as missionaries in an Islamic nation that we will not mention here. During their time overseas, I visited with them and had the chance to conduct and record an extensive interview with Bryan that was, in my opinion, pure gold. Sitting in a living room, with the Middle Eastern air already hot by midmorning, we discussed one of our favorite topics: the ongoing centrality of Israel in the plans of God. Bryan quickly turned to one of his areas of specialty, a crucial issue of which very few believers today are aware:

"This idea that Israel is significant according to the prophets and according to the testimony of the Scripture in reference to the last days is not novel," he told me. "Not only is it the plain reading of the Scripture itself, but in the mid to late 1800s, men were proclaiming that masses of Jews would come to Palestine and would even come into the formulation of a state. Many great historic preachers and theologians anticipated this, such as Charles Spurgeon, Adolph Saphir, David Baron, J. C. Ryle, [and] Horatius Bonar, great preachers, missionaries, and theologians."

This point that many great teachers of the Scriptures had predicted the last-days reestablishment of the State of Israel by the Jewish people is a profoundly powerful support for the literalist and futurist interpretation of Scripture. Many of them did this hundreds, or in one case, *over a thousand* years before the fact. When one surveys many of the books written by those who espouse replacement theology, those who reject and often even mock the idea that biblical prophecy is for today, or that national Israel has any place in the ongoing plans of God, they excel in highlighting the various failed prophecies and misguided date-setters throughout Church history. They love to point out false prophets like Edgar C. Whisenant (author of *88 Reasons Why the Rapture Will Be in 1988*) or Harold Camping (who said that Judgment Day would take place on May 12, 2011), but never will they acknowledge the very confident and accurate predictions of these many teachers who declared that a day was coming when the Jews would return to their land to reestablish a state. Let us then go back to draw out and shine a light on some of these too-often-forgotten treasures.

DAVID BARON (1855–1926)

David Baron was a Messianic Jewish believer who ministered in the late 1800s and early 1900s. After coming to faith, he went on to write several excellent books and cofounded the Hebrew Christian Testimony to Israel missionary organization in London. His most famous work is his classic 1918 commentary on the prophecy of Zechariah, *The Visions and Prophecies of Zechariah*, which is still widely published and used today. In addressing Zechariah 14, Baron wrote:

> First of all we have to suppose a restoration of the Jews in a condition of unbelief—not a complete restoration of the whole nation, which will not take place till after their conversion, but of a representative and influential remnant . . . It seems from Scripture that in relation to Israel and the land there will be a restoration, before the Second Advent of our Lord, of very much the same state of things as existed at the time of His First Advent, when the threads of God's dealing with them nationally were finally dropped, not to be taken up again "until the times of the Gentiles shall be fulfilled."[1]

This prediction of a Jewish return to their land, primarily in unbelief, was made thirty years before its actual fulfillment. But this was not Baron's first prediction. Twenty-seven years earlier, in 1891, Baron published a book titled *The Jewish Problem: Its Past, Present and Future*. I have an original copy, now more than 120 years old. The rather small book is an expositional argument in favor of a coming restoration of the Jews to their land. Consider Baron's comments concerning Jeremiah 30:3:

> The restoration here is a complete one: "I will bring again the captivity of my people Israel and Judah" and the number who return shall be "a great company," so that even the whole of the promised land will not be large enough for them. The same appears in that remarkable prophecy of Isaiah [11], which . . . is admittedly future in its application, where the "outcasts of Israel" and "the dispersed of Judah" are to be gathered together . . . Many more passages might be cited which speak of a complete Restoration of the entire nation in terms most unequivocal and minute; which certainly could not be said to have received their fulfillment in the—comparatively speaking—mere handful who returned from Babylon.[2]

Baron went on to state that "after the Restoration predicted in this and other prophecies, Israel is to enjoy at least national independence, if not supremacy."[3] Baron's predictions, of course, were made fifty-seven years before the State of Israel was officially founded.

NATHANIEL WEST (1826–1906)

Moving slightly back in time, Nathaniel West was born in Sunderland, England, in 1826, but moved to the United States to attend seminary. He went on to pastor several churches in Cincinnati, Pittsburgh, and Brooklyn. Later, he became a professor at Danville Theological Seminary. He was also the author of several books, including the classic *Studies in Eschatology: The Thousand Years in Both Testaments*, written in 1890. Although West believed the full restoration would occur during the thousand-year reign of Jesus, in this work he clearly predicted a future restoration of Israel as a nation:

> The solution of the great problem of Israel's future, sprung from the breach in David's Kingdom, is the solution of the Millennial Kingdom, and comes with Israel's future acceptance of David's Son as their Lord, the closing up of the ancient breach in David's Kingdom, the union of Israel and Judah into one nation, on the mountains of the fatherland forever;—in short, Israel a converted people and nation, acknowledged by Christ in person, the nations applauding.[4]

This prediction, published in 1890, was made fifty-eight years before Israel actually became a nation.

J. C. RYLE (1816–1900)

Jumping back another twenty-three years, we turn to the writings of J. C. Ryle. Ryle was a Reformed preacher who held to a literalist, futurist, and premillennial interpretation of Scripture. Several of Ryle's comments concerning what was yet a future regathering of the Jewish people to their land are truly striking in their clarity. For instance: "I believe that the Jews shall ultimately be gathered again as a separate nation, restored to their own land, and converted to the faith of Christ, after going through great tribulation (Jer. 30:10–11; 31:10; Rom. 11:25–26; Dan. 12:1; Zech. 13:8–9)."[5]

Or consider Ryle's rather direct claims elsewhere:

> But time would fail me, if I attempted to quote all the passages of Scripture in which the future history of Israel is revealed. Isaiah, Jeremiah, Ezekiel, Hosea, Joel, Amos, Obadiah, Micah, Zephaniah, Zechariah all declare the same thing. All predict, with more or less particularity, that in the end of this dispensation the Jews are to be restored to their own land and to the favor of God. I lay no claim to infallibility in the interpretation of Scripture in this matter. I am well aware that many excellent Christians cannot see the subject as I do. I can only say, that to my eyes, the future salvation of Israel as a people, their return to Palestine and their national conversion to God, appear as clearly and plainly revealed as any prophecy in God's Word.[6]

Again, Ryle's predictions concerning the reestablishment of the Jewish state were made in 1867, eighty-one years before Israel officially became a state.

SEPTIMUS SEARS (1819–1877)

Yet another Reformed preacher, Septimus Sears, was renowned in England as one of the country's most outstanding pastors and preachers. He began his ministry at age twenty, before becoming pastor of Clifton Strict Baptist Church, which he led until his death in 1877. In his book *The Things Which Shall Be Hereafter or God's Testimony about the Future, Gathered from Holy Scriptures*, Sears clearly predicted the future reestablishment of the State of Israel. Under the chapter heading "The Restoration of the Jews," Sears began by stating:

> The Jews will return to Jerusalem unconverted to Christ. For it is after they are returned to their own land that the following

Scripture will be fulfilled:—"For I will take you from among the heathen, and gather you out from all countries, and will bring you into your own land. Then I will sprinkle clean water on you and you will be clean: from all your filthiness, and from all your idols, will I cleanse you: I will take away the stoney heart out of your flesh, and I will give you a heart of flesh, and I will put my spirit within you, and cause you to walk in my statues, and ye shall keep my judgments, and do them. (Ezekiel 36:24–27)[7]

Sears went on to quote several other prophecies indicating that the Jews would return to their own land. Following these things, according to Sears, would be the time of "Jacob's Trouble,"—a terrible national calamity followed by the national conversion of the Jews and finally their ultimate and permanent restoration to the land. Let us note that Sears's predictions, like Ryle's, were published in 1867, eighty-one years before Israel officially became a state.

CHARLES SPURGEON (1834–1892)

Charles Haddon Spurgeon, sometimes referred to as "the Prince of Preachers," was a British Baptist. He remains a highly influential figure among a wide range of Christians today. Spurgeon was prolific in numerous ways. Although he was not a frequent commentator on the issue of the end times, from those occasions when he did discuss these matters, it is clear that he was a classic premillennialist who fervently believed that any plain reading of the Scriptures would lead one to look for the Jewish return to the land of Israel according to the promises of God. Consider the following very direct statement from the legendary Spurgeon as he commented on the latter chapters of the prophecy of Ezekiel:

Israel is now blotted out from the map of nations; her sons are scattered far and wide; her daughters mourn beside all the rivers of the earth. Her sacred song is hushed; no king reigns in Jerusalem; she brings forth no governors among her tribes. But she is to be restored; she is to be restored "as from the dead." When her own sons have given up all hope of her, then is God to appear for her. She is to be reorganized; her scattered bones are to be brought together. There will be a native government again; there will again be the form of a political body; a State shall be incorporated, and a king shall reign. Israel has now become alienated from her own land. Her sons, though they can never forget the sacred dust of Palestine, yet die at a hopeless distance from her consecrated shores. But it shall not be so forever, for her sons shall again rejoice in her.[8]

Notice that Spurgeon saw a future "native government," a "political body," when a "State shall be incorporated." Elsewhere, Spurgeon rightly exhorts us all:

I think we do not attach sufficient importance to the restoration of the Jews. We do not think enough about it. But certainly, if there is anything promised in the Bible it is this. I imagine that you cannot read the Bible without seeing clearly that there is to be an actual restoration of the Children of Israel . . . For when the Jews are restored, the fullness of the Gentiles shall be gathered in; and as soon as they return, then Jesus will come upon Mount Zion with his ancients gloriously, and the halcyon days of the millennium shall then dawn; we shall then know every man to be a brother and a friend; Christ shall rule with universal sway.[9]

Not only do far too many Christians today not "attach sufficient importance to the restoration of the Jews," but they actually strive to deny that such a restoration will ever occur. Yet according to Spurgeon, if we simply "read the Scriptures aright," then we will fully understand the fact that

the Jews have a great deal to do with this world's history. They shall be gathered in; Messiah shall come, the Messiah they are looking for—the same Messiah who came once shall come again—shall come as they expected him to come the first time. They then thought he would come a prince to reign over them, and so he will when he comes again. He will come to be king of the Jews, and to reign over his people most gloriously; for when he comes Jew and Gentile shall have equal privileges, though there shall yet be some distinction afforded to that royal family from whose loins Jesus came; for he shall sit upon the throne of his father David, and unto him shall be gathered all nations.[10]

Spurgeon's predictions of a restored Jewish state were made in 1864, eighty-four years before it actually took place.

ADOLPH SAPHIR (1831–1891)

Adolph Saphir was a Hungarian Jew who later embraced Jesus as Messiah when the Scottish Free Church sent missionaries to the Hungarian Jews. Saphir became ordained in the Irish Presbyterian Church and emerged as a man renowned for his exposition of the Word and moving lectures. In his great work *Christ and Israel*, Saphir spent a great deal of time expositing the Scriptures to determine what they said concerning the regathering of Israel. Saphir saw Israel's regathering as a yet-to-be future reality that was not in question. The section that addresses this subject is titled "The Phases of the Restoration, Culminating in the Coming of the Great King." Commenting on Isaiah 66:19, 20, Saphir said:

> Here it is declared that there shall be a second and more general ingathering of Israel out of all nations, and that after the light of Israel is come, and the glory of the Lord is risen upon her, and after the great judgments on the ungodly. There are thus two restorations- one before, the other after the great crisis; one partial, the other complete; one which provokes the enmity of the nations, the other in which the nations rejoice and even co-operate.[11]

Saphir was very specific that the Jews would return to Israel largely in an unbelieving state, not having yet turned to their true Messiah. Here are his comments concerning Ezekiel 22:17–22:

The Jews return in an unconverted state. They are to be brought to Jerusalem, in order to be judged. "And the word of the Lord came unto me, saying, Son of man, the house of Israel is to me become dross: all they are brass, and tin, and iron, and lead, in the midst of the furnace; they are even the dross of silver. Therefore, thus saith the Lord God: Because ye are all become dross, behold, therefore, I will gather you into the midst of Jerusalem. As they gather silver, and brass, and iron, and lead, and tin, into the midst of the furnace, to blow the fire upon it, to melt it, so will I gather you in Mine anger and My fury, and I will leave you there, and melt you. Yea, I will gather you, and blow upon you in the fire of My wrath, and ye shall be melted in the midst thereof. As silver is melted in the midst of the furnace, so shall ye be melted in the midst thereof; and ye shall know that I the Lord have poured out My fury upon you." If they had returned to their own land in a converted state, it is impossible that God would pour out upon them His wrath.[12]

Saphir's predictions were made in 1864, the same year Charles Spurgeon had come to precisely the same conclusion, eighty-four years before Israel became a state.[13]

HORATIUS BONAR (1808–1889)

Horatius Bonar, yet one more great Reformed preacher, was also a committed revivalist, author, and hymn writer from the Free Church of Scotland. In the following extensive citation of his work *Prophetical Landmarks, Containing Data for Helping to Determine the Question of Christ's Pre-millennial Advent*, we see that Bonar was a firm believer in the fact that the future would bring about the return of the Jews to the land of Israel. I encourage you to carefully consider the fullness of Bonar's very timeless words:

I am one of those who believe in Israel's restoration and conversion; who receive it as a future certainty, that all Israel shall be gathered, and that all Israel shall be saved. As I believe in Israel's present degradation, so do I believe in Israel's coming

glory and preeminence. I believe that God's purpose regarding
our world can only be understood by understanding God's purpose as to Israel. I believe that all human calculations as to the
earth's future, whether political or scientific, or philosophical or
religious, must be failures, if not taking for their data or basis
God's great purpose regarding the latter-day standing of Israel. I
believe that it is not possible to enter God's mind regarding the
destiny of man, without taking as our key or our guide His mind
regarding the ancient nation—that nation whose history, so far
from being ended, or nearly ended, is only about to begin. And
if any one may superciliously ask, What can the Jews have to do
with the world's history?—may we not correctly philosophize on
that coming history, and take the bearing of the world's course,
leaving Israel out of the consideration altogether? We say, nay;
but O man, who art thou that repliest against God? Art thou
the framer of the earth's strange annals, either past or future?
Art thou the creator of those events which make up these annals,
or the producer of those latent springs or seeds of which these
arise? He only to whom the future belongs can reveal it. He
only can announce the principles on which that future is to be
developed. And if He set Israel as the great nation of the future,
and Jerusalem as the great metropolis of earth, who are we, that,
with our philosophy of science, we should set aside the divine
arrangements, and substitute for them a theory of man? Human
guesses of the future are the most uncertain of all uncertainties;
and human hopes, built upon these guesses, are sure to turn out
the most disappointing, if not the most disastrous, of all failures.
*I believe that the sons of Abraham are to re-inherit Palestine, and
that the forfeited fertility will yet return to that land; that the wilderness and the solitary places shall be glad for them, and the desert
will rejoice and blossom as the rose.* I believe that, meanwhile, Israel
shall not only be wanderers, but that everywhere only a remnant,
a small remnant, shall be saved; and that it is for the gathering
in of this remnant that our missionaries go forth. I believe that
these times of ours (as also all the times of the four monarchies
[Dan. 2]) are the times of the Gentiles; and that Jerusalem and
Israel shall be trodden down of the Gentiles, till the times of the
Gentiles be fulfilled. I believe that, with the filling up of these
times of the Gentile pre-eminence, and the completion of what

the apostle calls the fullness of the Gentiles, will be the signal for the judgments which are to usher in the crisis of earth's history, and the deliverance of Israel, and the long-expected kingdom.[14]

Bonar's predictions were published in 1847, 101 years before the reestablishment of the State of Israel.

SAMUEL PRIDEAUX TREGELLES (1813–1875)

Samuel Prideaux Tregelles was a brilliant biblical exegete, scholar, and theologian from the Plymouth Brethren movement. Tregelles, having worked as an ironworker while he learned Greek, Hebrew, Aramaic, and Welsh, like my pastor friend Bryan Purtle, was indeed a scholar with well-calloused hands. He is also one of my favorite exegetes from this period.

Long before it could have ever been predicted, Tregelles confidently declared, like those before him, that the land of Israel would someday be resettled by the Jewish people. In speaking of the prophecies of Daniel, Tregelles predicted: "From the mention of "the daily sacrifice" and the "sanctuary" . . . plain that at [that time], these things will be found in existence—a portion of the Jews will have returned in unbelief to their own land."[15]

Before any of the previous nineteenth-century exegetes, Tregelles made his predictions in 1846, 102 years before Israel was reestablished.

JONATHAN EDWARDS (1703–1758)

Few are aware that prior to the nineteenth century, a vast number of Reformed theologians, Pietist Lutherans, and Puritans also believed in a future restoration of Israel. Among these various groups, however, there were many differences of opinion. Some believed that the Jews would return to the land only at the return of Jesus. Others believed that they would return and come to faith in Jesus as Messiah long before He returned. Many were postmillennialists, a deeply optimistic version of amillennialism.

One of the most well known restorationists is Jonathan Edwards, arguably America's most important and original philosophical theologian, and one of its greatest intellectuals and most important revivalists. He was a thoroughly Reformed theologian with a Puritan heritage. Having been so instrumental in the First Great Awakening, Edwards, like so many theologians of his time, had a profoundly optimistic postmillennialist view of the future, believing that the Jews would not only be restored to their land but would also embrace Jesus as their Messiah before the return of Jesus. In his *History of the Works of Redemption*, Edwards spoke at length about the future restoration of the Jews to their land and to faith in Jesus:

> Jewish infidelity shall then be overthrown. However obstinate they have now been for above seventeen hundred years in their rejecting Christ, and instances of conversion of any of that nation have been so very rare ever since the destruction of Jerusalem, but they have against the plain teachings of their own prophets continued to approve of the cruelty of their forefathers in crucifying [Christ]; yet when this day comes the thick veil that blinds their eyes shall be removed (II Cor. 3:16), and divine grace shall melt and renew their hard hearts, "And they shall look on him whom they [have pierced, and they shall mourn for him, as one mourneth for his only son, and shall be in bitterness for him, as one that is in bitterness for his firstborn]" (Zech. 12:10, etc.). And then shall all Israel be saved [Rom. 11:26]. The Jews in all their dispersions shall cast away their old infidelity, and shall wonderfully have their hearts changed, and abhor themselves for their past unbelief and obstinacy; and shall flow together to the blessed Jesus, penitently, humbly, and joyfully owning him as their glorious king and only savior, and shall with all their hearts as with one heart and voice declare his praises unto other nations [Isa. 66:20; Jer. 50:4]. Nothing is more certainly foretold than this national conversion of the Jews is in the eleventh chapter of Romans. And there are also many passages of the Old Testament that cannot be interpreted in any other sense, that I cannot now stand to mention.[16]

Edwards went on to acknowledge that while he didn't know the precise timing of when these things would happen, he was confident that the Scriptures spoke of their future restoration which would result in "life from the dead" among the Gentile nations of the earth. Edwards predictions were made in 1739, 209 years before Israel was officially declared to be a nation. Half of Edwards vision has been fulfilled, but exactly when the fullness of that nation will be fully restored through coming to faith in Jesus has yet to be seen.

SIR ISAAC NEWTON (1642–1727)

Sir Isaac Newton needs little introduction. Newton was a physicist and mathematician who died in 1727. He was also a devout student of the Bible. Although Newton largely held to a historicist interpretation of the Bible, he did strive to interpret it literally. In his commentary on the book of Revelation, Newton spoke of the coming time when we would see "the ruin of the wicked nations, the end of weeping and of all troubles, the return of the Jews [from] captivity and their setting up of a flourishing and everlasting kingdom . . . At that time is also predicted the end of the king of the North, the fall of the great Apostasy, the return of the Jewish captivity and the great tribulation."[17]

Although Newton wrongly believed that Israel's return to their land would coincide with the return of Jesus, he was adamant in his view that a future restoration of the Jewish people to their land was predicted in Scripture. This debate, whether the Jews would be converted before or at the time of the return of Jesus, was widely discussed among numerous Christians leaders and commentators in the roughly hundred or so years before Newton. Although the return of the Jews to their land obviously did not coincide with the return of Jesus, Newton did accurately predict a future restoration of the Jewish people to their land some two hundred fifty years before it happened.

WILHELMUS À BRAKEL (1635–1711)

Wilhemus à Brakel was a leading figure in what is called the Dutch Reformed movement (*De Nadere Reformatie*) who ministered in Rotterdam, Holland during the late seventeenth and early eighteenth centuries. This movement was a pietistic movement greatly influenced by English Puritanism. In his influential multi-volume magnum opus, "The Christian's Reasonable Service," written in 1700, Brakel said the following concerning a future regathering of Jews to their homeland:

> One more question remains to be answered: Will the Jewish nation be gathered together again from all the regions of the world and from all the nations of the earth among which they have been dispersed? Will they come to dwell in Canaan and all the lands promised to Abraham, and will Jerusalem be rebuilt?
>
> We believe that these events will transpire. We deny, however, that the temple will be rebuilt, and that the previous mode of worship will be observed, which prior to Christ's coming was of a typifying nature and would then be of a reflective nature. . . . They will be an independent republic, governed by a very wise, good-natured, and superb government. Furthermore, Canaan will be extraordinarily fruitful, the inhabitants will be eminently godly, and they will constitute a segment of the glorious state of the church during the thousand years prophesied in Rev 20.[18]

Though Brakel was a post-millennialist and thus had a much more optimistic view than most premillennialists today, his predictions should not be ignored. Though he made it clear that he was not expecting a rebuilt Jewish Temple and also believed the citizenry of Israel would largely have all become believers in Jesus the Messiah, his general conviction concerning a future return to the land was accurate. Brakel made this prediction in 1700, nearly 250 years before it came to pass.

THOMAS BRIGHTMAN (1562–1607)

Among the Puritans, there was a strong belief in Jewish restorationism. Thomas Brightman was an English clergyman who wrote much on this theme in his books, *A Revelation of the Revelation* (or *Apocalypse*) (written in 1611), and *Shall They Return to Jerusalem Again?* (written in 1615). In pondering the question as to whether or not the Jews shall return to their land, Brightman said, "What, shall they return to Jerusalem again? There is nothing more certain; the prophets do everywhere confirm it and beat upon it."[19]

Brightman's works were highly influential among his fellow Puritans. Many others from this period shared his restorationist perspective. His confident assertions were made in 1611, 337 before Israel was officially reestablished as a nation.

ISHODAD OF MERV (FL. 850)

If all of the previous predictions are not satisfactory to prove that these men were not influenced by natural trends or ideas popular in their day, then consider this one final prediction that dates back as far back as the ninth century. Ishodad of Merv was a Christian bishop over the city of Hadatha near modern-day Tiberius. In his commentary on Micah 5:3, he wrote, "'He shall give them up until the time when she who is in labor has brought forth.' This is what the prophet calls Jerusalem. This means He will abandon them to the afflictions of captivity until the time of the return. This means that these predictions will not come true before they are back from their captivity."[20]

When did Ishodad declare this? It was written in AD 850, *eleven hundred years before the modern Jewish state was born!*

IT WAS FORESEEN

Many others not mentioned here also made similarly confident predictions. It is important to state that these were not predictions based on international trends toward a Jewish return to the land.

This is an important point because some of the more determined scoffers among those who espouse replacement theology argue that these men were only mirroring the aspirations of the early Zionist movement of the late nineteenth and early twentieth centuries. But this argument is seen to be rather desperate, as the dates simply do not line up! Theodor Herzl, who is largely considered to be the modern father of the Zionist movement, was not even born until 1860. The founding of Herzl's World Zionist Organization at the First Zionist Congress in Basel, Switzerland, did not take place until 1897. The earliest signs of any discernible Zionist movement appear to be the *Hovevei Zion*, or the Lovers of Zion, who created about twenty Jewish settlements in the land between 1870 and 1897. But of the predictions just cited, many were made long before 1870, when this small stirring of Jews returning to Israel even began. And every one of the predictions cited here were made before the First Zionist Congress, when Zionism truly began to impact popular theological thought. Simply stated, *these expositors knew about Zionism even before the early Zionists knew about it!* In fact, it can be fairly said that Christian (or biblical) Zionism long preceded secular or Jewish Zionism. Supersessionists seem determined to deny this fact. Carl Medearis, who we have cited several times throughout this book, articulated the common supersessionist claim when he said of Christian Zionism "[is] a very recent heresy that's only risen in the last 100 years or so." Though obviously far from the truth, this claim has been widely repeated among supersessionist polemicists seeking to undermine the rich tradition of restorationism among Christians, including many from a non-Dispensationalist, Reformed tradition. How frequently one may hear the claim that restorationism and Christian support for Israel is a relatively new phenomena, allegedly having begun with John Nelson Darby and the Dispensationalist movement. Instead, as we have seen it was not long after many protestant believers turned to a diligent study of the Bible that numerous great men of the Church, began recognizing the ongoing calling and election of Israel through the prophets. These expectations of an Israeli state didn't come from sensationalism, political trends or visionary encounters. They came simply from a simple and straightforward reading of the testimony of the biblical prophets.

CONCLUSION

In closing this chapter, I would like to return to some comments made by the Messianic Jewish scholar David Baron, the first nineteenth-century theologian cited in this chapter. In commenting on how we should interpret Scripture, whether in the face-value manner of premillennialism (the view taken in this book) or in the allegorical manner of replacement theology, Baron said:

> Like thousands more, the writer has in the infinite grace of God been brought out of the darkness of Rabbinical Judaism into the marvelous light and liberty of the glorious gospel of Christ. He accepted Jesus of Nazareth as the Messiah of Israel and Saviour of the world, on the ground of a literal interpretation of the prophecies that concerning Him; and he cannot consistently, without doing outrage to his convictions, accept one principle of interpretation from one set of prophecies which have already been fulfilled, and another principle of interpretation for another set of prophecies not yet fulfilled. Rather, he honestly believes that manner of fulfillment of those prophecies which are now history, supplies the only sound basis of interpretation with regard to Israel and the kingdom which yet await their fulfillment.[21]

Let us also cite Dr. Walter C. Kaiser Jr., who made a very similar, yet profoundly simple comment concerning those who espouse replacement theology and who continue to argue that God is no longer committed to fulfilling His land promises to the Jewish people: "Look, it's already too late to argue about that because there are already six million Jewish people back in the land. So if you are going to argue, you've got to erase six million people that are back in the land, which you cannot do. So it's time to shape up the theology in connection with what reality shows."[22]

The Scriptures predicted it, many men of God using only the Scriptures as their guide both saw and predicted it, and now that miracle has taken place before the eyes of all the world. Pastor Purtle, in summarizing how the discerning Church should relate to this profound reality, said it best: "So we've got to pay attention to this. This is one of the Lord's great thunderclaps. It's almost as if He Himself is prophesying to the nations and saying, 'I have not abandoned or forgotten my covenant with this people or with this land, so pay heed to it.'"

The State of Israel stands before us, having been firmly established before all the world. When those who espouse replacement theology deny the Lord's hand in all of this, when they determinedly deny that it was prophesied beforehand and has been fulfilled before us, they are engaging in a deliberate hardening of the heart and closing of the ears to these profoundly clear signs. And if it was the simple studying of the Scriptures that empowered these men to know the future, then what else might a straightforward study of the prophets reveal? What kind of knowledge of the future might the Church gain if she would return to a simple reading of the words of the prophets? And what kind of information is being ignored by those segments of the Church that disdainfully look down upon the study of biblical prophecy? For in truth, the trumpet blasts from heaven are not primarily to remind us what has happened but to remind us of what is about to transpire. *Oh, that the Church would hear what the Spirit is saying to His people in this hour!* As we finish this chapter, would you pray the following prayer with me?

> *O Lord, let us not be found among those who turn a deaf ear to what You are doing right now among the nations. May the Church awaken not only to what You are doing now in the earth but also what the Scriptures say You are about to do. Show us what lies ahead for Your covenant people, Israel, and for all the nations. Wake us up, Lord! Awaken Your people. And having discerned all these things ahead of time, may we also make ourselves ready for all that is about to take place. Let us truly be a people prepared. Amen.*

15

SATAN'S RAGE AGAINST JEWISH

FULFILLMENT

For anyone who seeks to gain an understanding of the history of Christian hatred and persecution of the Jewish people, there are dozens upon dozens of books dedicated to this subject. I truly believe that all Christians should take it upon themselves to learn about and wrestle through the heartbreaking and shameful implications. None of these works, however—at least none that I am aware of—also address the future of Israel. Most of these books are academic works that explore the issue only from a historical, theological, or sociological angle. For our purposes, however, it is essential that we also address what the Bible says with regard to Israel's future. Understanding the future may actually be even more important than the past. The future, after all, is where our part in the story will be written.

To fully grasp the unfolding biblical story of redemption, it is critical to recognize the coming culmination of Satan's rage against the Jewish people and their fulfillment. Not only has Satan raged against the Jewish people throughout history, but the Scriptures are also clear that in the last days, just before Jesus returns, Satan will utilize his influence over the nations to muster all of his available troops and vent his rage against the Lord's covenant people. In the book of Revelation, we read, "Woe to the earth and the sea, because the devil has come down to you, having great wrath, knowing that he has only a short time" (Rev. 12:12). This will be the devil's final swan song indeed. The reason for this, of course, is very simple. Because the Lord's plans to establish His kingdom on the earth are so fundamentally Israel-centric, the primary thrust of Satan's final resistance will be focused on Jerusalem and Israel as a whole. It is crucial that we consider and familiarize ourselves with the overwhelming emphasis the Bible places on the land of Israel as ground zero for the final clash between Satan and the plans of God to fulfill all of His redemptive purposes for the whole earth.

THE LAST-DAYS INVASION OF ISRAEL IN MICAH

That Jerusalem will be the geographic center of the primary events that will unfold in the last days is a much-repeated theme throughout the prophets. The prophet Micah, for example, spoke very clearly of the day when the Antichrist would invade the land of Israel. In the famous messianic prophecy concerning the Messiah's place of birth, Micah wrote: "But as for you, Bethlehem Ephrathah, too little to be among the clans of Judah, from you One will go forth for Me to be ruler in Israel. His goings forth are from long ago, from the days of eternity" (5:2). The Gospels record that the chief priests and scribes referred to this very verse when King Herod inquired of them as to where the Messiah was to be born. Their answer was unequivocal; He would be born in Bethlehem of Judea (Matt. 2:4–5). This coming Messiah was to be a sign to the Israelites that an epoch had ended, and from that time forward, they would live securely under His leadership: "And He will arise and shepherd His flock in the strength of the LORD, in the majesty of the name of the LORD His God. And they will remain, because at that time He will be great to the ends of the earth" (Mic. 5:4). Israel would no longer have to fear her enemies, and the greatness of this Messiah's authority would reach the whole world. But it is the next verse where we are told that this very Messiah will specifically deliver Israel from the invasion of "the Assyrian": "This One will be our peace. When the Assyrian invades our land, when he tramples on our citadels . . .

He will deliver us from the Assyrian when he attacks our land and when he tramples our territory" (vv. 5–6). Obviously, there has been no point in history when Jesus delivered Israel from any Assyrian invasion. This passage is referring to the day when Jesus Himself will ultimately deliver Israel from the invasion of the Antichrist's forces, represented here by ancient imperial Assyria. So according to Micah, the Antichrist is the one who "invades our land . . . attacks our land and . . . tramples our territory." There can be no question that the geographic end-time thrust of Satan will be against the State of Israel.

THE LAST-DAYS INVASION OF ISRAEL IN EZEKIEL

Using terms that perfectly reflect the restored nation of Israel as it exists today, the prophet Ezekiel, in one of the most dramatic eschatological passages in the Old Testament, also prophesied concerning the last-days gathering of the nations against "the mountains of Israel":

> And the word of the LORD came to me saying, "Son of man, set your face toward Gog of the land of Magog . . . After many days you will be summoned; in the latter years you will come into *the land that is restored from the sword, whose inhabitants have been gathered from many nations to the mountains of Israel which had been a continual waste; but its people were brought out from the nations, and they are living securely, all of them.* You will go up, you will come like a storm; you will be *like a cloud covering the land,* you and all your troops, and many peoples with you." (Ezek. 38:1–2, 8–9; emphasis added)

Gog and all of his armies will invade Israel and cover the land like a cloud. In one of my previous books, *Mideast Beast: The Scriptural Case for an Islamic Antichrist,* I demonstrate that Gog is the Antichrist. One portion of the prophecy that strongly infers this is Ezekiel 38:17 where the Lord declares that Gog is the same invader spoken of by the previous prophets: "Thus says the Lord God, 'Are you the one of whom I spoke in former days through My servants the prophets of Israel, who prophesied in those days for many years that I would bring you against them?'" (Ezek. 38:17).[1] Various prophets who came before Ezekiel had been "for many years" declaring that at the end of the age, the Lord would bring a Gentile invader and his armies against Israel. Needless to say, the prophets that came before Ezekiel and clearly pointed to a last-days invasion of Israel are Jeremiah, Zephaniah, Habakkuk, Isaiah, Micah, and Amos. While these prophets were very often speaking to the threats in their immediate or near future, they spoke through these events, with their ultimate subject being the final invasion of Israel by the Antichrist and His defeat by Jesus the Messiah.

IS THE BATTLE OF GOG OF MAGOG A SUCCESSFUL INVASION OR A FAILURE?

There is a common belief among many students of prophecy that the Battle of Gog of Magog is a complete failure of an invasion and that the invading hordes are supernaturally devastated almost immediately as they enter the land of Israel. No sooner do they enter than they are utterly overcome—completely wiped out, even—or so we have been frequently told by various prophecy teachers. For years, I also believed this, as the descriptions of the destruction of the armies may seem at first glance to reflect such a scenario. But when one considers what the text actually says concerning the state of Israel at the onset of the invasion versus what it says concerning Israel's state at the conclusion of the invasion, then it becomes all too clear that the invasion is in fact entirely successful, resulting in a significant defeat for Israel.

As the oracle begins, the Lord is directly addressing Gog the Antichrist and describing the people of Israel as unsuspecting and living in a state of relative ease. They have been gathered together there from among the nations, to resettle the former ruins, and are now living richly, with livestock and an abundance of goods. In essence, it is a perfect description of Israel as it exists today:

"This is what the Sovereign LORD says: On that day thoughts will come into your mind and you will devise an evil scheme. You will say, 'I will invade a land of unwalled villages; I will attack a peaceful and unsuspecting people—all of them living without walls and without gates and bars. I will plunder and loot and turn my hand against the resettled ruins and the people gathered from the nations, rich in livestock and goods, living at the center of the land.'" (Ezek. 38:10–12 NIV)

So this is the condition of Israel when Gog the Antichrist begins to plan his assault. Later, however, after the destruction of Gog's armies, Ezekiel describes much of the people of Israel as being held captive, as prisoners among the surrounding nations, which are described as "their enemies' lands." It is from these lands that the Lord will deliver the prisoners and return every last one safely back to Israel. Ezekiel specifically contrasts their future condition of being enslaved among the nations with their former condition in the land, at ease and living in unfaithfulness to the Lord:

> Therefore thus says the Lord GOD: "Now I will bring back the captives of Jacob, and have mercy on the whole house of Israel; and I will be jealous for My holy name—after they have borne their shame, and all their unfaithfulness in which they were unfaithful to Me, when they dwelt safely in their own land and no one made them afraid. When I have brought them back from the peoples and gathered them out of their enemies' lands, and I am hallowed in them in the sight of many nations, then they shall know that I am the LORD their God, who sent them into captivity among the nations, but also brought them back to their land, and left none of them captive any longer." (Ezek. 39:25–28 NKJV)

Obviously, the invasion of Gog of Magog is a success, leading to a great number of Israelites being taken captive. It is in Israel's darkest hour, however, that the hand of God will intervene and the armies of Gog of Magog will be completely destroyed. This will take place when Jesus returns, which, to the shock of some, Ezekiel actually talks about.

EZEKIEL 38–39: THE PAROUSIA OF THE OLD TESTAMENT

Ezekiel actually reveals that at the conclusion of Gog's destruction, Jesus the Messiah will be physically present on the ground in the land: "For in my jealousy and in my blazing wrath I declare, on that day there shall be a great earthquake in the land of Israel. The fish of the sea and the birds of the heavens and the beasts of the field and all creeping things that creep on the ground, and all the people who are on the face of the earth, shall quake at my presence" (38:19–20 ESV). The word used for *presence* is the Hebrew word *panim*, a reference to the actual face of a person. When God says that the people of the earth will quake at His *panim*, He is saying that they will be terrified because of His actual, visible, face-to-face manifestation before them. Concerning the word *panim*, *The New Unger's Bible Dictionary* says, "The presence (face) of Jehovah is Jehovah in his own personal presence."[2] *The New International Encyclopedia of Bible Words* says, "In the OT, being in God's or another's presence is indicated by a preposition (l) prefixed to the Hebrew word *panim* ('face'). The thought is to be 'before the face of' the person."[3]

Ezekiel's description of people hiding from God's actual face reveals that at the conclusion of the Battle of Gog and Magog, Jesus the Messiah, God incarnate, will be physically present on the earth, in the land of Israel.

Further evidence for the physical presence of Jesus at the conclusion of this battle is seen in Ezekiel 39:7: "And my holy name I will make known in the midst of my people Israel, and I will not let my holy name be profaned anymore. And the nations shall know that I am the lord, the Holy One in Israel" (ESV).

This is the only time the phrase "the Holy One in Israel" is used in the Bible. It is the Hebrew *qadowsh qadowsh baYisra'el*. A similar phrase, "the Holy One of Israel" (*qadowsh qadowsh Yisra'el*), is used thirty-one times in Scripture (e.g., Isa. 12:6; 43:3; 55:5; 60:9). But here, the Lord is not envisioned merely as the Holy One of Israel; He is actually portrayed as present in the land and on the ground! While many have claimed in the past that this passage concludes several years before the return of Jesus, this verse makes this an absolute impossibility.

In conclusion then, there is no way that Ezekiel's prophecy could speak of anything apart from the last-days assault of Satan against the State of Israel and the Jewish people.

THE LAST-DAYS INVASION OF JERUSALEM IN ZECHARIAH

The prophet Zechariah also quite clearly spoke of the gathering of the nations in the last days, specifically, to take Jerusalem: "Behold, I am going to make Jerusalem a cup that causes reeling to all the peoples around; and when the siege is against Jerusalem, it will also be against Judah. It will come about in that day that I will make Jerusalem a heavy stone for all the peoples; all who lift it will be severely injured. And all the nations of the earth will be gathered against it (Zech. 12:2–3). And again in chapter 14:

> Behold, a day is coming for the LORD when the spoil taken from you will be divided among you. For *I will gather all the nations against Jerusalem to battle*, and the city will be captured, the houses plundered, the women ravished and half of LORD will go forth and fight against those nations, as when He fights on a day of battle. *In that day His feet will stand on the Mount of Olives, which is in front of Jerusalem on the east.* (vv. 1–4; emphasis added)

It is essential to take note of the fact that the Lord Himself says that He will actually personally engage in battle with these many nations that invade Israel and come to Jerusalem. "In that day," His feet will actually rest upon the Mount of Olives. This can be none other than Jesus Christ, God the Son, manifest on the earth, physically present at the time of His return. That which Ezekiel described was also described by the prophet Zechariah. Many of the prophets, in fact, referred to this specific time period. They were all emphasizing and indicating the undeniable reality. It is a point that cannot be emphasized enough: Jesus is going to return to Jerusalem.

THE LAST-DAYS INVASION OF JERUSALEM IN JOEL

Like the prophets before him, Joel also prophesied concerning the eschatological invasion of Israel by the surrounding nations:

> For behold, in those days and at that time, when I restore the fortunes of Judah and Jerusalem, I will gather all the nations and bring them down to the valley of Jehoshaphat. Then I will enter into judgment with them there on behalf of My people and My inheritance, Israel, whom they have scattered among the nations; and they have divided up My land . . . Let the nations be aroused and come up to the valley of Jehoshaphat, for there I will sit to judge all the surrounding nations. (Joel 3:1–2, 12)

While the motivation of the invading nations will be to seize Israel for themselves, the Lord's purpose in drawing them there will be to execute His judgments against them. The context of this end-time prophecy is "Judah and Jerusalem." But specifically, "the Valley of Jehoshaphat" is a reference to the Kidron Valley, which runs along the eastern edge of Jerusalem. The name Josaphat, a variant of Jehoshaphat, actually means "Yahweh judges." In the gospel of Matthew, as Jesus sat on the Mount of Olives looking down at this valley, he harkened back to this prophecy of Joel's and spoke of the time when He will judge all the nations: "But when the Son of Man comes in His glory, and all the angels with Him, then He will sit on His glorious throne. All the nations will be gathered before Him; and He will separate them from one another, as the shepherd separates the sheep from the goats" (Matt. 25:31–32).

As we have already seen in discussing the Davidic covenant, the "glorious throne" that Jesus will sit upon will be none other than the throne of David in Jerusalem, which God Himself repeatedly promised would one day be occupied by His Messiah, Jesus, the son of David.

THE PRETERIST PROBLEM

The fact that at the end of the age, just before the return of Jesus and the resurrection of the dead, Satan's rage is primarily focused on the State of Israel, the Jewish people, and Jerusalem, is an absolutely insurmountable problem for preterism. Remember, preterists believe that most prophecy has already been fulfilled in the events that unfolded in AD 70. If, however, the dissolution of the nation of Israel, the destruction of the Temple, and the dispersion of many of the Jewish inhabitants of the land were all God's way of very publicly declaring His *permanent* divorce from Israel, then it would make no sense whatsoever to have Satan continuing to direct all of his rage against that specific people and that specific land at the end of the age, two thousand years into the future. Or reworded, preterism's glaring problem is this: If Israel is now just like any other nation, and if the Jews are no different from any other people, then something must be wrong, *for Satan clearly hasn't received the memo.* If the Lord has rejected and divorced Israel from her corporate calling and as His special people, then there would be no reason for Satan to place such a great emphasis on and expend so much energy at the end of the age to assault Jerusalem and the Jewish people. This simply wouldn't make any sense.

Preterism has three profound witnesses against its case. First, Satan's rage has been vented against the Jewish people throughout the past *two thousand years.* In fact, it is entirely fair to say that no other people have been persecuted by such a wide variety of peoples, in such a wide range of locations, over such a long span of time, so consistently, so persistently, and so vehemently. Second, Satan continues to rage against Israel in our day, through the rising tide of anti-Semitism spreading throughout the earth. The examples are too numerous to list. At the time of this writing, in the very heartland of America, in Overland Park, Kansas, a man killed three people at a Jewish community center and shouted, "Heil Hitler" as he was being arrested. In France, hundreds marched and shouted slogans demanding that all Jews leave the country. In Paris, a Swiss imam stood at a mainstream Islamic conference and declared, "All the evil in the world originates from the Jews."[4] Tomorrow, no doubt, new stories will replace these. And third—and most important—the Scriptures thoroughly testify that as this present age reaches its climax, Satan's rage will be specifically focused on the land and the people of Israel. There is a principle at work here that supersessionists and preterists seem determined to ignore, but which they must be honest about. When I interviewed Rabbi Jonathan Cahn for my documentary, *End Times Eyewitness*, he explained it this way: "The enemy has been trying to wipe out the Jewish people with all hell for two thousand years, I mean crazily, supernaturally. Hitler—a position that makes no sense, except supernaturally. But this only proves God, because if the enemy is trying to wipe out this particular people, if he is trying to fight over this particular land, what it tells you is that God has something for this particular people and God has something for this particular land, and it is marking the spot, and saying, 'Here, Hey, guys, it's going to happen here.' So by default Satan ends up bearing witness to God and the purposes of God."

If only the larger Church, and specifically supersessionists and preterists, could talk with such common sense. In Satan's fury against Israel and the Jewish people, we should all see evidence of the Lord's deep and abiding love and calling upon them. And of course, we also see that replacement theology and preterism are simply untenable and should cast these methods of interpretation into the trash heap of erroneous theological ideas.

Because preterism seeks to shift the overwhelming emphasis of biblical prophecy to the events that surrounded AD 70, it takes many passages that speak of the vindication of Israel and the fulfillment of the Abrahamic, Davidic, and new covenants and applies them to one of the greatest catastrophes that Israel has ever experienced. Here is the profound difference between restorationism and replacement theology.

Restorationism-futurism is thoroughly *parousia-centric*—its overwhelming emphasis is the return of Jesus and the events that immediately surround His return. It is chiefly concerned with the Lord's deliverance of Israel out of her darkest hour, the judgment of her enemies, and her subsequent restoration. Preterism, on the other hand, is thoroughly centered on God's alleged divorce from Israel, the destruction of the land, and the accompanying loss of approximately 1.5 million Jews. Its chief concern is the vindication and triumph of Israel's enemies. It is for this reason that I say that preterism as a system of interpretation is not only irreconcilable with the Scriptures but also thoroughly anti-Semitic. It must be rejected by all Christians with good consciences and a healthy sense of discernment.

CONCLUSION

The Scriptures thoroughly testify that the geographic heart of Satan's rage and resistance against the unfolding plans and purposes of God will be the land of Israel, and specifically, Jerusalem. The fact that it all happens there is proof that the Lord is not done with His people Israel and is still faithful to His covenant promises. The very simple reason that all the nations of the earth will gather against Jerusalem is because Satan is committed to resisting God's plans to reestablish a glorified Jewish kingdom through which He will vindicate and glorify His own name and bless the whole earth. Satan wishes to annihilate the very people through whom God will vindicate Himself among the nations. Satan knows that the grand crescendo, the icing on the cake, the cherry on top of the Lord's magnificent plan of redemption is the salvation of the Jewish people. Therefore he is going to vent His full wrath against the very people the Lord has chosen and the city He will establish as the global capital of His coming kingdom.

This final period of time wherein Satan will make a final effort to thwart the glorious plan of God is known by most Christians as "the great tribulation." Elsewhere this short period is referred to as "the time of Jacob's trouble." It will be the final and greatest hour of testing for all mankind. We will devote the next chapter to this subject, and in the final chapter, we will discuss what our response as followers of Jesus must be.

16

JACOB'S TROUBLE

n the previous chapter, we reviewed the testimony of four of
the Old Testament prophets, all of whom spoke of Israel and
Jerusalem as the primary focus of satanic resistance against God's
plans during the final period immediately before the return of
Jesus. In this chapter, we will examine Jesus's sermon known as
the "Olivet Discourse," to gain a solid understanding of what Jesus
taught concerning the immensely difficult subject of "Jacob's distress"
or "Jacob's trouble" (KJV). As we will see, Jesus has shown us that a
tragedy of earthshaking significance is yet to happen in our future.

To understand exactly what Jacob's distress or trouble is, we
must first turn to Jeremiah 30, for it is in this passage that the term
"Jacob's distress" is first found. The prophecy begins with the word
coming to Jeremiah, informing him that in time, God would reestablish the Jewish people in their homeland: "'For behold, days are
coming,' declares the LORD, 'when I will restore the fortunes of My
people Israel and Judah . . . I will also bring them back to the land
that I gave to their forefathers and they shall possess it'" (vv. 1–3).

Immediately, however, the prophecy takes an immensely painful
turn. Something takes place in Israel so terrible that men are seen
gripping their stomachs as if in labor: "For thus says the LORD, 'I
have heard a sound of terror, of dread, and there is no peace. Ask
now, and see if a male can give birth. Why do I see every man with
his hands on his loins, as a woman in childbirth? And why have all

faces turned pale?" (vv. 5–6). Then comes the critical phrase: we are told that unparalleled days of trouble are in store for Israel: "*Alas! for that day is great, there is none like it; and it is the time of Jacob's distress*" (v. 7a). Yet, despite the unrivaled nature of this time of distress for the Jewish people, Israel is assured that they "will be saved from it" (v. 7b). The Lord will destroy all of the nations that bring oppression to Israel in that day: "I will break his yoke from off their neck and will tear off their bonds; and strangers will no longer make them their slaves" (v. 8). Verse 9 makes it clear that He is speaking of the time of Jesus's return, when He restores the Jewish kingdom: "But they shall serve the LORD their God and David their king, whom I will raise up for them."

"A TIME OF DISTRESS SUCH AS NEVER OCCURRED . . ."

With Jeremiah's prophecy as the backdrop, in Daniel 12:1 we find the angelic messenger informing Daniel concerning precisely the same time. According to the messenger, at that time the angel Michael, "who stands guard over" the Jewish people, "will arise" and just as we see in Jeremiah, there will be "a time of distress such as never occurred since there was a nation until that time." But then, again as in Jeremiah, the angel goes on to say that the righteous of Israel will be saved out of this time of tribulation: "Everyone who is found written in the book, will be rescued. Many of those who sleep in the dust of the ground will awake, these to everlasting life, but the others to disgrace and everlasting contempt." Because this time of unparalleled tribulation is so closely related to the resurrection of the dead, it again becomes obvious that this great "distress" will take place immediately before the return of Jesus.

JESUS'S OLIVET DISCOURSE

Having established the Old Testament backdrop concerning "Jacob's distress," we now turn to the words of Jesus. Shortly before His arrest and crucifixion, while sitting on the Mount of Olives with

His disciples, Jesus delivered His longest and most detailed sermon on the subject of the end times. The sermon is repeated in the three synoptic Gospels, in Matthew 24–25, Mark 13, and Luke 21. Needless to say, these passages are the subject of a tremendous amount of debate among scholars. Many seek to take large segments, or even all of the sermon, and apply it the events of AD 70. As we will see, however, a careful reading of the text, with a proper understanding of Jesus's various allusions to the prophets throughout His sermon, proves that He was not at all speaking of the events of AD 70. Rather, he was speaking entirely of the last days. There are several phrases interspersed throughout Jesus's sermon that prove this beyond any doubt. There is the reference is to "the beginning of birth pains," to the "abomination that causes desolation," to "Jacob's distress," and Jesus's statement: "And then the sign of the Son of Man will appear in the sky, and then all the tribes of the earth will mourn, and they will see the Son of Man coming on the clouds of the sky with power and great glory." Needless to say, it doesn't get much more clear than this. But let us unpack the first three phrases, starting with the reference to "the beginning of birth pains" (Matt. 24:8).

THE BEGINNING OF BIRTH PAINS

It's difficult to convey the magnitude of what Jesus was saying to His disciples when He stated that the Temple was going to be destroyed. For an American, this would be like touring the White House and the various national monuments in Washington, D.C., and then having the tour guide turn and say, "Assuredly I tell you, all of these things will be completely destroyed; they will become absolute rubble." This would be a complete shock for any American. For any Jew, the Temple was the center, the very heart, of Israel. Thus, after Jesus made the truly shocking statement to the disciples that the Temple would be destroyed, it was no doubt with a slightly panicked tone of urgency that they asked Him, "When will these things happen, and what will be the sign of your coming, and of the end of the age?" (Matt. 24:3).

So, Jesus sat down and began to lead them through the various signs of the end of the age and of His return.

He began with a litany of somewhat general events: "Many will come in My name, saying, 'I am the Christ,' and will mislead many. You will be hearing of wars and rumors of wars. See that you are not frightened, for those things must take place, but that is not yet the end. For nation will rise against nation, and kingdom against kingdom, and in various places there will be famines and earthquakes" (vv. 5–7). Then Jesus finished His statement by saying, "But all these things are merely the beginning of birth pangs" (v. 8).

As we saw in the last chapter, the reference to birth pains is clearly an allusion to Isaiah 26, and the disciples would have immediately recognized it as such. In that section of Isaiah's prophecy, Israel laments the fact that despite their great suffering as a nation, suffering so severe that it is likened to the pains of childbirth, they had *not* given birth, as it were, to the redemption of the world: "We were pregnant, we writhed in labor, we gave birth, as it seems, only to wind. We could not accomplish deliverance for the earth, nor were inhabitants of the world born" (v. 18). But the Lord assured Israel that the day will come when their great suffering will in fact bring about the resurrection of the dead: "Your dead will live," He told them. "Their corpses will rise. You who lie in the dust, awake and shout for joy, for your dew is as the dew of the dawn, and the earth will give birth to the departed spirits" (v. 19). Because the birth analogy is used to point to the resurrection, when bodies will rise from out of the earth, it is clear that Isaiah was speaking about the end of this present age. This also makes it crystal clear that when Jesus said that "all these things are merely *the beginning* of birth pangs" (v. 8; emphasis added), He was specifying that the events He had just spoken of would occur shortly before but not quite at the time of the end. The term "the beginning of birth pains," in modern scientific terms, is what we refer to as *Braxton Hicks contractions*. These may occur weeks before the actual birth. Braxton Hicks contractions, however, are not the actual, full-fledged contractions that occur in the final hours of labor. Jesus was using very natural analogies from human experience to describe the events that were leading up to His return and the resurrection of the dead.

After describing those preliminary, Braxton Hicks–type events, Jesus then shifted and began to speak of the actual contractions, the final events that would lead to His return. The turning point from the preliminary contractions to the final birth pangs begins with what Jesus referred to simply as "tribulation":

> "Then they will deliver you to tribulation, and will kill you, and you will be hated by all nations because of My name. At that time many will fall away and will betray one another and hate one another. Many false prophets will arise and will mislead many. Because lawlessness is increased, most people's love will grow cold. But the one who endures to the end, he will be saved. This gospel of the kingdom shall be preached in the whole world as a testimony to all the nations, and then the end will come." (Matt. 24:9–14)

THE ABOMINATION THAT CAUSES DESOLATION

Next Jesus makes a very clear reference to Old Testament prophecy, specifically, "the abomination that causes desolations as described by the prophet Daniel" (Matt. 24:15; cf. Dan. 9:27; 11:31; 12:11), and places it in the future. Ironically, many Christian commentators attempt to apply Jesus's words to Emperor Titus and the events of AD 70. But this is impossible. A careful consideration of the angelic interpretation found in Daniel chapter 12 makes it abundantly clear that the abomination of desolation and the ceasing of offerings will take place in the context of the final three-and-a-half years before Christ's return, when the Jewish people will go through a time of unparalleled suffering that will be followed by the resurrection of the dead. Beyond that, it is also specifically referred to five times as the *end times* (Dan. 8:17, 19, 26; 12:9, 13). Once it has been established that the "abomination of desolation" to which

Jesus referred takes place not in AD 70 but in the future, during the last days, then we understand that the remainder of the Olivet Discourse also concerns the last days. The disturbing implications, however, become clear when we see that along with the desolating abomination in the Jewish Temple comes the need for all in Judea to straightaway run for their lives:

> "Therefore when you see the abomination that causes desolation which was spoken of through Daniel the prophet, standing in the holy place (let the reader understand), then those who are in Judea must flee to the mountains. Whoever is on the housetop must not go down to get the things out that are in his house. Whoever is in the field must not turn back to get his cloak. But woe to those who are pregnant and to those who are nursing babies in those days! But pray that your flight will not be in the winter, or on a Sabbath." (Matt. 24:15–20)

JACOB'S TROUBLE: THE GREAT TRIBULATION

If Jesus's reference to the abomination that causes desolation was not sufficient to establish the thorough end-times context of His sermon, then the next phrase He used put the matter completely to rest. Once more, Jesus reached back into the book of Daniel and, drawing out the angel's words, He expanded upon them: *"For then there will be a great tribulation, such as has not occurred since the beginning of the world until now, nor ever will.* Unless those days had been cut short, no life would have been saved; but for the sake of the elect those days will be cut short" (Matt. 24:21–22; emphasis added; cf. Dan. 12:1).

This is truly fascinating. First, we had Jeremiah the prophet describing a time of unparalleled distress for Israel (for which *Jacob* is simply a synonym). Then the angel expanded on Jeremiah's words, again reiterating the historically unparalleled nature of the coming distress. And finally, Jesus paraphrased the angel's words and then expanded even further, again emphasizing that this "tribulation" would be not only historically unparalleled, but unparalleled even into the future. This would be the worst tribulation that the world has known or will ever know. Consider the progression:

1. Jeremiah: "Alas! For that day is great, there is none like it; and it is the time of Jacob's distress." (Jer. 30:7)

2. Angel: "And there will be a time of distress [for "your people"] such as never occurred since there was a nation until that time." (Dan. 12:1)

3. Jesus: "For then there will be a great tribulation, such as has not occurred since the beginning of the world until now, nor ever will." (Matt. 24:21)

The point that must be noted is that the "Great Tribulation," as it is most often known within Christian circles, actually finds its original context in texts that are all very much Israel centered. This is not to say that the last three and a half years before Jesus's return will not also be a time of tremendous tribulation for Christians in general throughout the earth, as Jesus also spoke of tribulation for *all* those who carry His name. They would be hated by all nations, He said (Matt. 24:9–10; cf. Rev. 13:15). But the fact remains that many Christians have taken Jesus's very Israel-centered statements about the Great Tribulation and largely ripped them out of their context. The warning to flee to the mountains is specifically for those in Jerusalem and Judah (Luke 21:21) who are running from the invading armies. It is not a directive for anyone and everyone *globally* to run to the nearest mountain range the moment they hear that the abomination of desolation has been erected in the Jewish Temple.

A CONTROVERSY ARISES

As Jesus reached the conclusion of this portion of His sermon on the Mount of Olives, He began to describe the actual time of His return:

"But immediately after the tribulation of those days the sun will be darkened, and the moon will not give its light, and the stars will fall from the sky, and the powers of the heavens will be shaken. And then the sign of the Son of Man will appear in the sky, and then all the tribes of the earth will mourn, and they will see the Son of Man coming on the clouds of the sky with power and great glory. And He will send forth His angels with a great trumpet and they will gather together His elect from the four winds, from one end of the sky to the other." (Matt. 24:29–31)

Having seen the various texts that Jesus was alluding to in His sermon, it should be clear that the primary emphasis of Jesus's sermon was the final period of time immediately before His return and not the events of AD 70. While many expositors agree with that statement, one text that the majority ascribe to AD 70 is a portion of Jesus's Olivet Discourse that is found in the gospel of Luke. Let's examine that passage to understand why it remains so controversial.

LUKE'S VERSION OF THE OLIVET DISCOURSE

Unlike the accounts in Matthew and Mark, in Luke 21 Jesus speaks of Jerusalem being surrounded by the Gentile nations in a military siege: "But when you see Jerusalem surrounded by armies, then recognize that her desolation is near" (v. 20). Though this detail is not mentioned in the accounts in Matthew or Mark, as we saw in the last chapter, this is precisely what the prophets Zechariah, Joel, Ezekiel, and Micah saw during the days just before the return of Jesus. The next statement, however, is exactly what is found in the other gospel accounts. Jesus warned that "those who are in Judea must flee to the mountains, and those who are in the midst of the city must leave, and those who are in the country must not enter the city; *because these are days of vengeance*, so that all things which are written will be fulfilled" (vv. 21–22).

Unlike the other synoptic accounts, here in Luke Jesus also spoke specifically of many of the inhabitants of Israel either falling by the sword in the invasion or being taken as prisoners of war to the surrounding nations: "For there will be great distress upon the land and wrath to this people; and they will fall by the edge of the sword, and will be led captive into all the nations; and Jerusalem will be trampled under foot by the Gentiles until the times of the Gentiles are fulfilled" (vv. 23–24). Here is where the controversy lies. First, no one wants to entertain the idea that this could yet happen again in the future in Israel. This, of course, is entirely understandable. Second, because this passage conjures up such strong imagery that seems to resemble the historical siege of Jerusalem by the Roman legions under Titus in AD 70, many interpreters are determined to argue that Luke is referring to that long past catastrophe. But there are at least four insurmountable problems with this view.

THEY WILL SEE THE SON OF MAN COMING ON THE CLOUDS . . .

The first and most obvious problem with placing this section of Luke in history is the simple fact that in a seamless flow, the passage continues to describe the cosmic signs that are repeatedly used to refer to the imminence of the Day of the Lord (e.g., Isa. 13:10; Joel 2:10, 31; Matt. 24:29; Mark 13:24; Rev. 6:12). For instance, we find a very direct reference immediately following which speaks of the return of Jesus on the clouds of heaven:

> "There will be signs in sun and moon and stars, and on the earth dismay among nations, in perplexity at the roaring of the sea and the waves, men fainting from fear and the expectation of the things which are coming upon the world; for the powers of the heavens will be shaken. Then they will see the Son of Man coming in a cloud with power and great glory. But when these things begin to take place, straighten up and lift up your heads, because your redemption is drawing near." (Luke 21:25–28)

THE DAYS OF VENGEANCE

The second reason to understand Luke's account as pertaining to the last days and not AD 70 is because of the phrase, "these are days of vengeance, so that all things which are written will be fulfilled" (v. 21). This specific phrase, used primarily by the prophet Isaiah, always refers to the ultimate deliverance of Israel from their enemies in the end times. Any Old Testament–literate Jew of Jesus's day would have recognized it. Consider the repeated usage of this phrase throughout Isaiah's prophecy to refer to the end times, the Day of the Lord, the vindication of Israel, and the destruction of her enemies:

> For the LORD has a day of vengeance, a year of recompense for the cause of Zion. (Isa. 34:8)

> Say to those with anxious heart, "Take courage, fear not. Behold, your God will come with vengeance; the recompense of God will come, but He will save you." (Isa. 35:4)

> He put on righteousness like a breastplate, and a helmet of salvation on His head; and He put on garments of vengeance for clothing and wrapped Himself with zeal as a mantle. (Isa. 59:17)

> To proclaim the favorable year of the LORD and the day of vengeance of our God; to comfort all who mourn . . . (Isa. 61:2)

> "I have trodden the wine trough alone, and from the peoples there was no man with Me. I also trod them in My anger and trampled them in My wrath; and their lifeblood is sprinkled on My garments, and I stained all My raiment. For the day of vengeance was in My heart, and My year of redemption has come." (Isa. 63:3–4)

We must recognize that the phrase "the day of vengeance" is not merely a general reference to the end times; rather, it is a very specific phrase speaking of the Lord's retribution against Israel's enemies and the ultimate triumph of Israel. Although the Scriptures are clear that Israel will experience a very great purging immediately before this time, "the day of vengeance" is specifically "for the cause of Zion" (Isa. 34:8). It is always a reference to the Lord coming in revenge *to save Israel from her enemies in her darkest hour and to execute a decisive and final judgment against them.* There is absolutely no way anyone can say that this describes the events of AD 70. That year marked a historical catastrophe of the greatest kind for Israel. But it was not followed by any sort of deliverance. Jerusalem and the Temple were destroyed, much of the nation was devastated, and roughly 1.5 million Jews were killed. In no way was it a time of vengeance against Israel's enemies; there was no vindication or salvation for Israel. It was precisely the opposite. It was *a great triumph for Israel's enemies.* The events of AD 70 simply do not align with the scriptural criteria and cannot be said to be the fulfillment of what Jesus was speaking about. Jesus was most certainly pointing back to Isaiah and was speaking of the last days, which still remain in our future.

SYNOPTIC MISFIRE?

Third, it must be acknowledged that, again, this sermon is the same one recorded in Matthew 24 and Mark 13 and known as the Olivet Discourse. The claim that Jesus was primarily speaking of the distant last days in only two of the synoptic passages and speaking of AD 70 in the third is simply inconsistent. To recognize just how similar this prophecy is to the parallel passages found in Matthew and Mark, consider the following chart:

MATTHEW 24	MARK 13	LUKE 21
"Therefore when you see the abomination of desolation which was spoken of through Daniel the prophet, standing in the holy place (let the reader understand) . . ." "But when you see the abomination of desolation standing where it should not be (let the reader understand) . . ."	"But when you see the abomination of desolation standing where it should not be (let the reader understand) . . ."	"But when you see Jerusalem surrounded by armies, then recognize that her desolation is near."

MATTHEW 24	MARK 13	LUKE 21
"Then those who are in Judea must flee to the mountains."	"Then those who are in Judea must flee to the mountains."	"Then those who are in Judea must flee to the mountains."
"But woe to those who are pregnant and to those who are nursing babies in those days!"	"But woe to those who are pregnant and to those who are nursing babies in those days!"	"Woe to those who are pregnant and to those who are nursing babies in those days."
"For then there will be a great tribulation, such as has not occurred since the beginning of the world until now, nor ever will. Unless those days had been cut short, no life would have been saved; but for the sake of the elect those days will be cut short."	"For those days will be a time of tribulation such as has not occurred since the beginning of the creation which God created until now, and never will. Unless the Lord had shortened those days, no life would have been saved; but for the sake of the elect, whom He chose, He shortened the days."	"For there will be great distress upon the land and wrath to this people; and they will fall by the edge of the sword, and will be led captive into all the nations; and Jerusalem will be trampled under foot by the Gentiles until the times of the Gentiles are fulfilled."

Although Luke exchanged the phrase "when you see the abomination of desolation" for "when you see Jerusalem surrounded by armies," it is clear that Matthew, Mark, and Luke are relaying the same sermon. Although Luke gives us some elements that both Matthew and Mark leave out, this is nonetheless the same sermon, and Jesus is obviously referring to the same end-time events.

HOW THE SIEGE OF AD 70 ACTUALLY HAPPENED

Fourth, a brief review of the manner in which Titus's siege of Jerusalem unfolded will show that Jesus could not have been speaking of these events. The historical record shows that the vast band of Roman legions and auxiliaries led first by Vespasian, the Roman general in charge of the campaign against Jerusalem, and then by his son Titus made its way to Jerusalem quite gradually over a period of years. But Jesus described the assault of Jerusalem as an event that is to unfold rather suddenly, leaving no time even to gather one's basic items.

The advisors to Vespasian had actually directed him to attack the city in AD 66. But because the city was already in the thick of a drastic internal civil war, Vespasian determined to simply let the Jews destroy themselves, as they seemed to be doing a much faster job than he himself could have done. Vespasian also didn't want an invasion to bring unity against a common enemy to the deeply divided city. So for almost three years, Vespasian took various cities in northern Galilee, but he avoided directly laying siege to Jerusalem. During this time, it was quite easily discernible that thick storms clouds of an invasion were gathering on the horizon. In both AD 67 and AD 68, there were two substantial Roman campaigns launched from Caesarea in the north that saw the fall of several cities through the land. In June of AD 68, Emperor Nero died, Vespasian returned to Rome, and his son Titus took over the campaign.

It was not until May of AD 70 that the assault of Jerusalem finally began. Titus established a camp on Mount Scopus, just northeast of the city. Initially, to test the resolve of the Jews, he led a small detachment of a mere six hundred troops to the city. But defenders rushed out of the city walls, divided Titus's troops, and nearly captured Titus himself. After that, Titus, utilizing the full force of all of his legions and auxiliaries, erected three camps around the city and set up a siege line. Jerusalem was surrounded by troops. By that time fleeing the city for the mountains was not an option. In fact, many who did attempt to flee at that point were captured or slaughtered in the process. Surrender or victory were the only options.

My point is this: if Jesus was warning about the siege of AD 70 in the Olivet Discourse, then He actually gave some truly terrible advice. Notice that Jesus did not say that when armies begin marching toward Jerusalem, then it is time to flee. He did not say when the Romans come for the first preliminary assault, then it is time to flee. He did not say that when troops enter into the land of Israel, then it is time to prepare an escape. No, Jesus specifically warned that "when you see Jerusalem surrounded by armies" *that* was the time to flee. He even expressed pity for those "who are pregnant and to those who are nursing babies in those days! For there will be great distress upon the land and wrath to this people" (Luke 21:23). In other words, once one sees the armies, the urgency to flee at that moment would be immense. And so I repeat, if Jesus's warning in Luke 21:20–21 concerned Titus's destruction of Jerusalem, as so many commentators argue, then He gave some truly poor advice. Anyone in Jerusalem who waited until the city was surrounded to attempt to flee would have been taken prisoner or killed.

Some have suggested that Jesus's warning to flee Jerusalem was fulfilled in AD 66 when Cestius Gallus surrounded the city for a brief time before withdrawing. The problem with this claim, however, is that when we consider Jesus's words it is with extreme urgency that He warned those in the city to flee. So urgent was the warning that He commanded those who would heed His words not to turn around to even grab anything. Just flee. Yet it was four full years from Cestius's brief siege before Jerusalem actually fell. This can hardly be said to be the fulfillment of Jesus's warning. Jesus's warning speaks of minutes to flee, not months or years.

Others point out that many of the Christians in the city, upon seeing Cestius's troops, chose to flee to the city of Pella that year. According to the *Zondervan Pictorial Encyclopedia of the Bible* "The city earned its name in church history in AD 66 when Pella became a refuge for Christians who were fleeing Jerusalem because the Roman army was coming to quiet a Jewish revolution."[1] There are two problems with claiming that these events fulfilled Jesus's prophecy. First, as was just mentioned, this was four years before the actual fall of Jerusalem and thus it cannot at all be made to correlate to the urgent nature of Jesus's warnings.

Second, according to the historical record, the Christians did not flee due to seeing the Roman armies but because of some kind of divine revelation. According to Eusebius, the Christians had actually fled prior to the war even began:

> The whole body, however, of the church of Jerusalem, having been commanded by a divine revelation, given to men of approved piety there before the war, removed from the city, and dwelt at a certain town beyond the Jordan, called Pella. Here those that believed in Christ, having removed from Jerusalem, as if holy men had entirely abandoned the royal city itself, and the whole land of Judea; the divine justice, for their crimes against Christ and His apostles finally overtook them, totally destroying the whole generation of these evildoers from the earth.[2]

In the end, there is nothing about the events of the fall of Jerusalem that we can rightly point to, claiming that "this is that" which Jesus warned of. The historical events simply do not conform to the nature of His warnings.

If, on the other hand, Jesus's warning pertained to the last-days assault against Jerusalem by the Antichrist, then it is far more realistic to imagine a surge of troops being mobilized rather suddenly around Jerusalem. A few possible scenarios could explain this.

Perhaps it will happen during a time when the city will be divided (see Joel 3:2) and shared by the Israelis and Palestinians and perhaps even policed by some form of international "peacekeeping" forces. In such a case, it would be quite possible for a sudden surge of troops to gather against Jerusalem in a rather abrupt and unexpected manner exactly as Jesus described. While it is difficult to know precisely how the events will unfold, it seems that there will come a moment at the center of the final seven years before Jesus returns when the Antichrist will remove his mask of tolerance and, using his troops, many of whom will have already been in the land to carry this out, will demand full control of the city of Jerusalem, including the Temple. This is the aforementioned abomination that causes desolation wherein the Antichrist will sit in and desolate the Temple of God (see 2 Thess. 2:4). And of course, all of this will be accompanied by terror for Israel's inhabitants, many of whom "will fall by the edge of the sword, and will be led captive into all the nations," (Luke 21:24) a time of tribulation so severe that Jesus described as unparalleled throughout all of world history—and beyond.

UNPARALLELED TRIBULATION AND THE HOLOCAUST

When considering the information we have just reviewed, we are immediately confronted with the glaring and truly terrifying reality that if Jeremiah, an angelic messenger (possibly Gabriel), and Jesus Himself all spoke of a time of unparalleled tribulation just before the return of Jesus, this would indicate that what is to come in Israel could be even worse than the Holocaust. While this certainly seems to be the case, I would suggest that we should not try to quantify the suffering to come or calculate the lives that will be lost. I see little fruit in engaging in such endeavors. If I am to be honest, I myself am simply not capable of truly exploring an event of such magnitude and horror. It is a pit too deep and terrifying. I cannot bring myself to peer over the edge. The point is that something terrible is coming and we need to get ready.

I'd also like to issue a warning specifically to those who are generally very interested in the subject of Bible prophecy. Sometimes apocalyptic matters are looked at in a factual, yet deeply detached and emotionless manner. While it is impossible to feel the full weight of these things as we discuss them, it is essential that we tread oh so carefully, never failing to recognize that we are not speaking of chess pieces or dots on a prophetic map. We are speaking of real families, real people, real lives. If discussing these things does not fill our hearts with sorrow and drive us to our knees in prayer, then it is clear that we are not seeing them through the eyes of the Father or His Son, Jesus.

I'll end this chapter simply by saying that those of us who desire to follow Jesus, in acknowledging the magnitude of what is coming, must begin preparing our hearts to truly and fully embrace the cross. Only hours before Jesus chose to endure the torture of His body and soul, He made a very deliberate point to communicate one of the clearest and most solemn warnings in all of Scripture. How we as the body of Messiah, both individually and corporately, respond to this information could very well be the single greatest test we will ever face. This is not an overstatement. In the next chapter, we will begin to discuss what a proper response might look like for the Church that seeks to live according to the words of Jesus in the last days.

17

DIETRICH BONHOEFFER, CORRIE TEN BOOM, AND THE JUDGMENT OF THE NATIONS

I n the previous chapter, we examined portions of Jesus's Olivet Discourse, His longest and final sermon on the end times. We didn't actually finish examining the whole sermon, however. While Matthew 24 details the events that led up to Jesus's return, the sermon actually continues in chapter 25. At the conclusion of His sermon, Jesus went on to describe what will happen after His return, when He will gather the nations for judgment. This passage is one of the most important, yet widely misunderstood passages in all of the Gospels. Let's begin by carefully reading Jesus's words:

"But when the Son of Man comes in His glory, and all the angels with Him, then He will sit on His glorious throne. All the nations will be gathered before Him; and He will separate them from one another, as the shepherd separates the sheep from the goats; and He will put the sheep on His right, and the goats on the left. Then the King will say to those on His right, 'Come, you who are blessed of My Father, inherit the kingdom prepared for you from the foundation of the world. 'For I was hungry, and you gave Me something to eat; I was thirsty, and you gave Me something to drink; I was a stranger, and you invited Me in; naked, and you clothed Me; I was sick, and you visited Me; I was in prison, and you came to Me.' Then the righteous will answer Him, 'Lord, when did we see You hungry, and feed You, or thirsty, and give You something to drink? And when did we see You a stranger, and invite You in, or naked, and clothe You? When did we see

You sick, or in prison, and come to You?' The King will answer and say to them, 'Truly I say to you, to the extent that you did it to one of these brothers of Mine, even the least of them, you did it to Me.' Then He will also say to those on His left, 'Depart from Me, accursed ones, into the eternal fire which has been prepared for the devil and his angels; for I was hungry, and you gave Me nothing to eat; I was thirsty, and you gave Me nothing to drink; I was a stranger, and you did not invite Me in; naked, and you did not clothe Me; sick, and in prison, and you did not visit Me.' Then they themselves also will answer, 'Lord, when did we see You hungry, or thirsty, or a stranger, or naked, or sick, or in prison, and did not take care of You?' Then He will answer them, 'Truly I say to you, to the extent that you did not do it to one of the least of these, you did not do it to Me.' These will go away into eternal punishment, but the righteous into eternal life." (Matt. 25:31–46).

WHO ARE JESUS'S BRETHREN?

The most critical and yet most commonly misinterpreted portion of the prophecy is the phrase "My brothers"—or, "my brethren" in the King James Version—used twice by Jesus, in verses 40 and 45. According to Jesus, the destiny of nations in the Day of Judgment, whether they are cast away or welcomed into the kingdom of God, is largely contingent upon their treatment of His brethren. Jesus even went so far as to say that how the nations treated His brethren *is how they treated Him.* He deeply identifies with this people group, taking their mistreatment as His mistreatment. Surely determining the identity of who Jesus was referring to is absolutely crucial.

Interpreters have suggested three different ways to understand this term. Some have argued that Jesus was speaking of the Jewish people, His actual blood "brethren." Others argue that Jesus was speaking about His disciples or anyone who willingly follows Jesus. Still others say that Jesus was simply referring to the poor, the suffering, and the oppressed in general. Now, while Christian care for the poor and the oppressed is certainly a central feature of the

Christian faith, it is not what this passage is speaking about. Samuel Clough, a Bible teacher who has written and taught extensively on this text, observed, "These brethren are not Jesus's brethren because they are suffering; instead they are suffering because they are Jesus's brethren."[1] When we see Matthew 25 in its actual full context, it becomes clear that when Jesus spoke of His "brethren," He was referring to the inhabitants of Jerusalem and Judea who will suffer during the time of "Jacob's distress," which He had just described in chapter 24. Consider the following larger context of Jesus's sermon:

> **MATTHEW 23:** Overwhelmed with emotion, tears, weeping, and mourning, Jesus cried out, "O Jerusalem, Jerusalem!" (v. 37 NKJV)

> **MATTHEW 24:** Jesus warned of a tremendous time of unparalleled distress and loss of life in Jerusalem and Judea in the last days.

> **MATTHEW 25:** Jesus taught that the nations will actually be judged based on how they treated His brethren in the time of their great distress.

There is a very clear and logical flow that we miss if we do not acknowledge the fuller context of Jesus's words.

THE VALLEY OF JEHOSHAPHAT

The debate concerning exactly who Jesus was speaking about is completely put to rest once we understand that Jesus was simply expanding on the prophecy of Joel 3. Let us carefully consider Joel's prophecy:

> "For behold, in those days and at that time, when I restore the fortunes of Judah and Jerusalem, I will gather all the nations and bring them down to the valley of Jehoshaphat. *Then I will enter into judgment with them there on behalf of My people and My inheritance, Israel,* whom they have scattered among the

nations; and they have divided up My land. They have also cast lots for My people . . . Let the nations be aroused and come up to the valley of Jehoshaphat, for there I will sit to judge all the surrounding nations." (vv. 1–3, 12; emphasis added)

The Valley of Jehoshaphat stretches from the north to the south between the Temple Mount and the Mount of Olives. It is precisely the valley that Jesus was overlooking as He delivered the Olivet Discourse. Understand that while Joel's prophecy speaks of YHVH God as the judge, Jesus spoke of Himself as the judge, thus directly declaring Himself to be YHVH God. Certainly the disciples would have recognized this tremendously dramatic point that Jesus was making, particularly since Jesus was sitting in the exact location where Joel says the judgment of the nations will take place. Thus, as Jesus sat on the Mount of Olives, looking down at the Valley of Jehoshaphat, when He said that He would gather the goats to His left, he was referring to the valley of *Gehenna*, which is the same term, in the Greek, that Jesus had consistently used elsewhere to refer to the place of eternal punishment (Matt. 5:22, 29, 30; 10:28; 23:15, 33; Mark 9:43, 45, 47; Luke 12:5; James 3:6). What's more, both Jesus and Joel made it clear that the nations will be judged because of their mistreatment of the Jewish people, whom the Lord calls "My people and My Inheritance" (Joel 3:2). So when Jesus used the phrase "my brethren," He was clearly pointing directly back to this reference.

THE LORD JUDGES ON BEHALF OF ISRAEL

We must also recognize that when Jesus taught that the nations would be judged based on their mistreatment of Israel, in no way was He making a new point. The wrath of God executed against Israel's enemies at the Day of Judgment is a theme that is repeated many times throughout the Prophets. Let's consider just a couple of the most obvious examples.

In Isaiah 34, the prophet speaks of the Day of the Lord as the day when the Lord's wrath and vengeance will be expressed toward the enemies of Israel: "For the LORD's indignation is against all the nations, and His wrath against all their armies; He has utterly destroyed them, He has given them over to slaughter . . . For the LORD has a day of vengeance, a year of recompense for the cause of Zion" (vv. 2, 8). Other translations use the phrase "the controversy of Zion." Surely today, throughout the earth, there is a controversy over Zion. Even within the Church, there is deep division between the Zionists (those who support Israel) and the anti-Zionists. According to Isaiah, after Jesus returns, on the Day of Judgment, Jesus will settle this controversy once and for all, and He will clearly judge on behalf of Israel concerning "the cause of Zion."

Later, in Isaiah 63, Jesus is portrayed as marching triumphantly out of Edom, the desert south of Israel, heading toward Jerusalem. His robes are described as being soaked with the blood of His enemies, whom He has trodden underfoot as grapes. This is one of the most dramatic and graphic passages describing Jesus after He has returned in all of Scripture:

> Who is this who comes from Edom, with garments of glowing colors from Bozrah, This One who is majestic in His apparel, marching in the greatness of His strength? "It is I who speak in righteousness, mighty to save." Why is Your apparel red, and Your garments like the one who treads in the wine press? "I have trodden the wine trough alone, and from the peoples there was no man with Me. I also trod them in My anger and trampled them in My wrath; and their lifeblood is sprinkled on My garments, and I stained all My raiment. For the day of vengeance was in My heart, and My year of redemption has come . . . I trod down the peoples in My anger and made them drunk in My wrath, and I poured out their lifeblood on the earth." (Isa. 63:1–4, 6)

Needless to say, this is certainly a far cry from the stereotypical painting of the gentle shepherd cradling a baby lamb over His shoulders. This is the Jesus of judgment and vengeance. We must understand, though, that the reason for His wrath is because of the Lord's great love for His people Israel:

I shall make mention of the lovingkindnesses of the LORD, the praises of the LORD, according to all that the LORD has granted us, and the great goodness toward the house of Israel, which He has granted them according to His compassion and according to the abundance of His lovingkindnesses. For He said, "Surely, they are My people, sons who will not deal falsely." So He became their Savior. In all their affliction He was afflicted, and the angel of His presence saved them; in His love and in His mercy He redeemed them, and He lifted them and carried them all the days of old (Isa. 63:7–9).

Another of the most prominent passages that describes the vengeance of God against the nations specifically because of how they treated Israel is the full chapter of Ezekiel 35. In fact, Jesus also alluded to this text in His Olivet Discourse. In this chapter, the Lord spoke through Ezekiel once more against Edom, which is also referred to as Mount Seir (the most prominent mountain in Edom). Because Edom is possessed with "everlasting enmity" or "perpetual hatred" (KJV) for Israel and will rejoice when Israel experiences the discipline of the Lord in the last days, He promises to judge Edom and make her perpetually desolate.

"Behold, I am against you, Mount Seir, and I will stretch out My hand against you and make you a desolation and a waste. I will lay waste your cities and you will become a desolation. Then you will know that I am the LORD. *Because you have had everlasting enmity and have delivered the sons of Israel to the power of the sword at the time of their calamity, at the time of the punishment of the end,* therefore as I live," declares the Lord GOD, "I will give you over to bloodshed, and bloodshed will pursue you; since you have not hated bloodshed, therefore bloodshed will pursue you. I will make Mount Seir a waste and a desolation . . . I will fill its mountains with its slain; on your hills and in your valleys and in all your ravines those slain by the sword will fall. I will make you an everlasting desolation and your cities will not be inhabited. Then you will know that I am the LORD." (Ezek. 35:3–9; emphasis added)

What makes this passage different from those in Isaiah is that this one specifically speaks of Edom mistreating Israel in the time of her punishment and distress in the last days. Thus, this passage features references to both Israel's end-time chastisement (which Jesus had just described in Matthew 24) and warnings concerning the judgment of the nations for how they treat Israel during this time (which Jesus then described in Matthew 25). It is also fascinating to recognize that the previous chapter, Ezekiel 34, is a prophecy that portrays the people of Israel as the Lord's sheep and the coming Messiah as the faithful shepherd: "Then I will set over them one shepherd, My servant David, and he will feed them; he will feed them himself and be their shepherd" (v. 23). No doubt, the imagery of Jesus acting as a just shepherd dividing the righteous sheep from the unrighteous goats was an allusion back to Ezekiel 34. So Jesus was harking back to both Joel 3 and Ezekiel 34–35 and working them both into His sermon.

There are several other passages throughout the Scriptures that also speak of the Lord returning to execute vengeance against the enemies of His people Israel (see Numbers 24:14–20; Psalms 102:13–20; Isaiah 25:8–11; Ezekiel 25:12–17; 30:1–5; 36:2–7; Obadiah 1:8–20; Micah 4:10–12; Zephaniah 2:2–11; Zechariah 1:14–17; 14:2–14). Though this is a well-established and foundational truth taught throughout the Old Testament and clearly reiterated and placed front and center by Jesus, it is a concept that is almost completely absent throughout the majority of the Church today. No doubt, the reality of this coming day must be recognized by discerning believers.

TWO SHINING EXAMPLES FOR OUR DAY

As we consider the truly profound implications of the fact that a time of unparalleled trouble is still ahead for Israel, there are two Christians whose testimonies have been well preserved for us that I believe this generation needs to look to as shining examples. Most

Christians have at least heard of Dietrich Bonhoeffer and Corrie Ten Boom. While there are quite a few books out there that tell about their lives as faithful and brave witnesses for Jesus during World War II under Nazi oppression, if you have not read anything about either of them, then I highly encourage you at the least to get the following two books: *Bonhoeffer: Pastor, Martyr, Prophet, Spy* by Eric Metaxas and *The Hiding Place* by Corrie Ten Boom. Although there were no doubt numerous other faithful witnesses during World War II who died without their stories ever being told, the stories of Dietrich Bonhoeffer and Corrie Ten Boom have been preserved for us, I believe, for a reason. Their stories contain profound lessons for us today, and particularly for those who live to see the events we discussed in the previous two chapters. Let us begin with Dietrich Bonhoeffer.

DIETRICH BONHOEFFER

Dietrich Bonhoeffer was many things: a German poet, a musician, an author, a pastor, a theologian, a philosopher, an anti-Nazi dissident, and finally, a martyr who died in 1945. Apart from his theological writings, Bonhoeffer also became best known for his outspoken opposition to the German church's compromise with Nazism and the persecution of the Jews.

In 1933, even in the early days of the Nazi takeover of Germany, Bonhoeffer was already outspoken in his resistance. Two days after Hitler was installed as chancellor, Bonhoeffer delivered a radio address in which he attacked Hitler and warned Germans against slipping into idolizing the Führer (leader), who he said could very well turn out to be *Verführer* (mis-leader or seducer). He was cut off the air in mid-sentence. He also began publicly raising his voice for active Christian resistance to Hitler's persecution of Jews, declaring that the Church must not simply "bandage the victims under the wheel, but jam the spoke in the wheel itself."[2]

In that same year, the German Lutheran Church held an election, wherein an overwhelming majority of key positions went to

Nazi-supporters within the church known as the German Christian (*Deutsche Christen*) movement. Shortly thereafter, Bonhoeffer was deputized by opposition leaders in the church to draft what was called "the Bethel Confession," a statement of faith that both opposed the German Christian movement and affirmed the ongoing calling and election of the Jewish people. Although the document did partially affirm a supersessionist perspective, stating, "The place of the Old Testament people of the Covenant has not been taken by another nation, but rather by the Christian church, called out of, and within, all nations," it also made a very strong and rare concession concerning the Jews as the chosen people whose fulfillment is yet future:

> God has given proof of overflowing faithfulness in remaining faithful to Israel, according to the flesh from which Christ was born in the flesh, despite all Israel's unfaithfulness and even after the crucifixion. God still wants to complete with the Jews the plan for redeeming the world that began with the calling of Israel (Romans 9–11). This is why God has preserved, according to the flesh, a sacred remnant of Israel . . . This sacred remnant has the character *indelebilis* of the chosen people.[3]

Revisions of the Confession were later so watered down that Bonhoeffer himself refused to sign it.

As a response to the virtual takeover of the Church by Nazi-sympathizers, Bonhoeffer and his friend and colleague Martin Niemöller soon formed the *Pfarrernotbund,* a Christian movement that would evolve into what became known as "the Confessing Church." The Confessing Church was a breakaway, schismatic church movement that stood opposed to the nazification of the larger German Protestant church. The Confessing Church adopted the Barmen Declaration, a document that insisted that Christ, not the Führer, was the head of the German church, and that the German Christians had corrupted church government by making it subservient to the state and had compromised the Gospel by aligning with Nazism.

In 1935, Bonhoeffer began and led an underground seminary for training Confessing Church pastors. Two years later, in July 1937, as the Nazi suppression of the Confessing Church intensified, Niemöller, Bonhoeffer's close associate and friend, was arrested. In 1937, the Gestapo closed the seminary and arrested twenty-seven pastors and former students. It was around this time that Bonhoeffer published his best-known book, *The Cost of Discipleship: A Study on the Sermon on the Mount*, in which he not only attacked "cheap grace" as a cover for ethical laxity but also preached "costly grace."

Bonhoeffer spent the next two years secretly traveling from one village to another to train pastors in what was called "seminary on the run." Most of Bonhoeffer's students were illegally ministering in small parishes.

In April 1943, after ten years of active ministry and resistance to the Nazis, Bonhoeffer was arrested. For a year and a half, he was held at Tegel military prison, awaiting trial. In February 1945, he was secretly moved to Buchenwald concentration camp, and finally to Flossenbürg concentration camp. Bonhoeffer was executed by hanging at dawn on April 9, 1945. He died just two weeks before American soldiers liberated the camp, three weeks before Hitler's suicide as the Soviets captured Berlin, and a month before the final capitulation of Nazi Germany. According to the account of a doctor who witnessed Bonhoeffer's execution:

> I saw Pastor Bonhoeffer . . . kneeling on the floor praying fervently to God. I was most deeply moved by the way this lovable man prayed, so devout and so certain that God heard his prayer. At the place of execution, he again said a short prayer and then climbed the few steps to the gallows, brave and composed. His death ensued after a few seconds. In the almost fifty years that I worked as a doctor, I have hardly ever seen a man die so entirely submissive to the will of God.[4]

CORRIE TEN BOOM

Nearby, in the Nazi-occupied Netherlands, another witness for Christ, Corrie Ten Boom, and her family were working to help Jews escape the Nazi Holocaust during World War II. In 1940, the Nazis invaded the Netherlands and soon began arresting Jews and sending many to concentration camps. The Ten Boom home had always been an open house for anyone in need. So in May 1942, when a Jewish woman whose husband had been arrested and whose son went into hiding, came to the Ten Booms's home in fear, looking for a place to stay, Corrie's father, Casper, immediately agreed. Casper was an ardent student of the Old Testament prophets who thoroughly rejected all forms of supersessionism. "In this household," Casper declared, "God's people are always welcome."

As the grip of the Nazi occupation tightened, the Ten Boom home soon became a refuge for both Jews and Dutch underground resistors. During 1943 and into 1944, there were usually six to seven people living illegally in their home. Additional refugees would stay with the Ten Booms sometimes for a few hours or days until another safe house could be located. Corrie and her sister, Betsie, became active leaders in the underground resistance in Haarlem, locating other courageous Dutch families willing to take in refugees. Corrie and Betsie spent much time during these years attending to the needs of the refugees once they went into hiding. To accommodate their Jewish guests, the Ten Booms provided kosher food and honored the Jewish Sabbath. They had built a secret room, only thirty inches deep but a few feet wide, where several people could stand quietly if there was an inspection or raid of the house. They called this small space "the hiding place."

In February 1944, a Dutch informant told the Nazis about the Ten Booms's work. The entire Ten Boom family was arrested. When the Nazis raided the Ten Boom home, there were six people in the hiding place. They remained there for nearly two days. When asked if he knew he could die for helping Jews, Casper replied, "It would be an honor to give my life for God's ancient people." Casper, who was eighty-four at the time of his arrest, died after only ten days in Scheveningen Prison.

Corrie and Betsie spent a total of ten months in three different prisons, the last of which was the infamous Ravensbrück concentration camp located near Berlin. Even in the concentration camp, Corrie and Betsie continued to spend their time bearing witness to Jesus and sharing the Gospel, leading many women to Christ during their imprisonment there.

Betsie died in Ravensbrück on December 16, 1944. Before her death, she told Corrie, "There is no pit so deep that He [God] is not deeper still." Corrie was released on December 28, 1944, the only one of her immediate family who survived to tell their story. The Jews whom the Ten Booms had been hiding at the time of their arrests remained undiscovered, and all but one, an elderly woman, survived. It is estimated that the Ten Boom family and the network they helped foster saved more than eight hundred lives.

ROLE MODELS FOR THE LAST-DAYS CHURCH

Both Dietrich Bonhoeffer and Corrie Ten Boom are prophetic role models for today's Church—which could very well be the last-day's Church. There can be no question that when we look at the Christian Church today, so much of what we see is but a faint shadow of what the Church is truly called to be. So little of it is a true reflection of the Church of the apostolic age. When I listen to so many of the sermons that emanate from the pulpits of the largest and most popular churches in my nation, what I see bears almost no resemblance whatsoever to the faith described in the pages of the New Testament. Few preach the call to take up our crosses. Fewer still preach the need to repent from sin. Few hold firm concerning the exclusive claims of Jesus as the only means to attain salvation. And even fewer preach the call of Jesus to lay down our lives in order that we will live with Him in the age to come. When we consider how many teach concerning the coming restoration of the Jewish kingdom, there are nearly none. Even among those churches and ministries that consider themselves to be more conservative and orthodox in expression, I still see a tremendous measure of compromise with the spirit of this age. It is here that the lives of Bonhoeffer and the Ten Booms stand out as such shining examples. Both Bonhoeffer and Ten Boom bucked the popular trends within the Church of their day. Despite the widespread acceptance of supersessionism, the Ten Booms were unapologetic restorationists who were so firm in their convictions that they were willing to break any law of the land to obey the Word of God. So also was Bonhoeffer a prophetic voice, not only standing firm against the trends within the Church of his day, but seeing clearly what was coming years in advance, he was able to lead a movement of resistors who held firm to the call of the Gospel. Let us consider just a few of the ways Bonhoeffer was an example for our time.

THE EXAMPLE OF DIETRICH BONHOEFFER

Prophetic voices are always mocked and marginalized, even within the Church, only later to be acknowledged and honored, most often long after their deaths. What is so fascinating about the life of Dietrich Bonhoeffer is that his vocal opposition to Nazism commenced many years before so many of his contemporaries even began to truly see the evil of what was overtaking Germany. Today, many Christians are unable to discern the multiple ways in which the spirit of this age has infiltrated the Church. Surely, one of the most significant signs this is taking place is that the Church increasingly tolerates and even celebrates those who seek not merely to look at Israel objectively, but to actually demonize her. Already, Satan is using confessing Christian leaders as his mouthpieces in his war against God's covenant people. But even as the deceiver has his own voices within the Church, so also is the Lord calling out for His own voices, for disciples like Dietrich Bonhoeffer, who will fearlessly stand against the waves of lies and deception that continue to breach the walls of His Church. So one of the premier ways in which Bonhoeffer was an example for the last-days Church, one which we should seek to emulate even now, was in his relentless determination to stand for truth and purity within the churches of God and to sound an alarm when he saw a clear and present danger on the horizon. No doubt, Bonhoeffer was accused of fearmongering in the early 1930s, but within less than a decade, his warnings were thoroughly vindicated. Today he is viewed as a prophet. As disturbing as it is to say, the storm clouds on the global horizon today are far darker and more ominous than they were in 1930. It is time for men and women of character to raise their voices and sound the alarm. A mighty storm is coming. Now is the time to prepare.

Another vital way in which Bonhoeffer was an example for the last-days Church was in his work forming the underground Church, including an underground seminary. When compromise with Nazism had reached the point where it had all but taken over his denomination, Bonhoeffer went underground and began to disciple, train, and father the true remnant Church, raising up other young leaders. So also in our day, as anti-Christian legislation and church corruption spreads, it will increasingly require an army of mature teachers, pastors, and spiritual fathers to go outside the camp and lead the remnant Church. In times of peace, the Church prospers, but in times of chaos, the true Church always goes underground. This is already the case in many nations around the world, but in the days ahead, I believe it will become the norm rather than the exception. Now is the time for the true apostolic leaders to arise.

THE EXAMPLE OF THE TEN BOOMS

It is in the lives of the Ten Booms, however, that we find an example that virtually any common Christian may look to. While not every Christian is called to walk in the level of leadership that Bonhoeffer walked in, all Christians can aspire to become the kind of servants that the Ten Boom family were. While Bonhoeffer was, in many ways, an example for the Christian leadership today, the Ten Boom family is one that I am convinced all Christians will need to look to as an example in the days ahead. Few today would ever consider preparing their homes and their hearts to hide or care for refugees in the days ahead, yet when we consider the merging of multiple trends and world events with the clear warnings of Scripture, this is actually a very natural conclusion.

Today, many within the Christian Church, and many even outside of the Church, have joined the movement known as "prepping." The idea is simple; in light of the meltdown of the global economy, the ever-increasing spread of terrorism, and the rise of natural disasters, there is wisdom in being prepared. There can be no question that there is tremendous wisdom in having the resources necessary to look to the future with peace of mind. From a Christian perspective, however, there is danger in preparing if one's primary focus is on self-preservation, with little or no emphasis on preparing to serve others and to give a very real demonstration of the Gospel in times of crisis. I believe the Lord will call His people throughout the world to open their homes as places of refuge during the great storm that lies ahead. But the willingness to do this requires preparing our hearts now. The days are coming when many of Jesus's brethren, the Jewish people, will once again be in a place of being hungry and thirsty. Are you prepared to give them something to eat and drink? Many will have nowhere else to stay. Will you invite them in? Jesus said in doing this, we will be inviting Him in.

It is fascinating to see that Revelation 12:6 speaks of Israel fleeing into "the wilderness" in the last days, where we are told that "she will be fed." If the woman is fed in the wilderness, we have to ask, who is it that will feed her? Some may seek to over-spiritualize this and simply say that God Himself will feed her. Of course, in the ultimate sense, this is true, but the Lord almost always uses His people to carry out His purposes. Jesus made this clear. I believe the Lord is even now awakening His people throughout the earth concerning their calling to be His provision to the Jewish people in the days ahead.

For most Christians, the practical reality of all of this may seem very difficult to connect with. When one actually ponders the matter, however, when we consider the global trend toward hatred of the Jewish people and the State of Israel, the radicalization of large portions of the Islamic world, and the withdrawal of American influence in the Middle East, it quickly becomes apparent, for all those with eyes to see, that this is actually a very reasonable matter of pressing significance.

In researching this subject, I interviewed Samuel Clough. Clough, as I mentioned earlier, is a very articulate Bible teacher who has given much thought to this particular issue and, I feel, approaches the subject in a very balanced and sober manner. Clough addressed the double standard of many within the Church today who on one hand judge the German Church for their failure to recognize early on the truth concerning Hitler and the Nazi Party, and on the other hand mock the idea that something very similar, if not far worse, could be looming on our own horizon:

"We go back and we say, 'Wow, the Germans were so blind in the late '30s. Couldn't they see it coming?' But right now, what's being said openly, particularly in the Middle East, but even all over the earth is far more virulent, far more aggressive than what was ever said publicly in Nazi Germany," he told me. And one of the great condemnations, I think, of this generation is that we study and celebrate and even exalt Bonhoeffer and men like him, and we appreciate their prophetic insight, but we are living in a generation where things are far surpassing what Bonhoeffer witnessed in terms of the language, the rhetoric, even the scale. We are not dealing with a localized nation within Europe; we are dealing with a global rising tide of radicalism making aggressive, open, genocidal threats.

"We celebrate Bonhoeffer," Clough continued, "and yet the idea of serving the Jew practically, or even preparing to in our generation, is not even thought of; it is completely dismissed. It is seen as a kind of a secondary issue that is not important. The fact that we do not even give this issue any attention is in itself a crisis in the Church. The German Church by and large did not respond properly to the crisis of their time. And we have judged the German Church harshly for that, and rightly so, because passivity in the face of that kind of wickedness and that kind of evil—passivity is the same as agreement. But in our generation we are confronted again with rabid anti-Semitism, again with radical Islam threatening to exterminate the Jews. "In light of our own passivity," he asked, "how do we expect to escape God's righteous judgment?"[5]

Clough is right in so many ways. Today, we are living in the first generation in human history that is witnessing the fulfillment of several of the signposts of the end of the age, such as the Gospel going forth to every tribe and tongue, the Jewish political state now reestablished in the biblical land of Israel, and the increasing threat against her on all sides, not only by radical Islam, but by the global rising tide of anti-Semitism. We have multiple signs, yet many seem determined to deny that the end of this age will ever come.

"How would the German Church judge us?" Clough asked me. "We've judged them harshly, but are we doing anything differently? We have more evidence, more rhetoric, it's more out in the open, we are more aware, and above it all, we have their example. The Holocaust was mostly plotted privately behind closed doors. Among the top of the SS is where they hatched plans for the final extermination, etc. In our generation, however, the rising tide of anti-Semitism is not being expressed behind closed doors among a few elite. It is being plotted openly on social media, openly on the Internet. It's being shouted from the mosques and other places. It is trumpeted openly. And still," he concluded sadly, "most are turning a blind eye."

When the Church of this generation stands before Jesus on the Day of Judgment, will any be able to honestly say that we didn't have any warning signs?

CONCLUSION

We began this book by citing the warnings of the apostle Paul concerning Gentile arrogance toward Israel. This warning was not like other warnings. Paul did not say that if Gentiles are arrogant toward Jews, they run the risk of missing an important truth or blessing. Paul was very clear that wrong attitudes held by Gentile believers toward the Jewish people, including unbelieving Jews, would result in Gentile believers being "cut off," a term that implies being eternally condemned and separated from God. Paul's statement was as strong a warning as one could make. As we surveyed the long and brutal history of Christian treatment of the Jewish people, we found that Paul's warning not only has not been heeded, but it has been downright trampled upon. Instead of shunning arrogance toward the Jewish people, the Church has championed, celebrated, and reveled in their degradation of them. The long history of Christian anti-Semitism is the truly great shame of Christendom. However, while Christians today cannot change the past, we can pay heed to Paul's warnings today, repenting of and rejecting all forms of supersessionism. We can relate to the Jews in a way that the Lord expects: by showing mercy, love, and honor. While the past cannot be changed, there is yet hope for the future.

We have also studied many of the passages that demonstrate that at the end of the age, the primary energy, resistance, and rage of Satan will be directed specifically against the people and the land of Israel. Though Christians are now, and will continue to be, targets of satanic rage throughout the world (Rev. 12:17), when we consider the overwhelming scriptural emphasis, it is placed almost entirely on Israel. Today, those who have eyes of discernment can see that the last days as described by the ancient Hebrew prophets are drawing near, perhaps even upon us.

The question that Christians must be most concerned with right now, however, is this: Where will the majority of the Church find itself at the end of the age and on the Day of Judgment? Will Gentile

Christians, who are called to walk in discernment and to stand with the Jewish people, instead see many from among their own ranks contend against Israel and give support to those who are working toward their destruction? Though it is difficult to imagine a greater tragedy, if the history of the Church, and several present trends within the Church, are any indicator, then sadly, this will, in fact, be the case. Like few other issues, Satan has directed His energies toward the spiritual battle for the heart of the Church, particularly as it pertains to how it relates to the Jewish people and the State of Israel. Wherever Satan finds even the slightest open doorway, he will exploit it for his own demonic ends. It is this demonic rage against the Abrahamic covenant—indeed, against the very plan of God for redemption—that is the primary spiritual catalyst driving so much of the conflict throughout the earth today.

Dalton Thomas, a friend and author of the *Controversy of Zion and the Time of Jacob's Trouble*, eloquently summarized exactly what is taking place not only throughout the earth today but even within the Church, and explained why it will only continue to grow:

"Today the controversy is mounting in an unprecedented way," he said to me in a personal interview. "We can explain it in geopolitical or historical terms and still miss the underlying reason. The underlying reason why there is so much controversy about the city of Jerusalem today is because God made a covenant about His son ruling and reigning from a specific piece of land at an appointed time. And as we draw closer to that appointed time, the powers and principalities and rulers of the air will get more urgent in their rage, their resistance, their opposition, and their contention, and they will use men like puppets to effect and to orchestrate their plans and purposes."[6]

Discerning Christians must do everything in their power to see to it that the abundant failures of the Church will not be repeated in the future. We must make sure that there is no open door for the enemy to exploit. This can only happen if the Church first thoroughly rejects the specific ideas and doctrines that have enabled, supported, and empowered the tremendous Jew-hatred that has dominated far too much of the Church for far too long. If the Church is to fulfill its calling in the last days and walk in truth, if it is to avoid partnering with the enemy, then it must rid itself of the false and destructive doctrines of supersessionism, preterism, and amillennialism and reclaim the biblical doctrines of restorationism, futurism, and premillennialism.

The highest calling of Gentile Christians in the days ahead is to give Israel a final shining witness of the cross—the very embodiment of the Father's love for His people. This can only done through identifying with them and laying our lives down for them. If Jesus the Messiah came and laid down His life for us, leaving us an example to follow (1 Peter 2:21), then how much more should we do the same for those whom He calls His brethren? The final generation will be judged largely based on their refusal or agreement to take up their crosses and to lay down their lives for the preservation of the Jewish people. Many Christians today desire to be grafted into Israel's glory and inheritance but want nothing to do with being grafted into her suffering. Jesus Himself fully identifies with the Jewish people in their suffering: "In all their affliction He was afflicted" (Isa. 63:9). How is it then, that so many Christians today believe they are above their Master (see John 15:20)? Christians today who desire to follow Jesus in the days ahead must identify with the Jewish people in their persecution, marginalization, and suffering. In the end, all who have truly joined themselves to the Jewish King must accept the fact that they are going to suffer with the Jewish people.

I understand that the idea of suffering is not something that anyone looks forward to. So much of our lives are dedicated to avoiding pain. Today, so many of the popular ideas taught within the western Church convey the idea that, as Christians, we are not even called to suffer. But I would remind everyone who has ears to hear that, "To this you were called, because Christ suffered for you, leaving you an example, that you should follow in his steps" (1 Peter 2:21). We are all called to imitate Jesus. But when we consider the glory and the beauty of the age to come, then we can endure the temporary afflictions that we experience now. As Paul reminded us, our "momentary, light affliction is producing for us an eternal weight of glory far beyond all comparison" (2 Cor. 4:17). The suffering and pain that we endure in this age, as we labor to live as His people, will be more than worth it. How quickly the pain of this age will be forgotten when we step into the beauty and the glory of the age to come.

In that day, there will be no more doubt, no more fear, no more disease, no more abortion, no more human trafficking, and no more war. Who among us doesn't long for the end of this present wicked system, for the end of all the things that make us groan and sigh? All of creation groans for that day. Yes, the day is coming, perhaps much sooner than most think, when Jesus Himself will come back from heaven in blazing fire, with all of His holy angels with him, to establish His glorious kingdom here on the earth. Oh, how I long for that day! How I long for the day when the knowledge of God covers the earth as the waters cover the sea, when we finally see Jesus face to face! How I long for that time—the day when *a Jew rules the world!*

NOTES

CHAPTER 1: THE WARNING: IGNORANCE AND ARROGANCE

1. Bruce Delmont, ed., *On the Jews and Their Lies by Martin Luther (1483–1546)* (Lulu.com), 165–66.

CHAPTER 2: RESTORATIONISM VERSUS SUPERSESSIONISM

1. Many would use the title "Covenantalists" here to refer to those who believe that God will yet fulfill His promises as made in the Abrahamic and Davidic covenants. In this book, however, I have chosen to use the title "restorationist" and the term "restorationism" to avoid any confusion with Reformed (Covenant) theology, which ironically denies the future literal fulfillment of the Abrahamic and Davidic covenants.
2. Knox Theological Seminary, "An Open Letter to Evangelicals and Other Interested Parties: The People of God, the Land of Israel, and the Impartiality of the Gospel," *If Americans Knew* (blog), http://www.ifamericansknew.org/cur_sit/wdoor.html; accessed July 10, 2014. The document was originally posted at the Knox Theological Seminary website in 2002. It has since been removed.
3. Alberus Pieters, *The Ten Tribes in History and Prophecy* (Grand Rapids: Eerdmans, 1934), 109.
4. N. T. Wright, *Jesus and the Victory of God* (London: SPCK: 1996), 446, 471; emphasis added.
5. Dalton Thomas, *The Divestment Theology of N.T. Wright.* Unpublished paper. Used with permission.
6. *Merriam-Webster Dictionary*, s.v. "subvert," http://www.merriam-webster.com/dictionary/subvert; accessed July 11, 2014.
7. J. C. Ryle, *Are You Ready for the End of Time?* (Fearn, Scotland: Christian Focus, 2001) 107–8; reprint of Coming Events and Present Duties.
8. Ibid., 157–59.

CHAPTER 3: THE ABRAHAMIC COVENANT

1. Gary M. Burge, *Jesus and the Land* (Grand Rapids: Baker Academic, 2010), 98.
2. Sam Storms, *Kingdom Come: The Amillennial Alternative* (Ross-shire, Scotland: Christian Focus Publications, 2013), 208. Sam is a former teacher of mine and is loved by everyone who knows him, myself included, though I disagree with him profoundly on this issue.
3. G. K. Beale, *The Temple and the Church's Mission* (Chicago: IVP, 2004), 352–53.
4. Carl Medearis, "Question #4: What is your position on Israel?" *Making Jesus Accessible* (blog), July 23, 2010, http://carlmedearis.com/2010/07/question-4-what-is-your-position-on-israel-as-youve-gotten-more-involved-there-im-often-concerned-that-you-may-be-anti-semitic/.

5. Carl Medearis, "My Take: Jesus would support Palestinian statehood bid," *Belief* (blog), September 21, 2011, http://religion.blogs.cnn.com/2011/09/21/my-take-jesus-would-support-palestinian-statehood-bid/; emphasis added.

CHAPTER 4: THE MOSAIC AND DAVIDIC COVENANTS

1. Robert W. Nicholson, "Evangelicals and Israel: What American Jews Don't Want to Know (but Need to)," *Mosaic*, October 2013, http://mosaicmagazine.com/essay/2013/10/evangelicals-and-israel/.
2. Gary Burge, *Whose Land? Whose Promise? What Christians Are Not Being Told about Israel and the Palestinians* (Cleveland: Pilgrim, 2004), 167.
3. Carl Medearis, "Question #4: What is your position on Israel?" *Making Jesus Accessible* (blog), July 23, 2010, http://carlmedearis.com/2010/07/question-4-what-is-your-position-on-israel-as-youve-gotten-more-involved-there-im-often-concerned-that-you-may-be-anti-semitic/.

CHAPTER 5: THE NEW COVENANT

1. Sam Storms, *Kingdom Come: The Amillennial Alternative* (Ross-shire, Scotland: Christian Focus Publications, 2013), 333–34.
2. Ibid., 334.
3. N. T. Wright, *Justification: God's Plan and Paul's Vision* (Downers Grove, IL: InterVarsity Press, 2009), 120.
4. Storms, *Kingdom Come*, 333–34.

CHAPTER 6: HOW SHOULD GENTILE BELIEVERS RELATE TO UNBELIEVING JEWS?

1. Jack Zavada, "What Is Messianic Judaism?" About.com, accessed July 15, 2014, http://christianity.about.com/od/messianicjewishmovement/a/What-Is-Messianic-Judaism.htm.
2. Statistics, "Current Estimates of the number of Messiancs [*sic*] (Jews proclaiming belief in Jesus) in Israel," Jewish Israel, 2014, http://jewishisrael.ning.com/page/statistics-1.
3. "Messianic Jews Are Not Jews," by Rabbi Jonathan Waxman, at http://israelnjudaism.blogspot.com/2011/04/messianic-jews-are-not-jews.html and "There Is No Such Thing as a 'Messianic Jew'," at http://5ptsalt.com/2013/01/02/there-is-no-such-thing-as-a-messianic-jew/.

CHAPTER 7: THE COMING KINGDOM OF GOD

1. "Abortions in the world—sources and methods," Worldometers, accessed July 15, 2014, http://www.worldometers.info/abortions/.
2. Randy Alcorn, "Heaven: Dreading It or Anticipating It?" Eternal Perspective Ministries, March 1, 2004, http://www.epm.org/resources/2004/Mar/1/heaven-dreading-it-or-anticipating-it/.

CHAPTER 8: THE RESTORATION OF THE JEWISH KINGDOM

1. Tom Wright, "Jerusalem in the New Testament" (originally published in *Jerusalem Past and Present in the Purposes of God*, P. W. L. Walker, ed., 2nd ed. [Carlisle: Paternoster; Grand Rapids: Baker], 53–77), http://ntwrightpage.com/Wright_Jerusalem_New_Testament.pdf, 11.
2. David Baron, *The Jewish Problem: Its Past, Present and Future* (1891; public domain), available online at http://preceptaustin.org/the_jewish_problem-david_baron.htm.
3. Narrated by al-Tirmidhi, 877; al-Nasaa'i, 2935.
4. Ibid.; Ahmad, 2792.
5. al-Tirmidhi, 959.

6. al-Tirmidhi, 961; Ibn Maajah, 2944.
7. THAYER'S GREEK LEXICON, Electronic Database. Copyright © 2002, 2003, 2006, 2011 by Biblesoft, Inc. All rights reserved. Used by permission. BibleSoft.com, at http://biblehub.com/greek/605.htm.
8. Gary Burge, Christ at the Checkpoint Conference, February 2014.
9. *Commentaries, Acts of the Apostles*, vol. 18, repr. (Grand Rapids: Baker, 1981), 43–44. The quotation is a translation and paraphrase by Dr. William Mallard, Candler School of Theology, of Calvin's commentary.

CHAPTER 9: CHRISTIAN JEW-HATRED: FROM INCEPTION TO THE FOURTH CENTURY

1. Ignatius of Antioch, Letter to the Magnesians, 8:1, 10:3, transl. J. B. Lightfoot, available online from the Early Christian Writings website, at http://www.earlychristianwritings.com/text/ignatius-magnesians-lightfoot.html.
2. Ibid.
3. Epistle of Barnabas, 4:6–8, trans. J. B. Lightfoot, http://www.earlychristianwritings.com/text/barnabas-lightfoot.html; emphasis added
4. Justin Martyr, *Dialogue with Trypho the Jew*, chap. 135.
5. Ibid.
6. Ibid., chap. 16.
7. R. Kendall Soulen, *The God of Israel and Christian Theology* (Minneapolis: Fortress, 1996), 29.
8. Hippolytus, "Expository Treatise against the Jews," pars. 1, 5, http://www.newadvent.org/fathers/0503.htm.
9. Ibid.
10. Leon Poliakov, *The History of Anti-Semitism* (New York, Schocken, 1965), 23.
11. Ibid.
12. Origen, Against Celsus, bk. 2, chap. 8; emphasis added.
13. "The Council of Elvira, ca. 306," http://faculty.cua.edu/pennington/Canon%20Law/ElviraCanons.htm; accessed July 16, 2014.
14. *Jewish History Sourcebook*: Jews and the Later Roman Law 315–531 CE, "Laws of Constantine the Great, October 18, 315: Concerning Jews, Heaven-Worshippers, and Samaritans," Fordham University, http://www.fordham.edu/halsall/jewish/jews-romanlaw.asp.
15. "Two millennia of Jewish persecution: Anti-Judaism: 70 TO 1200 CE," Religious Tolerance website, http://www.religioustolerance.org/jud_pers1.htm; accessed July 16, 2014.
16. Cyprian, *Three Books of Testimonies against the Jews*, in *Ante-Nicene Fathers*, vol. 5, *The Writings of the Fathers Down to AD 325* (Grand Rapids: Eerdmans).
17. "Anti-Judaism and the Council of Nicea," http://www.petahtikvah.com/Articles/ANTIJUDAISM.htm; accessed July 17, 2014.
18. *Jewish History Sourcebook.*
19. "A Brief History of 'Christian' Anti-Semitism," JewishRoots.Net, accessed July 17, 2014, http://jewishroots.net/library/anti-semitism/a-brief-history-of-anti-semitism-2.html.
20. Ronald Diprose, *Israel and the Church: The Origins and Effects of Replacement Theology* (Waynesboro, GA: Authentic Media, 2004), 22.
21. John Chrysostom, *Against the Jews*, Homily 1.2.7, http://www.tertullian.org/fathers/chrysostom_adversus_judaeos_01_homily1.htm.
22. Ibid., Homily 1.4.1.
23. Ibid., Homily 1.1.5.
24. Ibid., Homily 1.2.1.
25. Ibid., Homily 8.3.10, http://www.tertullian.org/fathers/chrysostom_adversus_judaeos_08_homily8.htm.
26. Ibid., Homily 1.3.1, http://www.tertullian.org/fathers/chrysostom_adversus_judaeos_01_homily1.htm.
27. Ibid., Homily 1.4.2.

28. Steven Katz, "Ideology, State Power, and Mass Murder/Genocide," in Peter Hayes, ed., *Lessons and Legacies: The Meaning of the Holocaust in a Changing World* (Evanston, Northwestern Univ. Press, 1991), 52.

29. Ambrose of Milan, "Letters about a Synagogue Burning," August 388, Council on Centers on Jewish Relations, http://www.ccjr.us/dialogika-resources/primary-texts-from-the-history-of-the-relationship/248-ambrose-of-milan-qletters-about-a-synagogue-burningq-aug-388.

30. Edward Gibbon, *The Decline and Fall of the Roman Empire*, vol. 4, chap. 47, http://www.sacred-texts.com/cla/gibbon/04/daf04038.htm.

31. *Jewish History Sourcebook*, "III. *A Law of Theodosius 11*, January 31, 439: Novella III: Concerning Jews, Samaritans, Heretics, and Pagans."

32. Philip Schaff, ed., *Nicene and Post Nicene Fathers*, series 1, vol. 8 (Christian Classics Ethereal Library, 2009), Augustine's exposition on Psalm 114.

33. Ibid., Augustine's exposition on Psalm 109.

34. Augustine, "On the Holy Trinity" in Philip Schaff, ed., *Nicene and Post Nicene Fathers*, series 1, vol. 3 (Christian Classics Ethereal Library, 2009).

35. "Two millennia of Jewish persecution: Anti-Judaism: 70 TO 1200 CE."

36. "Jerome, Ep. LXXXIV, 3; *Corpus scriptorum ecclesiasticorum latinorum*, cited in James Everett Seaver, *The Persecution of Jews in the Roman Empire* (Lawrence: University of Kansas, 1952), 51.

37. "Two millennia of Jewish persecution: Anti-Judaism: 70 TO 1200 CE."

38. *Jewish History Sourcebook*, "IV, A Law of Justinian, July 28, 531: Concerning Heretics and Manichaeans And Samaritans."

39. Fritz B. Voll, "A Short Review of a Troubled History," Jewish Christian Relations website, accessed July 17, 2014, http://www.jcrelations.net/A_Short_Review_of_a_Troubled_History.2267.0.html?id=720&L=3&searchText=a+short+review+of+a+troubled+history&searchFilter=%2A&page=0.

40. Ibid.

CHAPTER 10: CHRISTIAN JEW-HATRED: FROM THE FOURTH CENTURY TO THE HOLOCAUST

1. *The Jewish Encyclopedia*, s.v. "France," accessed July 17, 2014, http://www.jewishencyclopedia.com/articles/6262-france.

2. "Two millennia of Jewish persecution: Anti-Judaism: 70 TO 1200 CE," Religious Tolerance website, http://www.religioustolerance.org/jud_pers1.htm; accessed July 16, 2014.

3. Philip Schaff, Henry Wace, eds., *A Select Library of Nicene and Post-Nicene Fathers of the Christian Church*, vol. 14 (New York: Charles Scribner's Sons, 1900), 370.

4. Charles Herbermann, ed. *The Catholic Encyclopedia*, vol. 4 (New York: Robert Appleton, 1908), 294.

5. Charles Joseph Hefele, *A History of the Councils of the Church from the Original Documents*, vol. 5, trans. William R. Clark (Edinburgh: T& T Clark, 1896), 248.

6. Warren Treadgold, *A History of the Byzantine State and Society* (Stanford: University of Stanford Press, 1997), 350, 352–53.

7. Fritz B. Voll, "A Short Review of a Troubled History," Jewish Christian Relations website, accessed July 17, 2014, http://www.jcrelations.net/A_Short_Review_of_a_Troubled_History.2267.0.html?id=720&L=3&searchText=a+short+review+of+a+troubled+history&searchFilter=%2A&page=0.

8. Jonathan Riley-Smith, *The Crusades: A History* (Yale University Press, 2005), 50.

9. "Two millennia of Jewish persecution: Anti-Judaism: 70 TO 1200 CE."

10. Peter the Venerable, *Against the Inveterate Obduracy of Jews*, trans. Irven M. Resnick (Catholic University of America Press, 2013), 49.

11. Ibid., 211–12.

12. "Two millennia of Jewish persecution."

13. Richard Gottheil and Joseph Jacobs et al.,, eds., *Jewish Encyclopedia*, s.v. "The Crusades."

14. Will Durant, *Story of Civilization*, vol. 4: *The Age of Faith* (New York: Simon & Schuster, 2014), 391.

15. *Jewish History Sourcebook*, "The Expulsion of the Jews from France, 1182 CE," Fordham University, http://www.fordham.edu/halsall/jewish/1182-jewsfrance1.asp.
16. Ibid.
17. Ibid.
18. Jean Flori, *Richard the Lionheart: Knight and King*, trans. Jean Birrell (Edinburgh: Edinburgh University Press, 1999), 95.
19. "A Brief History of 'Christian' Anti-Semitism," JewishRoots.Net, accessed July 17, 2014, http://jewishroots.net/library/anti-semitism/a-brief-history-of-anti-semitism-2.html.
20. Jewish Encyclopedia, s.v. "Badge," http://www.jewishencyclopedia.com/articles/2317-badge; accessed July 17, 2014.
21. Bernard Lewis, *The Jews of Islam* (Princeton, Princeton Univ. Press, 1987), 25–26.
22. Jewish Encyclopedia, s.v. "Badge."
23. Wikisource, s.v. "Catholic Encyclopedia (1913), Fourth Lateran Council," accessed July 17, 2014, http://en.wikisource.org/wiki/Catholic_Encyclopedia_(1913)/Fourth_Lateran_Council_(1215).
24. Mortiz Stern, *Urkundliche Beiträge über die Stellung der Päpste zu den Juden* (Kiel, Germany: H. Fiencke, 1893), 13.
25. *Medieval Sourcebook*, "Twelfth Ecumenical Council: Lateran IV 1215," Fordham University, http://www.fordham.edu/halsall/basis/lateran4.asp.
26. Jewish Encyclopedia, s.v. "Bulls, Papal" http://www.jewishvirtuallibrary.org/jsource/judaica/ejud_0002_0004_0_03728.html; accessed July 17, 2014.
27. *Encyclopedia Judaica*, vol. 7, 2nd ed. (Farmington, MI: Keter, 2007), 522.
28. Ibid.
29. According to the timeline compiled by Elizabeth D. Malissa on the page titled "The Jewish Virtual World: Italy" on the website of the Jewish Virtual Library, accessed July 17, 2014, https://www.jewishvirtuallibrary.org/jsource/History/italytime.html.
30. *Jewish Encyclopedia*, s.v. England, http://www.jewishencyclopedia.com/articles/5764-england.
31. "An overview of 2,000 years of Jewish persecution: Anti-Judaism: 1201 to 1800 CE," Religious Tolerance website, http://www.religioustolerance.org/jud_pers3.htm; accessed July 17, 2014.
32. Ibid.
33. *Jewish Encyclopedia*, s.v. "Belgium," http://www.jewishencyclopedia.com/articles/2803-belgium.
34. A. James Rudin, "A Jewish View of Gibson's 'Passion.' The film may transmit negative attitudes, stereotypes and caricatures about Jews," Beliefnet, 2004, http://www.beliefnet.com/News/2004/02/A-Jewish-View-Of-Gibsons-Passion.aspx.
35. *Jewish Encyclopedia*, s.v. "Bavaria," http://www.jewishencyclopedia.com/articles/2677-bavaria.
36. Ibid., s.v. "Spain," http://www.jewishencyclopedia.com/articles/13940-spain.
37. Ibid., s.v. "Basel," http://www.jewishencyclopedia.com/articles/2609-basel.
38. Gerhard Falk, *The Jews in Christian Theology* (Jefferson, NC: McFarland, 1992), 83.
39. *Jewish Encyclopedia*, s.v. "Spain."
40. Ibid., s.v. "Portugal," http://www.jewishencyclopedia.com/articles/12299-portugal.
41. Ibid.
42. Ibid., s.v. "Ghetto," http://www.jewishencyclopedia.com/articles/6653-ghetto.
43. "An overview of 2,000 years of Jewish persecution."
44. Quoted in Robert Michael, *Holy Hatred: Christianity, Antisemitism, and the Holocaust* (New York: Palgrave Macmillan, 2006), 111.
45. Martin Luther, *On the Jews and Their Lies*, in *Luther's Works*, vol. 47, trans. Martin H. Bertram (Philadelphia: Fortress, 1971).
46. Ibid.; emphasis added.
47. Paul Johnson, *A History of the Jews* (New York: Harper Collins, 1987), 242.
48. John Calvin, "Ad Quaelstiones et Objecta Juaei Cuiusdam Responsio," in Gerhard Falk, *The Jew in Christian Theology* (Jefferson, NC; and London: McFarland, 1931).
49. Falk, *The Jew in Christian Theology* (Jefferson, NC; and London: McFarland, 1992), 96.
50. Robert Weinberg, *The Revolution of 1905 in Odessa: Blood on the Steps* (Indiana Univ. Press, 1993), 164.

51. "Jewish Massacre Denounced," *New York Times*, April 2, 1903.

52. A version of this chart originally appeared in Raul Hilberg, *Destruction of the European Jews* (New York: Holmes & Meier, 1985).

53. Martin Gilbert, The Holocaust (New York: Henry Holt, 1985), 399.

CHAPTER 11: SUPERSESSIONISM AND JEW-HATRED

1. Dalton Thomas, "The Divestment Theology of N. T. Wright," unpublished paper, used with permission.

2. Eva Fleischner, *Judaism in German Christian Theology*, repr. (1975), 31.

3. Albertus Pieters, The Seed of Abraham (Grand Rapids, Eerdmans, 1950), 123–124

4. Hans Küng, *On Being a Christian* (Garden City, NY: Doubleday, 1976), 169.

CHAPTER 12: ISLAMIC SUPERSESSIONISM

1. Moses Maimonides, Letter to Yemen, in Andrew G. Bostom, *The Legacy of Islamic Antisemitism: From Sacred Texts to Solemn History* (Amherst, NY: Prometheus, 2008), 11.

2. For a detailed and scholarly reference work on these matters, see Bat Ye'or, *The Decline of Eastern Christianity under Islam: From Jihad to Dhimmitude: Seventh–Twentieth Century* (Cranberry, NJ: Associated Univ. Presses, 1996).

3. Ahmad in the "Musnad," by Bayhaqi, in *Dala'il an-Nubuwwa*; and Ibn Kathir in his book *Mawlid Rasul Allah*.

4. The Hadith collection of Sahih Abu-Muslim, Kitab-ul-Hajj; Bab: Fadl-us-Salat bi Masjidi Mecca wal Medina.

5. The Hadith collection of Sahih Abu-Muslim, Kitab-ul-Fada'il, Bab-ul-Khatimin-Nabiyyin.

6. The Hadith collection of Sahih al-Bukhari 8:387.

7. Sahih Muslim, bk. 41, no. 6985.

8. Yunis Al Astal on Al-Aqsa TV, May 11, 2011.

CHAPTER 13: THE NEW CHRISTIAN ANTI-SEMITISM

1. Origen, as quoted in Leon Poliakov, *The History of Anti-Semitism* (New York: Schocken, 1965), 23.

2. Tom Wright, "Epilogue: The Holy Land Today" (originally published in *The Way of the Lord: Christian Pilgrimage in the Holy Land and Beyond* [Grand Rapids: Eerdmans; London: SPCK, 1999], 119-30), http://ntwrightpage.com/Wright_Holy_Land_Today.htm.

3. Melanie Phillips, "'Jesus Was a Palestinian': The Return of Christian Anti-Semitism," *Commentary* magazine, June, 1, 2014, http://www.commentarymagazine.com/article/jesus-was-a-palestinian-the-return-of-christian-anti-semitism/.

4   David Brog, "The End of Evangelical Support for Israel?" *Middle East Quarterly*, Spring 2014, http://www.meforum.org/3769/israel-evangelical-support; emphasis added.

5. "Protocol of Conference on the final solution (Endlösung) of the Jewish question." House of the Wannsee Conference. http://www.ghwk.de/fileadmin/user_upload/pdf-wannsee/texte/protocol.pdf.

6. *A moment of truth: A word of faith, hope, and love from the heart of Palestinian suffering* (2009), http://www.kairospalestine.ps/sites/default/Documents/English.pdf, 3.

7. "Adolf Hitler: Excerpts from *Mein Kampf*, Jewish Virtual Library, accessed July 18, 2014, https://www.jewishvirtuallibrary.org/jsource/Holocaust/kampf.html.

8. Jonathan S. Tobin, "Presbyterians Declare War on the Jews," *Commentary* magazine, February, 11, 2014, http://www.commentarymagazine.com/2014/02/11/presbyterian-church-usa-declare-war-on-the-jews-israel/.

9. The Church of Scotland, Church and Society Council, "The inheritance of Abraham? A report on the 'promised land,'" May 2013, http://www.israelpalestinemissionnetwork.org/main/ipmndocuments/Inheritance_of_Abraham_.pdf, 8.

10. Dennis Prager, "The Church of Scotland's scandel," *Jerusalem Connection Report*, May 14, 2013, http://www.thejerusalemconnection.us/blog/2013/05/14/the-church-of-scotlands-scandel.html.

11. Ibid.

12. As'ad AbuKhalil, "A Critique of Norman Finkelstein on BDS," *Al-Akhbar English* (blog), February 17, 2012, http://english.al-akhbar.com/blogs/angry-corner/critique-norman-finkelstein-bds.

13. Ahmed Moor, "BDS is a long term project with radically transformative potential," *Mondoweiss* (blog), April 22, 2010, http://mondoweiss.net/2010/04/bds-is-a-long-term-project-with-radically-transformative-potential.html.

14. Dan Diker, "The world from here: Hamas and BDS," *Jerusalem Post*, March 4, 2014.

15. The Investigative Project on Terrorism, "Hamas Supporter Speaking on London Campus," *For the Record* (blog), February 24, 2012, http://www.investigativeproject.org/3462/hamas-supporter-speaking-on-london-campus.

16. Ibid.

17. Paul Miller, "Jewish Depaul Student: 'I no longer felt safe on this campus,'" Breitbart, May 23, 2014, http://www.breitbart.com/Big-Peace/2014/05/23/Jewish-DePaul-Student-I-No-Longer-Felt-Safe-on-This-Campus.

18. Ben White, "Is It Possible to Understand the Rise in Anti-Semitism?" *CounterPunch*, June 18, 2002, http://www.counterpunch.org/2002/06/18/is-it-possible-to-understand-the-rise-in-anti-semitism/.

19. Stephen Sizer, question-and-answer session, Rivercourt Methodist Church, King Street, London, October 6, 2011, quoted in Ron Cantor, "Sizer Reaffirms: Messianic Jews in Israel an Abomination," *Charisma News*, March 13, 2014, http://www.charismanews.com/opinion/43110-sizer-reaffirms-messianic-jews-in-israel-an-abomination.

20. Stephen Sizer, "Christian Zionism: The New Heresy that Undermines Middle East Peace," *Middle East Monitor*, August 1, 2013, https://www.middleeastmonitor.com/articles/guest-writers/6743-christian-zionism-the-new-heresy-that-undermines-middle-east-peace.

21. March 9, 2014, https://twitter.com/stephensizer/status/442722828044210176.

22. Brian McLaren, "Four Points Toward Peace in the Middle East," *Sojourners* magazine, April 16, 2009.

23. An Open Letter to Evangelicals and Other Interested Parties: The People of God, the Land of Israel, and the Impartiality of the Gospel, initiated by Knox Theological Seminary; available online at http://www.ifamericansknew.org/cur_sit/wdoor.html.

24. Amiel Hirsch, "SodaStream and Scarlett Johansson: Three Comments," *HuffPost's The Blog*, February 11, http://www.huffingtonpost.com/rabbi-ammiel-hirsch/sodastream-and-scarlett-j_b_4759810.html.

25 Personal interview with author. Used with permission.

CHAPTER 14: THE PROPHESIED JEWISH RETURN TO THEIR LAND

1. David Baron, *Zechariah: A Commentary on His Visions and Prophecies* (Grand Rapids: Kregel, 2001), 492.

2. David Baron, *The Jewish Problem: Its Solution or Israel's Present and Future*, 4th ed. (London: Morgan and Scott, 1891), 18.

3. Ibid.

4. Nathaniel West, *Studies in Eschatology: The Thousand Years in Both Testaments* (Fincastle, CA: Scripture Truth, 1890), 9.

5. J. C. Ryle, *Prophecy* (Reading, UK: Cox and Wyman Ltd. 1991), 8; reprint of *Coming Events and Present Duties*, originally published in 1876.

6. Ibid., 213–14.

7. Septimus Sears, *The Things Which Shall Be Hereafter, or God's Testimony about the Future, Gathered from the Holy Scriptures*, 4th ed. (London: Sovereign Grace Advent Testimony, 1963), 17.

8. Charles Spurgeon, "The Restoration and Conversion of the Jews," a sermon preached June 16, 1864, available online at http://www.spurgeongems.org/vols10-12/chs582.pdf; emphasis added.
9. Spurgeon, "The Church of Christ," *The New Park Street Pulpit*, 6 vols. (London: Passmore and Alabaster, 1856–61; repr., Grand Rapids: Baker, 1990).
10. Spurgeon, "The Leafless Tree," *The New Park Street Pulpit*, 3:114.
11. Adolph Saphir, *Christ and Israel* (London: Morgan and Scott, 1911; repr., Jerusalem: Keren Ahvah Meshihit, 2001), 170.
12. Ibid., 168–69.
13. Cf. David Baron's comments in the introduction to Saphir, *Christ and Israel*, xii.
14. Horatius Bonar, "The Jew," *Quarterly Journal of Prophecy* (July 1870): 209–11, quoted in Barry E. Horner, *Future Israel: Why Christian Anti-Judaism Must Be Challenged* (Nashville: B&H Academic, 2007), 10; emphasis added. For a much fuller discussion of the subjects addressed in this chapter, Horner's book is absolutely the best work available on the subject and is highly recommended as an indispensable resource.
15. Samuel Prideaux Tregelles, *Tregelles on Daniel: Remarks on the Prophetic Visions in the Book of Daniel* (London: Sovereign Grace Advent Testimony, 1852; repr., Eugene, OR: Wipf & Stock, 2007), 87. Citations are to the Wipf & Stock edition.
16. Jonathan Edwards, Works. A History the Work Redemption. vol. 9. ed. John E Wilson (New Haven: Yale University Press, 1989), 469.
17. "Sir Isaac Newton predicted world would end in 2060 AD," OpentheWord.org, October 16, 2010, http://opentheword.org/2013/10/16/sir-isaac-newton-predicted-world-would-end-in-2060-ad/.
18. Wilhelmus à Brakel, The Christian's Reasonable Service, vol. 4, tran. Bartel Elshout, ed. Joel R. Beeke, (Grand Rapids, Reformation Heritage Books, 1992), 530, 531.
19. Baron, *The Jewish Problem*, 16.
20. Ancient Christian Commentary on Scripture, Volume XIV, The Twelve Prophets, General Editor Thomas Oden, (Intervarsity Press, Downers Grove, 2003), 166.
21. David Baron, The Jewish Problem, Its Solution, 4th edition, (Morgan and Scott, London, 1891), 15–16.
22. Dr. Walter C. Kaiser Jr. (President Emeritus; Colman M. Mockler Distinguished Professor Emeritus of Old Testament and Old Testament Ethics at Gordon Conwell), in an interview with the author, July 2013.

CHAPTER 15: SATAN'S RAGE AGAINST JEWISH FULFILLMENT

1. For a thorough examination of Ezekiel 38–39, see my book *Mideast Beast: The Scriptural Case for an Islamic Antichrist* (Washington, DC: WND Books, 2012).
2. *The New Unger's Bible Dictionary* (Chicago: Moody, 1988), 1028.
3. *The New International Encyclopedia of Bible Words* (Grand Rapids: Zondervan, 1999), 502.
4. JTA, "Major Islam conference said mired by anti-Semitism," Times of Israel, April 25, 2014 http://www.timesofisrael.com/major-islam-conference-said-mired-by-anti-semitism/.

CHAPTER 16: JACOB'S TROUBLE

1. Merrill C. Tenney, The Zondervan Pictorial Encyclopedia of the Bible, Volume Four, (Grand Rapids: Zondervan, 1974), 672.
2. Eusebius, The Ecclesiastical History of Eusebius Pamphilus, Bishop of Caesarea, (London: George Bell & Sons, 1894), 75.

CHAPTER 17: DIETRICH BONHOEFFER, CORRIE TEN BOOM, AND THE JUDGMENT OF THE NATIONS

1. Samuel Clough, "Who are the 'Least of These My Brethren'?" http://samuelclough.com/1109/who-are-the-least-of-these-my-brethren; accessed July 21, 2014.
2. Geffrey B. Kelly and F. Burton Nelson, eds., *A Testament to Freedom: The Essential Writings of Dietrich Bonhoeffer*, rev. sub. ed. (New York: HarperOne, 2009), 132.
3. The Bethel Confession of 1933, in *Dietrich Bonhoeffer Works*, vol. 12, *Berlin 1932–1933*, ed. Carsten Nicolaisen (Minneapolis: Fortress, 2009), 418.
4. Eberhard Bethge, *Dietrich Bonhoeffer: A Biography* (Minneapolis: Fortress, 2000), 927.
5. Samuel Clough, personal interview with author.
6. Personal interview. Used with permission.

INDEX